'WIT'S WILD DANCING LIGHT'

'Wit's Wild Dancing Light'

Reading the Poems of Alexander Pope

William Hutchings

https://www.openbookpublishers.com

©2023 William Hutchings

This work is licensed under an Attribution-NonCommercial 4.0 International (CC BY-NC 4.0). This license allows you to share, copy, distribute and transmit the text; to adapt the text for non-commercial purposes of the text providing attribution is made to the authors (but not in any way that suggests that they endorse you or your use of the work). Attribution should include the following information:

William Hutchings, *'Wit's Wild Dancing Light': Reading the Poems of Alexander Pope.* Cambridge, UK: Open Book Publishers, 2023, https://doi.org/10.11647/OBP.0372

Copyright and permissions for the reuse of this image is provided in the caption and in the list of illustrations. Every effort has been made to identify and contact copyright holders and any omission or error will be corrected if notification is made to the publisher.

Further details about the CC BY NC license are available at
http://creativecommons.org/licenses/by-nc/4.0/

All external links were active at the time of publication unless otherwise stated and have been archived via the Internet Archive Wayback Machine at https://archive.org/web

Digital material and resources associated with this volume are available at
https://doi.org/10.11647/OBP.0372#resources

ISBN Paperback: 978-1-80064-300-0
ISBN Hardback: 978-1-80064-301-7
ISBN Digital (PDF): 978-1-80064-413-7
ISBN Digital ebook (epub): 978-1-80064-414-4
ISBN XML: 978-1-80064-415-1
ISBN HTML: 978-1-80064-673-5

DOI: 10.11647/OBP.0372

Cover image: Michael Dahl, 'Alexander Pope' (ca. 1727),
https://commons.wikimedia.org/wiki/File:Alexander_Pope_by_Michael_Dahl.jpg
Cover design: Jeevanjot Kaur Nagpal

Contents

About the Author	1
A Note to the Text	3
Introduction	5
1. *Pastorals*	21
2. *Sappho to Phaon*	35
3. *An Essay on Criticism*	39
4. *Windsor Forest*	53
5. *The Rape of the Lock*	59
6. *Epistle to Mr Jervas*	79
7. *Eloisa to Abelard*	85
8. *Elegy to the Memory of an Unfortunate Lady*	93
9. Homer, *The Iliad*	99
10. *Epistle to Robert Earl of Oxford and Earl Mortimer; To Mr Addison; Epitaph on James Craggs, Esq*	113
11. *An Essay on Man*	121
12. *An Epistle to Richard Boyle, Earl of Burlington*	145
13. *An Epistle to Allen, Lord Bathurst*	155
14. *An Epistle to Sir Richard Temple, Lord Cobham*	165
15. *Epistle to Miss Blount with the Works of Voiture; Epistle to Miss Blount, on her Leaving the Town after the Coronation; An Epistle to a Lady*	169
16. *The First Satire of the Second Book of Horace Imitated*	181
17. *The Second Satire of the Second Book of Horace Imitated. To Mr Bethel*	197

18. *The Second Satire of the First Book of Horace. Imitated in the Manner of Mr Pope*   203

19. *Epistle to Dr Arbuthnot*   207

20. *The First Ode of the Fourth Book of Horace: To Venus*   217

21. *The Second Epistle of the Second Book of Horace Imitated*   221

22. *The First Epistle of the Second Book of Horace Imitated. To Augustus*   229

23. *The Sixth Epistle of the First Book of Horace Imitated. To Mr Murray*   239

24. *The First Epistle of the First Book of Horace Imitated. To Lord Bolingbroke*   245

25. *Epilogue to the Satires: Dialogues I and II*   257

26. *The Dunciad*   267

Bibliography   293

Index   299

About the Author

William Hutchings is an Honorary Research Fellow in English and American Studies at the University of Manchester. Previously, he was Senior Lecturer in English Literature and Director of the Centre for Excellence in Enquiry-Based Learning at the University of Manchester.

He is the author of *The Poetry of William Cowper* (1983), *Living Poetry* (2012), and *Living Fiction* (2014); and co-editor of *Thomas Gray: Contemporary Essays* (1993). Hutchings has published articles on, among others, William Collins, William Cowper, Sir John Denham, Thomas Gray, and James Thomson. In addition, he has published numerous articles on Enquiry-Based Learning. He has been lecturing to meetings of The Jane Austen Society for many years and is Patron of the Northern Branch.

A Note to the Text

Quotations are from the *Oxford World's Classics* text, edited by Pat Rogers (2006), with further modernisation and supplementation by the *Twickenham Edition*, the earlier *Oxford* text edited by Herbert Davis (1966), and later excellent editions (Valerie Rumbold's of *The Dunciad* (1999) and Tom Jones's of *An Essay on Man* (2016)).

References in parentheses are to works listed in the Bibliography.

Abbreviations:

OED – Oxford English Dictionary

TE – The Twickenham Edition

Introduction

Reading Pope

In her treatise on aesthetics, *Feeling and Form*, the twentieth-century philosopher Susanne K. Langer wrote that Wordsworth's 'Ode: Intimations of Immortality' conveys above all the joyous experience of having such a great idea as that which informs the poem—the 'excitement of it' (Langer 1963, p. 219). Wordsworth's 'Ode' is not so much an explication of the idea itself as an expression of the powerful feelings engendered by encountering the idea. As a student, my initial feelings on reading Alexander Pope were like that: I felt the excitement of meeting a poet whose writing expressed sheer verbal vitality. Gradually, as I gained more experience of reading and re-reading him, I came to see that his diversity of both subject-matter and genres was held together by this essential power. The world in which he lived supplied the material out of which he shaped his poetry. No poet was more a part of that world; no poet was more dynamically able to generate from it such exhilaration. I slowly realized that whatever attitude elicited the poem (be it satirical, laudatory, forensic, adulatory) was transformed by the intensity of his intellectual and artistic accomplishment. For example, the deterioration of his friendship with Joseph Addison into something close to enmity—however justified or unjustified, however rightful or shameful—was transfigured by what he made of it through his utter command of the materials of poetic language into the portrait of Atticus in his *Epistle to Dr Arbuthnot* (1735). That immense power was what I initially experienced, the excitement of verbal energy: what Pope defines in book 1 of *The Dunciad* (1728–29 and 1743) as 'wit's wild dancing light'. Chapter 26 will examine how this phrase's ironic context further dramatizes its vibrant significance. For the moment, let us consider the phrase for itself. The adjective 'wild' is guided by its position between the two nouns 'wit' and 'light' towards its positive sense of natural creativity (as in 'wild flowers'), rather than any tempestuous associations. 'Wit' carries, as it often did in eighteenth-century usage deriving from its Old English etymological root, the serious meaning of 'knowledge' or 'intellect', rather than superficial facetiousness. Like John Milton before him, Pope is ever conscious of language's vulnerability to the shifting sands of time. Language reflects the human condition of living with partial, not absolute, knowledge. The phrase's second adjective, 'dancing', brings in a feeling of movement as rendered by a present participle, and also an additional element of meaning. A couplet from Pope's earlier *An Essay on Criticism* defines one quality of good poetry: 'True ease in writing comes from art, not chance, / As those move easiest who have learned to dance' (lines 362–63). Nature and art both manifest beauty; and both lie at the heart of Pope's phrase, as definitions of the 'light' of knowledge. The phrase as an entity is held together by euphony of consonants (/w/,/d/, and /l/) and vowels (long and short /i/), and consists of parts set in an order which reflects and expresses its meaning: that enlightenment is achieved by a dynamic combination of natural and artistic vitality. The phrase is a compact cell, active within the body of the whole poem.

This book is an attempt to set out how, and how consistently, Pope so constructed the substantial edifice of his poetry. How could this best be done? Because 'the source, and end, and test of art' (*An Essay on Criticism*, line 73) is the nature of the poetic expression, I felt that my method had to be, at heart, a close reading of his work. So, I decided that I would take each of his major poems in chronological order (or approximately so) and examine in detail a number of extracts. I hope the result is that, to some degree, 'Parts answering parts' might 'slide into a whole' (*An Epistle to Burlington* (1731), line 66) as regards both the poem and the *oeuvre*. We have to learn how to read Pope before we can articulate with confidence an overall vision. Each chapter begins with a brief contextual explanation, and lists the passages selected for discussion. I hope that, by following Pope through individual poems and a whole career, a picture will emerge of a great artist at work.

The remainder of this Introduction will attempt to lay the foundations of the book by addressing the essential building blocks of Pope's poetry:

his use of the couplet, his forging of couplets into sustained verse-paragraphs, and the key forms of his writing in his final full decade, the 1730s. En route, some of the literary devices—figures, syntactic structures, and genres—he uses most often are defined and exemplified.

The Couplet

Nearly all Pope's poems are written in rhyming couplets of ten-syllable lines. These lines take the form of, or present variations upon, iambic pentameters: that is, five measures of alternating an unstressed and a stressed syllable. Pope begins his *Prologue* to Joseph Addison's play *Cato* (1713) with a regular example. The aim of tragedy, he says, is 'To wake the soul by tender strokes of art'. The line invites being read with stresses on 'wake', 'soul', 'ten-', 'strokes', 'art'. These are the important words: one verb, three nouns, and one adjective naturally stressed on its first syllable. The line appropriately sets the fundamental metrical pattern for the play it introduces. *Cato* is, like so much English drama, written in blank verse: unrhymed five-stress lines. Pope tells the audience what to expect from the play, and shows how it will sound.

But no play really consists of the unbroken sequence of such lines; nor does *Cato*'s *Prologue*. Here is Pope's full opening couplet:

> To wake the soul by tender strokes of art,
> To raise the genius, and to mend the heart.

The important words in the second line are 'raise', 'genius', 'mend', 'heart': two verbs and two nouns, the first of which ('genius') is naturally stressed on its first syllable. 'Genius' is here pronounced as two syllables rather than three in order to preserve the regularity of the metre. This practice of running adjacent sounds into one another, common among eighteenth-century poets, is called 'elision'. This line therefore has four stressed and six unstressed syllables. Pope gathers the stressed syllables in two matching compact structures: 'raise the genius' and 'mend the heart'. These are placed on either side of the line's caesura, its pause or break ('caesura' is Latin for 'cut'), indicated on the page by a comma and extended by the three successive weaker, unstressed syllables. The couplet's first line, in contrast, has no punctuation, thus inviting a smoother reading. An actor speaking the line might well pause very briefly after the word 'soul' but will mark the next line's caesura with a more extended pause.

This couplet, then, exemplifies a principle of variation within regularity that lies at the heart of the couplet form; as we shall see, this is further elaborated when couplets join together to make longer stretches of writing and, ultimately, complete poems. One further observation should be made at this stage. The creative poet—and Pope is the supreme artist of the pentameter couplet—will use variation for expressive purposes. Pope diversifies the opening couplet of this *Prologue* to *Cato* not only for aesthetic and aurally pleasing purposes, important though such aims are. Addison's play depicts in the figure of Cato a man of supreme principle who, through his commitment to virtue, embodies resistance to tyranny. *Cato* is not concerned to move an audience by appeals to human sympathy; it demonstrates an ideal of statesmanship in the face of despotism and brute force. The hero represents a state's proper 'genius' in the sense of its prevalent and distinctive spirit or character. Samuel Johnson appropriately described the play as 'unquestionably the noblest production of Addison's genius'. Its magnificence lies in its depiction of intellectual and ethical splendour in the face of adversity. *Cato* is, Johnson writes, 'a succession of just sentiments in elegant language' (Johnson, I, 1925, p. 354).

Pope therefore adapts his language to match these qualities and to prepare an audience for what will be required of them: a commitment to virtue and principled idealism commensurate with that shown by the play's hero. *Cato* is about abstract values, and Pope's couplet also focusses on abstracts. The first line sets 'soul' within the elegance noted by Johnson ('tender strokes of art'); the second raises its rhetoric, in the original senses of eloquence and persuasion, through its stronger, more marked structure, while retaining abstract locution. A trio of infinitive verbs ('To wake', 'To raise', 'to mend') holds together the syntax of both lines. The rhyming nouns connect manner of writing ('art') to its object ('heart' in multiple senses, particularly courage). The full *Prologue* continues to define such idealism, both in individual lines, such as 'A brave man struggling in the storms of fate', and in vocabulary. The word 'virtue', for example, appears four times in its forty-six lines.

***

The dual form of the couplet constantly prompts the reader to ask what, precisely, the relationship is between the individual lines and their constituent parts. Do they complement one another, or do they—to some degree—present contrast? In the former case, the rhyme that locks the two lines together serves as an auditory sign of congruence, a satisfying resolution of stages of the argument. Such a balanced structure is a civilized, thoughtful procedure: argument by concurrence, by reflective harmony. The mind, like the poetry, is at ease with itself. In the case of a contrast, the same structure becomes an antithesis, a sharpening of ideas by means of differing meanings. These may range from subtle shifts of emphasis, to fuller qualifications, to outright denial and contradiction.

The following couplet, from the fourth epistle of *An Essay on Man* (1733–34, lines 323–24), occurs within a passage seeking to define how virtue demonstrates itself in human actions:

> Never elated, while one man's oppressed;
> Never dejected, while another's blessed.

Some individual words in the two lines express difference: 'Elated'/'dejected'; 'one man's'/'another's'; 'oppressed'/'blessed'. Others are repetitions: 'Never', 'while'. The syntax and metre are exactly parallel in all four half-lines, with the slight exception of 'one man's' nearly equal stresses against 'another's' stress on the middle syllable alone. The full lines are yoked together at their beginning and end. The repetition of 'Never' is an example of a device commonly employed in Pope's poetry, known technically as *anaphora*: repetition of a word or set of words in successive clauses. Here, inversion of normal iambic rhythm, so that the first syllable receives strong emphasis, adds force to the parallel, driving the two lines along. Then the rhyming words bring the couplet together. The joint result of how the couplet is written is a resolution of potential differences. In our lives, we meet or hear of instances when people are weighed down by adversity or distress; on the other hand, more happily, fortune can smile on people. In either case, we should temper our responses accordingly. Each line sets a limit, with a resultant concord that we may define as moderation or due proportion.

***

When Sir Isaac Newton died in 1727, Pope wrote an epitaph intended for his tomb in Westminster Abbey. It is in two parts. Firstly, a Latin portion has time, nature, and heaven bearing witness to his immortality, followed by the stone itself acknowledging his mortality. Secondly, Pope appends an English couplet:

> Nature and Nature's Laws lay hid in Night.
> GOD said, *Let Newton be!* And all was Light.

The elemental rhyme here is a perfect manifestation of the creative power to harmonize opposites. Given Newton's work on optics, in addition to his mathematical analysis of the structure of the known universe, the resultant enlightenment is doubly appropriate. 'Nature' and '*Newton*' are the only disyllables in the couplet, and also happily match each other phonetically and metrically. The exclamation itself alludes to the divine fiat of Genesis 1.3 ('Let there be light'), perhaps a step too far for the intended ecclesiastical setting. Nonetheless, the couplet reads clearly as a supreme panegyric: an elevated testimony of praise.

And yet, as Pope was of course fully aware, he had earlier, in *The Rape of the Lock*, written a daringly comic paraphrase of the same biblical verse in his account of a game of cards: 'Let spades be trumps! She said, and trumps they were' (canto 3, line 46). There is no reason to believe that the Newton epitaph is anything other than sincere; but it is also true that Pope's muse repeatedly draws his poetry towards the comic, sometimes even in the darkest of contexts. Would it be going too far to suggest that the sheer ease of the couplet—exemplified in the simple conjunction 'and' and the sense of inevitability it smoothly enacts—risks dallying with glibness? God the great magician, plucking a Newton like a white rabbit out of a hat?

That it is possible to raise such questions should help to counter a charge sometimes made about Pope's poetry: that it is always *didactic*, teaching lessons and providing instructions for living. A couplet may take on the quality of an *aphorism*: that is, a concise generalization. But aphorisms themselves are more open to further questioning and scrutiny than is commonly assumed. Chapter 11 will examine the term further. The main point is that the process of condensing ideas into a brief single statement inevitably excludes possible qualifications, complications or consequences. It should therefore initiate, not foreclose, further thought.

A full reading of Pope's poetry actually necessitates a reader's inquiry: it is a challenge, as properly intellectual writing should always be.

The Verse-Paragraph

Pope's couplets are rarely literary items by themselves. His epitaph on Newton is one of a relatively small number. His regular procedure is to build couplets into larger units: the equivalents of prose sentences taking their place in the development of a paragraph. We shall begin with an example of his inclination to find the comic in his world: the opening paragraph of canto 3 of *The Rape of the* Lock (1714).

> Close by those meads, for ever crowned with flowers,
> Where Thames with pride surveys his rising towers,
> There stands a structure of majestic frame,
> Which from the neighbouring Hampton takes its name.
> Here Britain's statesmen oft the fall foredoom
> Of foreign tyrants, and of nymphs at home;
> Here thou, great ANNA! Whom three realms obey,
> Dost sometimes counsel take—and sometimes tea.

The paragraph is divided into two halves by the full-stop. In his first four lines, Pope adopts the roles of pastoral and topographical poet, and of cultural tourist guide. All good pastoral poetry has its fair share of 'meads' (an alternative form of 'meadow' from its earliest appearances in medieval writing, handy for poets needing a monosyllable); and flowers as crowning the ground is a nice elevation and ornamentation. For example: 'The turf with rural dainties shall be crowned'. Author? Pope himself. It is line 99 of 'Spring' from his Pastorals, the group of four poems whose appearance in Jacob Tonson's *Miscellanies* (1709) marked Pope's entrance into the field of poetry. The verb is very neat in the paragraph above because it is building up to a royal palace—'a structure of majestic frame'—in a phrase matching the grandeur implicit in the root meaning of 'majestic'. Hampton Court is a source of 'pride', indeed, as a personified Father Thames recognizes.

Pope is, self-consciously and deliciously, leading us up the primrose path to his second *quartet* (that is, group of four lines), linked by the anaphora of 'Here' and taking up from 'Where' and 'There'. Each couplet sustains an elevated level until its final half line, where metrically matching phrases ('nymphs at home'; 'sometimes tea'—tea was then pronounced 'tay') act as limp afterthoughts, demeaning, questioning and belittling the assumed dignity that precedes them. The two phrases together reflect equivocal social attitudes inhabiting the world of Hampton Court, apparently in thrall to brittle sentiments: that value lies in 'cups and spoons' (canto 3, line 105), and that young women may legitimately be called 'nymphs'. This word, liberally scattered through the poem, originally derived from a classical term for female spirits positively animating the natural world. In some English poetry from the Elizabethan period onwards, however, it began to acquire dubious associations, often in order to prettify, and so patronize. Such language sits uneasily alongside the statesmanlike tasks of opposing tyranny and offering the monarch mature advice. It is notably absent from *The Rape of the Lock*'s principal ethical voice, that of Clarissa, who delivers her speech at the start of canto 5, although it is ironically used by the narrator to introduce her. This is the last passage Pope wrote, adding it to the 1717 version 'to open more clearly the MORAL of the poem', as a note from its editor, William Warburton, says (see Chapter 5).

These are examples of *bathos*. Pope's mock-serious *Peri Bathous: or, Martinus Scriblerus, His Treatise of the Art of Sinking in Poetry*) was one of the principal products of the Scriblerus Club. He invents the term *bathous* as a parody of *Peri Hypsous*, a guide to the sublime style usually attributed to the third-century critic Longinus. Bathos signifies a sudden descent from dignified language to the banal or commonplace. This, Martinus Scriblerus/Pope informs us, is 'the natural Taste of Man, and in particular, of the present Age' (Cowler 1986, p. 188). The Scriblerus Club, formed in 1713, was a group of like-minded writers: Pope, Dr John Arbuthnot, John Gay, Thomas Parnell, Jonathan Swift, and the politician Robert Harley. Their aim was to subvert the pretensions and pedantry of contemporary writing and bring it down to—preferably beneath—earth. The chief target of *Peri Bathous* is bad writers who cannot tell the difference between registers of language. In *The Rape of the Lock*, the issue is more than linguistic: Pope is using humour to raise questions about current social and ethical attitudes of those in positions of power.

***

The comic is an essential component of satire, the genre of writing with which Pope has become most commonly associated. This, I hope the chapters constituting the main body of this book will show, is both true— up to a point—and misleading, if by satire we understand a consistently hostile and demeaning approach to the people and ideas with which his poetry engages. But, yes, Pope is a master of the satirical mode as properly understood. Here is a paragraph from his *Epistle to Burlington* (lines 133–40), a witty and excoriating analysis of the grotesque lengths to which the ignorant rich will pursue their misplaced idea of taste: more money than sense, let us say. The second half of the poem describes the villa and gardens of one such man, 'Timon', including his library:

> His study! with what authors is it stored?
> In books, not authors, curious is my lord;
> To all their dated backs he turns you round:
> These Aldus printed, those Du Suëil has bound.
> Lo some are vellum, and the rest as good
> For all his Lordship knows, but they are wood.
> For Locke or Milton 'tis in vain to look,
> These shelves admit not any modern book.

Pope's couplets are an ideal form for satire because their dual or antithetical structure echoes, and often expresses, satire's conceptual core: that exposure of vice and folly is predicated on belief in their opposites, virtue and wisdom. The first couplet of this paragraph sets that principle out in clear terms. Its first line poses the kind of question any visitor might ask, Pope's voice adopting that of general enquiry. The second line then comes in with a reply which gets directly to the heart of the issue, and of the satirical judgement, through a distinction between 'books' and 'authors'. Authors are the writers, the people who are seeking to inform, present ideas or entertain. By 'books' Pope means books as objects. The second couplet explains: their value for Timon lies in the quality and monetary value of their production. Aldo Manutio ('Aldus') was a highly respected and historically significant Venetian printer of the late fifteenth and early sixteenth centuries. Augustin Deseuil ('Du Suëil') was a French bookbinder of the early eighteenth century and, so, a well-regarded contemporary. Books are Timon's equivalent of the exotic and rich objects which crowd Belinda's dressing-table in *The Rape of the Lock* ('the various offerings of the world'; canto 1, line 130). They are the accoutrements of (in Belinda's case) fashionable living and (in Timon's) ostentatious wealth. Books are commodities, of value for their material presence and not for their contents.

The third couplet adds a joke about the habit some such collectors acquired of filling shelves with painted 'books' of wood in order to give the impression of a well-stocked library. All they achieve is to demonstrate the superficiality and stupidity of their owners' minds and taste: wooden 'books' for wooden heads. The final couplet further exemplifies the problematic matter of value: John Locke and Milton represent high points in recent (late seventeenth-century) philosophical writing and epic poetry. They are voices of considerable force within modern culture but of no consequence as objects of historical significance. They lack 'dated backs', elegant printing and fine binding. Throughout the lines Pope's satirical observation is that, in every way, Timon's taste manifests the opposite of a proper value system. Books are, or should be, conveyors of a vibrant intellectual world. A fundamental irony underlies the satire. The truth is the opposite of Timon's display: books are sources of ideas, stimulators of thought, products of the human mind.

A concern with the nature of good writing and useful books runs through Pope's work from his early *An Essay on Criticism* (1711) to *The Dunciad* (1728–29 and 1743). This is a natural enough subject for a critical poet such as Pope, for whom the purpose and quality of writing are to a large extent that of which his life consists. The particular force of his engagement is conveyed by a constantly vigorous display of his own artistry: he shows in his work what poetry should be—a free play of the committed mind—within both satire and panegyric. He does more than expose and comment on cultural contests: he takes part in them. So, in this paragraph, the sheer vivacity and lucidity of his writing represent the true values denied by Timon's perversion of them. We can point to the lines' rhythmic variety, where an opening couplet marked by 'irregularity' (syllabic structures of 3/7 and 2/3/5) suitable to an exclamatory and questioning tone gradually gives way to a very smooth and elegant fourth couplet. We can see how repetition and echo provide connections: the reiteration of 'authors' in lines one and two; the 'books'/ 'backs' internal pararhyme (that is, chiming of consonants accompanied by variation in vowels), followed up by a similar pattern in the seventh line's 'Locke'/ 'look'; the singular form of 'books' with which the paragraph ends. We can note the satisfying balance of syntax in the fourth line ('These Aldus printed, those Du Suëil has bound'), whose five/five syllabic structure is followed in the very next line ('Lo some are vellum, and the rest as good'), so providing harmony at the heart of the paragraph and as the peak of the comedy is reached. This is virtuoso, alert, writing.

Genres: Epistle, Imitation

The *Epistle to Burlington* is one of a whole series making up a significant proportion of Pope's *oeuvre*. The genre dominates his work in the 1730s. For Pope, verse epistles are organized, civilized communications which bind together key figures in his circle: Henry St John, Viscount Bolingbroke, his 'guide, philosopher, and friend' (epistle 4, line 390), to whom the large-scale *An Essay on Man* is addressed, aristocrats such as Richard Boyle, Earl of Burlington and Allen, Lord Bathurst, long-term friends such as Martha Blount, and professionals such as Dr Arbuthnot. Friendship is the principal connection and the central theme. The epistles as an ensemble represent a valued group of (mainly) like-minded enlightened people. They form an antidote to the nation's Timons.

These epistles allow Pope to pursue arguments and ideas in a relatively relaxed, but still intellectually structured, way.

> On human actions reason though you can,
> It may be reason, but it is not man.
>
> *An Epistle to Cobham*, lines 25–26

Pope is here responding to Richard Temple, Lord Cobham's hostile stance towards those who spend too long 'to books confined' (line 1). He agrees, but also proposes a qualification, that it is possible to go to an opposite extreme by relying wholly on observation of people's actual behaviour: 'Men may be read, as well as books, too much' (line 10). Why is this the case?

The couplet provides a compact, forceful answer: you can apply reason to a study of people's actions, but this is to assume that reason can explain human behaviour. If you think it can, you've got your wires crossed, confusing reason with human nature. To express this, Pope deploys one of his favourite literary devices, a *chiasmus*. Chiasmus is the Greek for 'crossing', and signifies a pattern in which the word-order of the first part of a statement (or sentence, or clause, or line of verse) is reversed in the second. Here, 'human actions' correspond to 'man' ('man' is, indeed, part of 'human'), the word 'reason' is repeated within the lines, and two simple auxiliary constructions connect the two parts of the statement ('you can', 'It may be'). We can represent the full structure algebraically: a b c b a ('human'/'reason'/'you can'/'It may be'/'reason'/'man'). The chiasmus does not just describe getting one's wires crossed: it enacts it verbally.

Chiasmus can be short and clear, as in the Cobham example, or complex, as in this example from the fourth epistle of *An Essay on Man*, where Pope is examining the limited and ephemeral nature of celebrity:

> What's fame? a fancied life in others' breath,
> A thing beyond us, even before our death.
> Just what you hear, you have, and what's unknown
> The same (my Lord) if Tully's, or your own.
> All that we feel of it begins and ends
> In the small circle of our foes or friends;
> To all beside as much an empty shade,
> An Eugene living, as a Caesar dead,
> Alike or when, or where, they shone, or shine,
> Or on the Rubicon, or on the Rhine.
>
> lines 237–46

The two examples of fame are Prince Eugene of Savoy, who commanded the Imperial Forces in alliance with the Duke of Marlborough during the War of Spanish Succession, and Julius Caesar. The latter, of course, is dead, whereas Prince Eugene was still living when the *Essay* was written and published. Pope's point is that fame is, and always has been, limited in range and in time, whichever way you look at it. If you do not agree, you are just confused. To express this, he gives us two overlapping examples of chiasmus, one representing time ('when'), the other place ('where'). Eugene's martial exploits were around the river Rhine; Caesar's famous action was crossing the Rubicon. Eugene is living and so should be represented by a present tense ('shine'); Caesar, as a figure from ancient history, needs a past tense ('shone'). So we have the following patterns: 'Eugene'/'Caesar'/'Rubicon'/'Rhine' (a b a), and 'living'/'dead'/'shone'/'shine' (c d c). Pope then integrates the two, resulting in the pattern Eugene (a), living (c), Caesar (b), dead (d), shone (d), shine (c), Rubicon (b), Rhine (a). By expanding chiastic style into a quartet, Pope slows the pace of the poem, adding weight to it. In comparison, the couplet in *An Epistle to Cobham* flows more rapidly. The internal rhyme of 'shone'/'shine', 'Rubicon', 'Rhine' is, we may additionally note, not a chiasmus: the past tense and present tense ('when') succeed each other in the same order as the places ('where') do: Caesar shone on the Rubicon, Eugene shine[s] on the Rhine. So, a further variety is included within the whole structure. *An Essay on Man* is, as its title indicates, a more formally intellectual poem than the more relaxed *Epistle to Cobham*. Pope chooses a relatively straightforward single chiasmus for the verse letter, and an intensely intricate structure for the essay. The styles of writing reflect the nature of the poems. *An Essay on Man* addresses hard questions seriously. The poetry challenges us to think seriously about them, here by expressing a form of controlled confusion.

***

Some of the epistles Pope wrote in the 1730s take their cue from satires and epistles by the first-century BCE Roman poet Horace. The result was a series of *Imitations of Horace* (1733–38), which constitute a group of their own, with particular aesthetic qualities. They differ from translations by being much freer, adaptations with contemporary addressees, references, and topical material. Pope's *Imitations* were published with the Latin originals on the verso (left) pages and the English version on the recto (right) pages. Horace referred to both his satires and epistles—he wrote two books of each—as 'sermones': that is, dialogues or chats. Pope adopts a similarly conversational, relaxed style and picks up Horace's themes of the state of society and personal identity. Crucially, Pope allows his poems to form a fluid relationship with the original, following and altering it as he sees fit.

For example, Pope's epistle to his young friend William Murray, a member of the political opposition to Robert Walpole's government, and a barrister who would go on to enjoy a highly successful career as Solicitor-General and Lord Chief Justice, takes the form of an imitation of the sixth epistle of Horace's first book. Horace's poem opens with the oft-quoted tag 'Nil admirari', which Pope—openly using the current standard translation by Thomas Creech—renders literally: 'Not to admire, is all the art I know, / To make men happy, and to keep them so.' Horace and Pope both recommend that we should not get carried away by any of the slick temptations to 'happiness' life offers—such as pursuit of wealth or (again) fame—all of which will ultimately prove to be vacuous. But Horace's economical 68 lines expand in Pope's version to 133, as is visually apparent in their original juxtaposed printing format, reproduced in the *Twickenham Edition* (Butt, ed., IV, 1939, pp. 236–46). Why? One reason is that Pope takes time to expose more fully and satirically the excesses of social corruption caused by selfish pursuit of gratification. Pope is more politically engaged than Horace.

Similarity to and diversion from the Latin poem invite readers who look across the pages as well as down them (or read Pope's poem alongside any of the easily available modern prose translations of Horace) to think about the relevance and effectiveness of more contemporary and precise social commentary. Pope's imitation brings ancient and modern together in their finales:

> If, after all, we must with Wilmot own,
> The cordial drop of life is love alone,
> And SWIFT cry wisely, 'Vive la bagatelle!'
> The man that loves and laughs, must sure do well.
> Adieu—if this advice appear the worst,
> Even take the counsel which I gave you first:
> Or better precepts if you can impart,
> Why do, I'll follow them with all my heart.

Pope's eight lines double Horace's four, each quartet representing two of Horace's lines. In accordance with this expansion of the original, Pope supplies two sources of advice. Wilmot is the Restoration poet John Wilmot, the Earl of Rochester, notorious for his amatory verses, discreetly glossed as recommending 'love' as the heart of good living. Jonathan Swift had told another Scriblerian, John Gay, that 'Long live trifles' was his maxim (Sherburn 1956, III, p. 298). The letter is dated July 1732. These are Pope's modern versions of Horace's single source (a certain Mimnermus) who proposed that nothing can be pleasurable without love and fun ('amore, iocisque'). Both poets then conclude by inviting their addressee to take their advice, unless he can come up with anything better. Horace and Pope come together in a convivial, nonchalant tone consistent with that advice ('Nil admirari'): 'let's not take things too seriously'. When all is said and done, they suggest, we should be relaxed in our attitude to life. Pope explores some pretty troubling areas and engages in serious ethical discussion, but, ultimately, his stance tends towards the comic. Even in—what may seem to us—dark political and cultural conditions, loving and laughing are our best resource. That is what friends are for—in ancient Rome and modern Britain.

A Map of Pope's Poems

(Numbers in brackets refer to chapters in the present book; some poems appear under more than one heading.)

Genres

Pastoral/Georgic: *Pastorals* (1); *Windsor Forest* (4)

Ovidian Epistles: *Sappho to Phaon* (2); *Eloisa to Abelard* (7)

Essays: *An Essay on Criticism* (3); *An Essay on Man* (11)

Epic/Mock-Epic (or Mock-Heroic): *The Rape of the Lock* (5); *Homer's Iliad* (9); *The Dunciad* (26)

Epistles: *To Miss Blount, with the Works of Voiture* (15); *To Mr Jervas* (6); *To Miss Blount, on her Leaving the Town after the Coronation* (15); *To Mr Addison* (10); *To Robert, Earl of Oxford* (10); *To Richard Boyle, Earl of Burlington* (12); *To Allen, Lord Bathurst* (13); *To Sir Richard Temple, Lord Cobham* (14); *To a Lady* (15); *To Dr Arbuthnot* (19); *The Second Epistle of the Second Book of Horace Imitated* (21); *The First Epistle of the Second Book of Horace Imitated. To Augustus* (22); *The Sixth Epistle of the First Book of Horace Imitated. To Mr Murray* (23); *The First Epistle of the First Book of Horace Imitated. To Lord Bolingbroke* (24)

Elegies/Epitaphs: *To the Memory of an Unfortunate Lady* (8); *Epitaph on James Craggs* (10); *Epitaph Intended for Sir Isaac Newton* (Introduction)

Satires: *Epistle to Dr Arbuthnot* (19); *The First Satire of the Second Book of Horace Imitated* (16); *The Second Satire of the Second Book of Horace Imitated*

(17); *The Second Satire of the First Book of Horace Imitated* (18); *Epilogue to the Satires: Dialogues I and II* (25); *The Dunciad* (26)

Imitations of Horace: *The First Satire of the Second Book of Horace Imitated* (16); *The Second Satire of the Second Book of Horace Imitated* (17); *The Second Satire of the First Book of Horace Imitated* (18); *The First Ode of the Fourth Book of Horace* (20); *The Second Epistle of the Second Book of Horace Imitated* (21); *The First Epistle of the Second Book of Horace Imitated. To Augustus* (22); *The Sixth Epistle of the First Book of Horace Imitated. To Mr Murray* (23); *The First Epistle of the First Book of Horace Imitated. To Lord Bolingbroke* (24)

Themes

Art, Language and Writing: *Prologue to Mr Addison's Tragedy of Cato* (Introduction); An *Essay on Criticism* (3); *Epistle to Mr Jervas* (6); *An Epistle to Richard Boyle, Earl of Burlington* (12); *The Dunciad* (26)

Friendship: *An Essay on Criticism* (3); *To Mr Jervas* (6); *To Robert Earl of Oxford* (10); *An Essay on Man* (11); *Epistle to Dr Arbuthnot* (19); *The First Ode of the Fourth Book of Horace* (20); *The First Epistle of the First Book of Horace Imitated. To Lord Bolingbroke* (24)

Nature and State of Humankind: *An Essay on Man* (11); *To Richard Boyle, Earl of Burlington* (12); *To Allen Lord Bathurst* (13); *To Sir Richard Temple, Lord Cobham* (14); *To a Lady* (15); *The First Satire of the Second Book of Horace Imitated* (16); *The Second Satire of the Second Book of Horace Imitated* (17); *The Second Satire of the First Book of Horace Imitated* (18); *The Second Epistle of the Second Book of Horace Imitated* (21); *The First Epistle of the Second Book of Horace Imitated. To Augustus*(22); *The Sixth Epistle of the First Book of Horace Imitated. To Mr Murray* (23); *The First Epistle of the First Book of Horace Imitated. To Lord Bolingbroke* (24); *Epilogue to the Satires: Dialogues I and II* (25); *The Dunciad* (26)

Women in Society: *To Miss Blount, with the Works of Voiture* (15); *The Rape of the Lock* (5); *To a Lady* (15)

1. *Pastorals*

Examples: 'Spring', lines 69–76; 'Summer', lines 73–84; 'Autumn', lines 23–30; 'Winter', lines 45–52

The art of writing pastorals is precisely that: an art. Pastorals come with their baggage neatly packed, labelled, and secured. Sources go back to the third century BCE Sicilian poet Theocritus, whose idylls (that is, 'little pictures', from the Greek *eidullion*) were contrived to represent an urban myth of rural life by 'artful mannerism' (Bulloch, p. 573). For Virgil, and so for Pope who began by modelling himself on Virgil's poetic progress, essays in the pastoral mode were base camp on a climb to the summit of Mount Helicon. Paradigms were presented by Theocritus and taken up by Virgil. Pope then incorporated these in his *Pastorals* (1709): for example, singing contests between two shepherds (Virgil's third and seventh eclogues, Pope's 'Spring'), laments for lost or unrequited love (Virgil's second and tenth eclogues, Pope's 'Autumn'). Earlier English examples abound, notably Edmund Spenser's *The Shepherd's Calendar* (1579). The youthful Pope recognised that a reader's over-familiarity with the genre necessitated both economy and a striking demonstration of the arrival of a new and assured voice. Hence, he reduced Virgil's ten and Spenser's twelve (one per month) to just four (one per season), and—for all his confession of immaturity in his notes to the 1709 text—clearly honed his artistry until he felt fully ready to make an appearance. Indeed, manuscript versions circulated for some years prior to their publication. As we shall see, Pope was eager to seek advice from established writers as well as to demonstrate the qualities of his own work and his independence of judgment (see 'Summer', lines 73–84, below).

His structural plan was relatively complex. The year's round is set alongside life from youth to age and day from morning to night. Keeping to four poems also allowed him to align each with one of the traditional four elements of, in order of appearance, air, fire, earth, and water—not too ostentatiously, but quietly. All this adds to the contrivance of the poems but also keeps readers on their toes in order to appreciate a satisfying arrangement of intersecting patterns. Further, as conventions become such because they do, after all, contain more than just seeds of truths underlying lived experience, so these poetic beginnings promise potential developments and, crucially, hint at a future where technical virtuosity can be relied on to run like a current through every line, every couplet, every paragraph.

'Spring', lines 69–76

We begin with a singing-contest:

> *Strephon*
> All nature mourns, the skies relent in showers,
> Hushed are the birds, and closed the drooping flowers;
> If Delia smile, the flowers begin to spring,
> The skies to brighten, and the birds to sing.
>
> *Daphnis*
> All nature laughs, the groves are fresh and fair,
> The sun's mild lustre warms the vital air;
> If Sylvia smiles, new glories gild the shore,
> And vanquished nature seems to charm no more.

The rules of the game are that Daphnis has to respond to Strephon by producing lines which are both the same as his and the opposite. So, 4 lines match 4 lines (the number 4 is a recurrent referent in these *Pastorals*); couplets maintain order through repetition ('All nature ...'; 'If Delia ... If Sylvia'), but, even there, difference crucially enters ('All nature mourns' / 'All nature laughs'; 'Delia / Sylvia'). Daphnis has to make quick decisions, too. Which element will he pick? Strephon offers him a choice between water ('showers') and air ('skies'). Daphnis is no fool. He recognizes he is in spring when days are lengthening and light increasing. The trajectory set by Strephon is upwards, so that 'drooping flowers' 'begin to spring'. Daphnis, then, has to rise to the challenge in order to match or better his opponent with reference to another natural process. Strephon's skies 'begin ... to brighten'; Daphnis's 'glories gild': he adds polish to 'brighten'.

At the core of the structure lies a contest between human forces, not just the singers but also those of whom they sing. Strephon's lines are about how Delia, inspiring nature thus, becomes its equal: his complex phonic patterning of chiming short and long vowel sounds weaves together Delia, flowers and birds in the sky, aligning human and natural worlds and the environment they share: 'If ... smile ... begin ... spring ... skies ... brighten ... sing'. Daphnis's response is to demonstrate how Sylvia not merely inspires nature (already quite a claim), but actually outshines her, and so a line that looks as if it is simply following the chiming vowels ('If/Sylvia/smiles/gild') contains at its core a promise of something more: 'new glories'. It then gives way to its rhyming partner in which nature confesses defeat (or, at any rate, 'seems' to: perhaps it would be too disrespectful to be excessively triumphalist?) and the language enters new phonic territory.

Both speakers perform with admirable artistic verve, precision, and economy. Harmony is therefore appropriately restored when Damon, who is judging the contest, declares both to be winners: 'Cease to contend' (line 93). But there is a further sense in which the poem is a singing match. Pope is showing off his ability—as creator of both Strephon and Daphnis—to defeat all rivals. The *Pastorals* were first published in Jacob Tonson's *Miscellanies* before taking their place in Pope's 1717 *Works*. Tonson placed them at the end of the *Miscellanies*, perhaps implying their status as the climax of the volume. A rival set of pastorals by Ambrose Philips appeared earlier in the volume. Just in case readers missed the implicit contest between the two poets, Pope wrote an amusingly ironic *Guardian* paper (no. 40, 27 April 1713) ostensibly in praise of Philips's verses but actually choosing to quote lines whose attempts at rendering a contemporary and native British version of pastoral frequently collapse into the ridiculous:

> O woeful day! O day of woe, quoth he,
> And woeful I who live the day to see.

Pope calls this, with his tongue firmly in his cheek, an instance of Ambrose Philips's 'beautiful rusticity', and praises as 'extremely elegant' the 'simplicity of diction, the melancholy flowing of the numbers, the solemnity of the sound, and the easy turn of the words' (Ault 1936, p. 103; Barnard 1973, pp. 67–68). A reader of Philips's couplet perhaps would have in mind a different meaning of 'simple'. Pope's willingness to enter into controversy in support of his own work does not bode well for a trouble-free literary career; but, for the moment, it is no contest.

'Summer', lines 73–84

It is summer time, and the loving is easy. In the heat of the noon-day—fire is the season's element—the shepherd Alexis sings of his unrequited love: 'The bleating sheep with my complaints agree, / They parched with heat, and I inflamed by thee' (lines 19–20). His paean to his beloved attains an ecstatic height in its penultimate paragraph, where Alexis calls on her to bless the scene with her presence as night falls:

> Where'er you walk, cool gales shall fan the glade,
> Trees, where you sit, shall crowd into a shade:
> Where'er you tread, the blushing flowers shall rise,
> And all things flourish where you turn your eyes.
> Oh! how I long with you to pass my days,
> Invoke the Muses, and resound your praise!
> Your praise the birds shall chant in every grove,
> And winds shall waft it to the powers above.
> But would you sing, and rival Orpheus' strain,
> The wondering forests soon should dance again,
> The moving mountains hear the powerful call,
> And headlong streams hang listening in their fall.

The twelve lines are divided by the punctuation into three couplet quartets (groups of four lines). The first of these has become well-known through Handel's opera *Semele* (1744), where they are set to a deliciously mellifluous tune. Pope's lines invite such musical treatment because they themselves flow with the smoothness of honey, the root meaning of 'mellifluous'.

A surviving manuscript here allows us a rare glimpse into the process of Pope's artistic creation (Audra and Williams, eds *TE*, I, 1961, pp. 477–82). In a first version, Pope has lines 73 and 75 as: 'Winds, where you walk, shall gently fan the glade' and 'Flow'rs, where you tread, in painted pride shall rise', together with marginal alternatives as 'Where'er you walk, fresh gales shall fan the glade' and 'Where'er you tread, the purple flow'rs shall rise'. Pope offered these alternatives to his early mentor, William Walsh (1663–1708), along with a different version of the entire passage. Walsh opted for the present lines, with the marginal alternatives. Pope rightly accepted the advice of his older fellow-writer, but not completely. The published text altered 'fresh gales' to 'cool gales', and 'purple flow'rs' to 'blushing flowers'. Maynard Mack comments approvingly on Pope's final choices. First, the 'insistent' alliteration of /f/ and /g/ ('fresh gales'/ 'fan the glade') is replaced by 'a subtler echo', and the juxtaposition of /k/ sounds in 'walk, cool' adds a slightly longer pause at the caesura, the mid-line break, to add to the musicality. Secondly, 'blushing flowers' assigns to the flowers 'a shy, deferential reticent responsiveness' (Mack 1985, p. 114). This is precise and perceptive commentary, and the analysis points to a mature, complementary set of qualities in the young Pope: deference to more experienced judgment, independence, and confidence which enable him to improve on the improver, and persistence in seeking better and better versions.

Later lines, in their turn, confirm Pope's sensitivity to euphony and understanding of semantic nuances, notably in the clause 'And winds shall waft it' (line 80). 'Waft', again, is a Handelian word: 'Waft her, angels, to the skies' runs a chorus at the emotional height of his last oratorio, *Jephtha* (1751), a work in which he also sets—much more grimly—Pope's aphoristic 'Whatever is, is right' from the closing line of *An Essay on Man*'s first epistle. 'Waft' in the context of the 'Summer' lines is particularly rich in meaning as well as sound. The *Oxford English Dictionary* cites the full couplet—'Your praise the birds shall chant in every grove, / And winds shall waft it to the powers above'—in illustration of 'waft' meaning to carry a sound or a scent through the air (*OED*, v. i, 5). Birds or other winged forms can themselves be wafted on the air, as Pope himself demonstrates in *The Rape of the Lock*, where he uses it to describe Belinda's guardians, the sylphs: 'Some to the sun their insect-wings unfold, / Waft on the breeze, or sink in clouds of gold' (canto 2, lines 59–60). Again, the *OED* compilers had Pope at their sides, citing the couplet to exemplify the intransitive use of the verb (6b). So, birds chanting the beloved's praise, which is then wafted by the winds, is doubly appropriate. Various forces of nature combine in an action of mellifluous sympathy. Pope will later inflict indignity on the word to convey the distinctly un-pastoral sounds of 'sonorous Blackmore's strain': 'Thames wafts it thence to Rufus' roaring hall, / And Hungerford re-echoes bawl for bawl' (*The Dunciad*, book 2, lines 265–66). *The Dunciad* is, in many ways, Pope's anti-pastoral. And, yes, the *OED* cites the couplet (5c).

The 'Summer' passage employs other song-like devices, too, in the service of serene and limpid musicality. Euphony stretches to link assonance to alliteration in 'cool gales shall fan the glade' ('gales' here in the poetical sense of 'breezes'). The couplets of the second quartet are linked by repetition of 'your praise' at the end of the first and the beginning of the second. The climactic third quartet concludes with strong parallelism: 'The wondering forests …', 'The moving mountains …', 'And headlong streams'. 'Headlong' here acts as an Anglicization of the common Latin term for wildly impetuous movement, 'praeceps' (from 'prae-caput', 'head-first'). Horace, and others, use it with 'amnis' and similar nouns to signify rushing rivers, headlong streams. Compare Spenser in *The Faerie Queene* (1590): 'Nor bounds nor banks his headlong ruin may sustain' (book 2, canto 11, stanza 18).

Particularly characteristic of Pope's metrical diversity and energy are the virtuosic rhythmic variations of the first quartet, examined by Winifred Nowottny (1962, pp. 11–12), whose fine analysis I develop in the following paragraphs. In this appeal to Alexis's beloved, Pope demonstrates mastery of poetic technique, a command of the materials of poetic expression. Further, and to an impressive level, he shows how a combination of elements—diction, rhythm, metre, rhyme, phonetics, grammar, syntax, metaphor, personification, structure—results in an intensity of expression that characterizes poetic language at its most communicative.

Structurally, the four lines place in a 'frame' a taut but varied network of syntactic variations. The frame, as that metaphor proposes, is set up at the beginning and rounded off at the end, but it is also reiterated within the overall picture. It consists of a sequence of subordinate clauses of place:

> 'Where'er you walk … where you sit … Where'er you tread … where you turn your eyes. '

Within this structure, the main clauses carry the principal meaning:

> 'cool gales shall fan the glade', 'Trees … shall crowd into a shade', 'the blushing flowers shall rise', 'And all things flourish. '

These main clauses describe the effect the poet's beloved will have on the natural environment she will inhabit. The tense is future: 'shall' is explicit in the first three clauses and implicit in the fourth. They amount to a splendid, heart-felt (even if, from another point of view, we could say hyperbolic) compliment to the beloved from the poet or, rather, the speaker. The speaker, though, is called Alexis, a name both of pastoral lineage and also close to Pope's own. There is a sophisticated game going on here.

Each of the four lines is metrically divided so as to contain both one of the subordinate and one of the main clauses. The proportions, location and grammatical form of subordinate and main clauses are varied.

Line 1 is divided by the cæsura at its comma into four and six syllables. The preposition in the subordinate clause is 'where'er', an elision of 'wherever' that comes from the stable of 'poetic' vocabulary. The subordinate clause is intransitive. The main clause, which occupies six syllables, is transitive.

Line 2 immediately varies the pattern. A subordinate clause inserted between the subject and predicate of the main clause appropriately pauses the line where the beloved is invited to sit. The subordinate clause's preposition is simpler, more prosaic ('where'), and it is intransitive. The predicate of the main clause has an indirect object—'into a shade'—rather than a direct object as line 1's does. The first two lines, of course, form a couplet, and so are brought together in harmony by the rhyme, which resolves in a satisfying manner the rhythmic variations of the two lines.

Line 3 repeats the opening formula of line 1. The main clause, which, as in line 1, occupies the longer half of the four/six syllable division, differs by containing an intransitive verb, 'rise'. This makes it the only line of the three to end on a verb rather than a noun, which raises the reader's anticipation of a resolution to come.

Line 4 differs from all the others by being divided equally into two five-syllable halves. This Pope effects by ending the main clause with a descending rhythm: 'flóurish'. The absence of any punctuation within the line does actually invite the reader to glide over the change from main to subordinate clause, giving this line a special lyrical smoothness. The subordinate clause is, for the only time, placed after the main clause and—again for the only time—is transitive in form: 'where you turn your eyes'. So, the couplet and the four lines as a whole conclude on a noun. The couplet begins and ends with balanced relative clauses ('Where'er you tread', 'where you turn your eyes'), with balanced main clauses ('the blushing flowers shall rise', 'all things flourish') nestling in between. The word-order resembles a comforting, harmonious embrace. The entire four lines also begin and end with relative clauses: 'Where'er you walk' 'where you turn your eyes'. The effect is doubly comforting and harmonious.

This amounts, certainly, to a bravura display of structural ingenuity, and we might imagine the youthful Pope's delight at demonstrating his technical prowess. 'You want proof that I'm a poet? Well, here you are!'. All right, Alexander, you've passed your apprenticeship. But it is much more than just a technical achievement. We may say that the plaintive lover is offering his beloved the gift of his high artistry. This is no slipshod or hesitant or merely prosaic statement of his love. It is a tribute to the power she holds over that love, even as it proposes the power she will have over nature. 'For, lady, you deserve this state, / Nor would I love at lower rate', as Andrew Marvell earlier addressed his 'coy mistress' ('To His Coy Mistress', 1681, lines 19–20). The artistry demonstrated in the quartet of lines represents a heightening of ordinary language and syntax to an expressive register fitting for the beloved, and forms a linguistic equivalent to her elevation over plain nature. 'Nature', usually the goddess, is now envisaged as bowing to the new goddess, the beloved. Such transference of value and power demands its equivalence from the speaker, and he rises—like the blushing flowers—to the occasion. Hyperbole it may all be, to return to an earlier point, but there are times when apparent hyperbole is really no more than the emotional truth. Pastoral invites this high level of sophistication because at its heart lies the paradox that a courtly description of 'simple' life is really a means of expressing complexity. To borrow from William Shakespeare, the truest love—like poetry—is the most feigning (*As You Like It*, III, iii). And, we might add, the most discreetly erotic.

Pope also ornamentally expands on mere praise in his individual and collective selection of vocabulary. 'Gales' in the sense of 'gentle breezes' is—like 'where'er' in the frame sections—conventionally 'poetic' diction. The following pastoral in his sequence, 'Autumn', reiterates this by including the word in its refrain of 'Go, gentle gales'. These cooling breezes play off against the 'blushing flowers' of the third line, which, in their varied colouring and in their embarrassment, 'rise' to that incomplete, anticipatory ending to the third line. Within the first line itself, 'gales' glides euphonically into 'glade', which becomes the rhyme-word satisfied by 'shade'. Shade is the result of the action of the 'trees' that open the second line (and which are given unique stress by the special, most complex, metrical structure of that line).

These remarkable actions to be performed by adulatory nature are permitted by personification, the attribution to nature of human powers. Cool gales shall 'fan' the glade like ladies at a ball. Trees that might, in a natural woodland, be randomly scattered shall 'crowd into a shade', thereby creating an opening, a glade. From here, the language looks ahead to the final line. The third line's subject, its equivalent of the gales and trees of the first couplet, is the blushing flowers whose euphonic match is the verb 'flourish'. The etymological root of 'flourish' is Latin 'flos', meaning 'flower'. Thus, the flowers, as it were, constitute their own flourish. The last line itself, as we earlier observed, is metrically the most lyrical or fluid; a satisfying rhythmic expression of the organic wholeness implied in the simple, but euphonious, word 'all'. The whole of nature, its final flourish, is a testimony to the inspiring power of the beloved's beauty as finally located in her look, her eyes. And all this is carried in the poetry by diction that is almost entirely monosyllabic. In the final line, indeed, 'flourish' is the only disyllable. Simplicity, again, lies at the heart of complex artifice. 'Simplex munditiis', as Horace memorably and famously described the 'simple elegance' with which Pyrrha tied back her blonde hair to receive her young lover (*Odes*, book 1, 5, line 5). Pope's lines have all the simplicity of great artifice.

The whole twelve lines are arranged in order to rise steadily—to be wafted—from graceful and gracious compliment to mythic near-apotheosis. The first quartet declares that, were the beloved present, all nature would in sympathy respond to her. Her beauty would animate Nature to address itself to her comfort. Her power is rendered through the repetition of 'you' at the beginning and end: 'Where'er you walk', 'where you turn your eyes'. Nature yields willingly to her control. The second quartet, fused into a whole by that 'your praise' repetition, asserts that Alexis's verses would be matched by Nature's own. Alexis and Nature are at one in their elevation of 'her praise' to 'the powers above'. In the third quartet, both Nature and Alexis are outdone. Your own song, it declares, would elevate you to the power of Orpheus, the mythical archetype of the ultimate power of music. Orpheus, granted a lyre by the god Apollo himself and taught by the Muses, was able to charm all animals, trees, and rocks so that they followed the sound of his lyre. All nature would be animated and charmed by the beloved's song. Nature would dance to her tune, hear her voice, and suspend all movement to attend her in absolute stasis. She is the apogee of all lyricism. It does not get better than that.

'Autumn', lines 23–30

'Autumn', modelled on Virgil's eighth eclogue, is made up of two love plaints, from Hylas and Aegon, sung as the sun sets. Whereas the love song in 'Summer' rises to heights of expression, the melancholy of these monologues matches the falling year and the falling day.

> Go, gentle gales, and bear my sighs along!
> For her, the feathered choirs neglect their song;
> For her, the limes their pleasing shades deny;
> For her, the lilies hang their heads and die.
> Ye flowers that droop, forsaken by the spring,
> Ye birds that, left by summer, cease to sing,
> Ye trees that fade when autumn-heats remove,
> Say, is not absence death to those who love?

Structurally and stylistically, we are now in familiar territory. Our extract consists of two quartets, each strongly marked by anaphora (repetition of words in successive clauses) in the last three lines of the first set and the first three lines of the second ('For her ...'; 'Ye ...'). The specific content of each triad is varied in order but covers the same elements of the natural world: birds, trees, flowers in the first; then flowers, birds, trees in the second. However, by topping and tailing the triads with the imperative, direct utterances of lines 23 and 30 (the question mark carries the rhetorical force of an exclamation), Pope converts the entire passage into another distinct structural unit, a chiasmus: imperative/anaphora/anaphora/ imperative. The middle lines are dense with vocabulary of departure, desertion, and decline. All Nature, that is (and with but sketchy acknowledgement of the variants in actual timings involved), conjoins in an act of ending. Meanwhile, the two imperative lines move the argument and mood along in a way that counters the tendency of chiasmus to represent stasis. Line 23 is 'pastoral' in language. 'Gales' is the Latinate word for soft 'breezes' (as in the 'cool gales' of 'Summer'), and 'sighs' is the conventional and sentimental language of love lyric. By contrast, the imperative of line 30 is blunter in conception. The thought is familiar enough, but the choice of language is more tragic, lacking the literary conventionality of line 23. The proposition—that absence of the beloved is as devastating as death to the lover—may be hyperbolic, but nevertheless contains some truth. If it is love that makes the lover's world go round, the round of the seasons has now brought him to the loss of that which moves and motivates him. Incidentally, this passage, like pastorals more generally, illustrates how the genre's perspective is universally male, with females as the object of lovers' declaration, desire (usually frustrated), and lament. When Pope moves on, as he soon will, to deepen—and sometimes darken—his 'pastoral' vision in *The Rape of the Lock* and *Windsor Forest*, female voices will become integral to, and often dominate, the language. Here, in 'Autumn', death is the universal to which all Nature yields and beneath which all Nature is subsumed. The first quartet begins in pastoral mode ('gentle gales') and ends in the death of flowers. The second quartet begins with flowers drooping, including the lilies that 'hang their heads' in line 26, and concludes with 'death' in the human world. There is no ultimate difference: the remorseless cycle of life, from morn to evening, bears all away.

'Winter', lines 45–52

In 'Autumn', death appeared in the human world in the form of absence. Now, in 'Winter', it is not hyperbole or metaphor; it is literal and brutal. The genre is elegy, as in Virgil's fifth eclogue, a lament for the dead Daphne:

> No grateful dews descend from evening skies,
> Nor morning odours from the flowers arise;
> No rich perfumes refresh the fruitful field,
> Nor fragrant herbs their native incense yield.
> The balmy zephyrs, silent since her death,
> Lament the ceasing of a sweeter breath.
> The industrious bees neglect their golden store;
> Fair Daphne's dead, and sweetness is no more!

These eight lines resound with negatives. 'No grateful dews ...Nor morning ...No rich ...Nor fragrant' open the first four lines in a pattern alternating the same blunt adjective and conjunction; then the remaining four lines enclose 'ceasing' and 'neglect' within the forthright repetition of 'death', 'dead' before the final plangency of 'no more'. The lines thus uncompromisingly depict a natural world in which all movement and vitality have been suspended. This is what the state of winter means—and the human world is included within Nature: we are not comfortably imaged by natural processes, but are Nature.

Water is the element of 'Winter'. Gone are the 'grateful dews' with which the human and animal worlds began their day in 'Spring': 'Soon as the flocks shook off the nightly dews, / Two swains, whom love kept wakeful, and the Muse, / Poured o'er the whitening vale their fleecy care, / Fresh as the morn, and as the season fair' ('Spring', lines 17–20). In their place are rains of winter (line 15) and tears of grief (line 66). 'Winter' laments the loss of animated life, but as part of a cyclical process: those rains are 'kind' because they 'swell the future harvest of the field' (lines 15–16). Humanity and the natural world are inextricably entwined within that all-encompassing process. 'Balmy zephyrs'—west winds, that is—are 'silent since her death' and lament 'the ceasing of a sweeter breath': their 'breath' is suspended, anthropomorphically, as is that of Daphne, Pope's female equivalent of Virgil's Daphnis.

***

Pope's *Pastorals* were published in the sixth part of Jacob Tonson's *Miscellanies* (1709) but had been circulating among celebrated elder statesmen of the arts since 1705. John Barnard's *Pope: The Critical Heritage* usefully brings together a set of extracts from private letters, which illustrate the enthusiasm with which the *Pastorals* were received

(Barnard 1973, pp. 59–61). George Granville (1667–1735), a Tory grandee, patron, and a respectable poet himself, hailed this first step onto the Virgilian pathway: 'If he goes on as he has begun, in the Pastoral way, as *Virgil,* first try'd his Strength, we may hope to see *English* Poetry vie with the Roman, and this Swan sing as sweetly as the *Mantuan*'. William Walsh, in a letter to the dramatist William Wycherley agreeing to meet Pope to offer advice, gave praise indeed: 'Tis no flattery at all to say, that Virgil had written nothing so good at his Age'. Walsh later wrote direct to Pope that he had 'read over your Pastorals again, with a great deal of pleasure'. Jacob Tonson, writing to Pope to offer publication in his *Miscellanies* series, described the poem as extremely fine, and noted that it was 'generally approv'd off [sic] by the best Judges in poetry'. Wycherley himself, after publication of the volume, wrote to Pope to assert that 'all the best Judges, of good Sense, or Poetry are Admirers of Yours', and that this 'first Success will make you, for all your Life a Poet'.

Much later in the century (1777–79), the ever-alert Samuel Johnson pointed out that the usually careful Pope had made his zephyrs somehow lament in silence. Well, one could argue in Pope's defence that his lines are intended to be an elliptical construction: The balmy zephyrs [which have been] silent since her death, / [Now] Lament the ceasing of a sweeter breath. The word order, that is, represents a time order. But it scarcely matters. Johnson authoritatively and correctly states that to 'charge these *Pastorals* with want of invention'—and so of the requirement to be scrupulously accurate in their descriptions—'is to require what was never intended' (Archer-Hind 1925, II, p. 215). Pope's aim, in his youthful first work, the same passage continues, is to show that he can 'copy the poems of antiquity with judicious selection' and that he has 'obtained sufficient power of language and skill in metre to exhibit a series of versification which had in English poetry no precedent, nor has since had an imitation'.

One further step we can take. 'Power of language' and 'skill in metre' result in art; but that art emerges, at the same time, as deeply expressive of feeling, in 'Winter' the emotion of grief. Repeated consonant motifs are woven through lines 45–52. /F/ sounds in the first quartet emphasize all that, in our winter landscape, is absent: 'flowers', 'fragrant herbs', and (lying between these intimations of sensory deprivation) the repression of natural reproduction concisely captured in 'fruitful field'. Instead, the second quartet relocates the /f/ sounds to a 'zephyrs'/'Daphne'—an echo (half-hidden from the eye but open to the voice) that brings together agents and the object of grieving. Alongside, /z/-sounding consonants begin with the rhyme words in the opening couplet, where long vowels augment softness by harmoniously stretching the syllables: 'skies' / 'arise'. Conversely, the second quartet begins by modulating from the warm 'zephyrs' of sympathetic nature to the blunt reality of 'silent since her death', a phrase whose uncompromising quality is echoed in the last line: 'Daphne's dead'. A similar repetition accompanied by a switch in grammar connects 'sweeter' to 'sweetness' (lines 50, 52), while admitting a pre-Keatsian collocation of 'ceasing' and 'bees' ('to set budding more, / And still more, later flowers for the bees, / Until they think warm days will never cease': Keats, *To Autumn*, lines 8–10). Pope's long 'e' and 'o' vowels are strongly counterpointed by the hard consonants and short, sharp vowels in 'Daphne's dead', themselves linking back to the first line's 'dews descend' and thus identifying night with death. Such euphonious and versatile language interlaces beauty with grief, inextricably binding one into the other, while never shirking the brutal actuality of grief's cause. 'Et in Arcadia ego': 'I, death, am also in Arcady' (Panofsky 1970, pp. 340–67 for the history and development of the Latin phrase).

Through learning a poetic craft and, at the same time, displaying a finished poem, Pope grows into mature reflection on the matter of art. As in all the best pastorals, seriousness seeps mellifluously into the fabric of apparent artificiality. The much-discussed maxim at the close of Keats's *Ode on a Grecian Urn* (1819), 'Beauty is Truth, Truth Beauty', asserts a deep identity between aesthetic splendour and severe reality. In his *Pastorals*, Pope finally establishes that, far from feigning, true art is a fusion of truth with form. The rest of his writing career will confirm and strengthen that initial perception.

2. Sappho to Phaon

Examples: Lines 143–48; 179–84

Pope's earliest venture into the erotically charged world of the Ovidian verse epistle is *Sappho to Phaon*, a translation of the fifteenth poem in the Latin poet's *Heroides*, a series of letters from legendary heroines to their lovers. In a surviving manuscript, Pope states that it was written in 1707 (Mack 1984, pp. 72–89). The poetic world it inhabits is that of his other early work, the *Pastorals*. *Sappho to Phaon* was published in March 1712, in the eighth edition of a collective translation of Ovid's *Epistles*, which had first appeared in 1680.

The legend was that Sappho, a sixth-century BCE Greek lyricist from the Aegean island of Lesbos, fell in love with Phaon, a boatman of Mytilene who had been granted beauty and youth by Aphrodite. Sappho's only extant complete poem is a hymn to Aphrodite, which may have suggested linking together the historical and the legendary. Phaon is said to have rejected Sappho's love and fled to Sicily, leaving her distraught: 'Phaon to Etna's scorching fields retires, / While I consume with more than Etna's fires' (lines 11–12). The somewhat frantic and over-heated tones of these early lines happily soon give way to something altogether richer and more moving. Or, it may be that Sappho is being depicted as gradually settling into elegiacs: broadly speaking, alternating lines of dactylic hexameters and pentameters (respectively six- and five-stress lines)—an unaccustomed form for a poet whose natural home is the stanzaic lyric. Sappho herself draws attention to this change: the 'lute neglected, and the lyric muse', she writes, love has taught her tears 'in sadder notes to flow' and tuned her heart 'to elegies of woe' (lines 6–8). Elegiac metre is distinctly different from the regular hexameters familiar from epic poetry. Indeed, Ovid devoted the first poem in his *Amores* to a playful demonstration of Cupid's ownership of the six-five form's alternating rhythms. However, Pope has in mind a longer-term goal than an attempt at specific metrical imitation. Dryden's Virgil translation, which appeared in 1697, had shown how a flexible and resourceful deployment of heroic couplets, occasionally diversified with triplets, could render epic hexameters successfully. Pope's aspirations, even at this stage, are targeted on finding a kind of heroic couplet suitable for his own serious aims. In this early Ovidian work, Pope manages his couplets in such a way as to express an intense empathy with the original, an immersion of the poet's voice within the emotions and situation of the epistle writer.

Lines 143–48

'Tis thou art all my care and my delight,
My daily longing, and my dream by night:
Oh night more pleasing than the brightest day,
When fancy gives what absence takes away,
And, dressed in all its visionary charms,
Restores my fair deserter to my arms!

These lines set up at the outset a tone of intimacy and simplicity: 'Tis thou'. There is no affectation of language or syntax in the largely monosyllabic line 143, so that the 'all' comes across as lacking any hyperbole. The smooth metrics produce a line of directness and flowing grace, making 'delight' an agreeably appropriate concluding word. The frank and ungarnished repetition of 'my' into the second line of the couplet continues these notes, but now with rhythmic variation so as to form a line metrically balanced to give weight to the totality of the speaker's commitment. The satisfying completion of 'daily' by 'night' is phonically effected by the alliteration of 'daily ... dream', set up in the last word of the first line ('delight'), leading naturally into 'dream by night'. Every part of Sappho's life is filled with 'thou'.

The next line reverses the day/night sequence to form a gentle chiasmus: 'My *daily* longing, and my dream by *night*: / Oh *night* more pleasing than the brightest *day*'. Night glides smoothly back to day, with only the slightest breath after 'pleasing' to dwell on an echo of the falling rhythm of 'longing'. The remaining lines explain why night is more pleasing than day: its release of the imagination in dream can restore the image of Phaon. Night supplies what day has removed. What might, in other contexts, have been a harsh oxymoron, 'fair deserter', is here accommodated into Pope's rhythmic and syntactic gentleness. 'Fancy' is not only Sappho's nocturnal dream: it is Pope's poetic imagination. Both are palliative, Pope's poetry merging with the comforting ease of her dream.

Lines 179–84

> A spring there is, whose silver waters show,
> Clear as a glass, the shining sands below:
> A flowery lotus spreads its arms above,
> Shades all the banks, and seems itself a grove;
> Eternal greens the mossy margin grace,
> Watched by the sylvan genius of the place.

The lamenting Sappho now situates herself within the world of Pope's *Pastorals*. 'Summer', for example, contains a 'crystal spring' that serves as a mirror, a 'watery glass' (lines 27–28). In particular, the lamenting songs of Hylas and Aegon in 'Autumn', one mourning an absent love, the other a faithless love, share similar moods. The voice of Sappho is thus subsumed into a pastoral world, but with a new intensity of the actual. She is, after all, a historical figure, even if one remote in time and, in this epistle, given a legendary role. Sappho's real presence derives from her foundational status within the love monody, the amorous lyric. Hers is the original voice of love poetry.

Other details reflect from *Sappho to Phaon* to the *Pastorals*. For example, Aegon's regret for his lost love prompts him to propose as a solution to his pains 'one leap from yonder cliff' ('Autumn', line 95). Sappho is called by a 'watery virgin' to throw herself off a cliff into the sea (lines 186ff). For the moment, though, the mood is softer, as becomes a pastoral. Honeyed indulgence extends over the scene, symbolized by Pope's Lotus tree whose fruit brings the forgetfulness that overwhelms Odysseus's men in book 9 of Homer's *Odyssey*. The green world stretches beyond the reach of time, and the whole scene is guarded by a 'sylvan genius of the place', a protective and nourishing spirit of the woods.

All this is rendered in rhythms that remain undisturbed and in euphonious diction that casts a graceful air over the landscape. For example, the rhyme word 'grove' echoes the long vowel in 'lotus', and varied long vowels ('greens ... genius', 'grace ... place') protract the third couplet, adding an element of dreaminess, counterpointed by not-too-intrusive consonantal chiming: 'mossy margin', 'greens ... grace'. The poetic voice is one of ease, easefully achieved. *Sappho to Phaon* re-appeared in the 1717 *Works,* but there it is accompanied by later poems where Pope's capacity to immerse his poetic voice with a female protagonist's is set a sterner test. In the pastoral tones of this translation, he is only warming up.

3. *An Essay on Criticism*

Examples: Lines 68–79, 88–91, 152–57, 223–32, 243–52, 289–300, 729–34

It is wonderful how rapidly Pope progressed from the *Pastorals*, an apprentice-piece designed to show off his grasp of traditional forms and his own particular style, to his first unarguable masterpiece, *An Essay on Criticism*, published in 1711. Or perhaps it is not so surprising, given the scale of his ambition and the proof of his technical command. *Windsor Forest* (1713) will endeavour to demonstrate a contemporary version of Virgil's amalgamation in his *Georgics* of national progress and rural activities, but *An Essay on Criticism* is an example of practical, didactic poetry with, as principal parts of its brief, the aim of tracing a lineage for its topic and setting out a methodology for its successful implementation.

And yet it is much more. Its academic and intellectual subject necessitated, or at least admitted, an extension of classical models to the Horatian—the *Ars Poetica*, the third of the epistles that constitute Horace's second book—and of time-scale to acknowledge and include the recent past, notably Boileau's *L'Art Poétique* (1674) and essays in verse by seventeenth-century English poets such as Dryden and Roscommon. Joseph Addison's laudatory notice of Pope's poem in *The Spectator* compared its manner of argument to Horace's (no. 253, 20 December 1711; Bond, II, pp. 481–86; Barnard, pp. 77–80). An expansion of models is a mark of contemporary engagement with tradition. Further, the quality that distinguishes Pope's poem is its expressive and imaginative force. Its title may sound, at first, somewhat arid and prescriptive, but it is worth recalling the root meaning of essay in the French 'essayer': *essai* means a trial, an attempt, an endeavour. Experimentation is as much a part of the term's signification as are statement and argument.

Lines 68–79

> First follow *Nature*, and your judgment frame
> By her just standard, which is still the same:
> Unerring NATURE, still divinely bright,
> One clear, unchanged, and universal light,
> Life, force, and beauty, must to all impart,
> At once the source, and end, and test of art.
> Art from that fund each just supply provides,
> Works without show, and without pomp presides:
> In some fair body thus the informing soul
> With spirits feeds, with vigour fills the whole,
> Each motion guides, and every nerve sustains;
> Itself unseen, but in the effects, remains.

'First follow Nature'. *An Essay on Criticism* did indeed follow on chronologically from the *Pastorals*, where the natural world—however idealized and mythologized—dictated the course of the poem as it does the course of the seasons. The *Essay* now asserts, in the aphoristic manner that will also characterize sections of Pope's later *An Essay on Man*, that a true critic takes the lead from the same source. As with similar imperatives there, such as 'Know then thyself', there is nothing remotely original about the injunction. On the contrary, its force and reliability derive from its status as a crisp, no-nonsense reiteration of an age-old adage. 'What oft was thought, but ne'er so well expressed' (line 298), we might say; or at least seldom so well expressed. As the art historian Hugh Honour wrote in an appropriately concise and disarming commentary on the term 'Nature', '[p]ractically every eighteenth-century belief, whether religious, moral, philosophical, economic or artistic, was supported by an appeal to the law of nature' (1977, p. 105).

But what exactly does it mean? Honour goes on in the same paragraph to assert that the primary connotation of Nature for the Enlightenment was uniformity, universality. *An Essay on Criticism* invokes this fundamental idea in order to set out rules for all judgment of poetry. Pope's own artistry then demonstrates how these rules may be, and should be, creatively applied.

'First follow *Nature*, and your judgment frame'. The opening clause is strongly marked and accented, with three stresses in five syllables ('Fírst fóllow Náture'), forceful alliteration, and imperative mood. The second half of the line is more relaxed in rhythm, with just two stresses ('and your judgment fráme'), and moves the topic from 'Nature' to 'judgment'. In the context of a poem entitled *An Essay on Criticism*—not 'An Essay on Nature'—this second clause represents firmer territory. What else is 'criticism' but the exercise of one's judgment on a work of art? Pope reverses normal word order here, with the verb 'frame' *following* its object 'judgment', so that the line encloses its two abstract nouns within two imperative verbs. To 'frame' in this transferred sense means to 'shape', 'construct', 'direct' thoughts or ideas to a certain purpose (see *OED*, 'frame' v. 5c), with a distinct implication of 'combination and fitting together of parts' (*OED*, 'frame' v. 7). The metaphor derives from a structure made by joining parts to form a whole window or building. The principal point, then, is not the 'meaning' of nature, but how judgment connects with nature to form a shape. And the line is itself formed as a 'frame': verb/noun/noun/verb. The two half-lines are connected in mood (imperative), and phonetically (the long vowels in 'nature' and 'frame' as well as the alliteration), and so 'fit together'. Take the whole line, and Pope's subject becomes, as David B. Morris writes, not the praise of nature but how to 'frame' one's judgment (Morris 1984, p. 53).

The remainder of the paragraph provides an explanation of what such a process entails. Now, this inevitably involves some consideration of what the qualities of 'nature' are; but the direction of travel is throughout towards the central questions: what is art, and how does one judge it? And 'nature' is defined not by the generalities and abstractions of *Rasselas*'s philosopher, but by artistic means: images and verbal dynamics. These work together to shape an essential paradox: that an entity which is in a state of perpetual rest ('still the same'—that is, always in the same state) is also and at the same time the cause and source of all motion and vitality. Nature's static being, its 'stillness'—the adverb, signifying 'always', is repeated in lines 69 and 70—is rendered by adjectives and adverbs: 'still divinely bright', 'clear', 'unchanged', 'universal'. Its production of vitality is rendered by verbs: 'impart', 'provides', 'works', 'presides', 'feeds', 'fills', 'guides', 'sustains'.

Description by itself is static, like nature itself; verbs inject it with active energy. Put the two together, conjoin them as in a frame, and one has the paradoxical whole. Nature thus operates as an unmoved mover. As the Twickenham editors, E. Audra and Aubrey Williams, note in their concise and authoritative review of the classical and medieval sources behind the implied cosmology, Pope is relying on a 'scarcely veiled analogy' between Nature and God, defined as a first cause (I, 1961, pp. 219–23).

At the heart of these lines Pope couples his two sentences together by repeating 'art'. Rhetoricians term this repetition of a word or phrase across a punctuation mark *anadiplosis*, from the Greek for 'doubling back':

> At once the source, and end, and test of art.
> Art from that fund each just supply provides.

The first of these lines sums up the role of Nature as the ordering principle operating cosmologically, and so at the heart of all endeavour, including human efforts. It is the source of everything: if there is no Nature, nothing exists. It is the end of everything, in the sense that it represents the goal of all endeavour, the model to which all activity aspires. And it is the test of all enterprise, in that it guides our judgment of activity. True artists, then, seek illumination ('light'), vitality ('Life'), energy ('force', quietly setting up an internal rhyme with 'source'), and aesthetic attraction and coherence ('beauty'). For critics, these are the 'test'; the paradigms against which they judge what they read. Does a poem cast light on what it presents? Does it present this energetically, so that it communicates vitally with the reader? Does it attract the reader with the beauty of its language and form?

Subsequent lines expand on how art, at its finest, operates and so define the principles by which we judge it. Great art possesses, like life itself, an 'informing soul'. The adjectival participle carries much weight here. To 'inform' means to impart life or spirit to; to inspire, animate, actuate. It is to fill the body with its 'anima', its spirit. But it is also to give form to, to provide it with its shape. This, indeed, is its earliest meaning, deriving from scholastic Latin 'informare' (*OED*, 'inform' v. ii 3). Pope's art fulfils both functions. He begins with a prepositional phrase containing the static object ('fair body'). Then he releases the subject ('informing soul') which governs all the invigorating verbs, beginning with 'feeds' and 'fills'. These verbs animate the object. The syntax of the sentence (object/subject/actions) follows the contours of the process, so that its form exemplifies on the page the action being described.

Lines 88–91

> Those RULES of old discovered, not devised,
> Are Nature still, but Nature methodized;
> Nature, like liberty, is but restrained
> By the same laws which first herself ordained.

'Rules' is the kind of word that can intimidate a modern reader, whose view of poetry is likely to favour imaginative freedom over regulations. But Pope has in mind a more profound and subtle meaning of what at first may sound unduly restrictive. Nature is the fundamental, always ('still': cf. 'her just standard, which is still the same', line 69, in the first extract discussed). Since Nature underlies everything, all else derives its existence and its vitality from Nature. This includes art, poetry and criticism (which is the judgment of art). Any 'rules' or 'laws' which art or criticism might extract from their activity must, therefore, also derive from Nature. This cultural circle may be likened to political processes: all laws derive their authority from their source; from a constitution that—written or derived from custom and tradition—is their foundation. Those laws, then, may be judged only with reference to that foundation. Just as laws are the principles of a society, put in order, arranged, reduced to method, so the principles of art are 'Nature methodized' (*OED*, 'methodize' v. 1 *trans*: 'To reduce to method or order; to arrange (thoughts, ideas, expression etc.) in an orderly manner'). Art is 'human skill as an agent, human workmanship (*OED*, 'art' sb. 2; adding: 'opposed to nature'). Art is the area of human craftsmanship, but, as human beings are actually part of Nature, its operations are not so much 'opposed' to Nature as constructed by processes analogous to Nature. Humanity is a synecdoche of nature, a part of a wider whole.

Each new work of art derives from the same source. But each new work also *adds* to the store of 'art'. It is a 'new' creation. Art is not a static entity, but an eternally increasing and developing one—at least, as long as humanity survives and goes on creating. Having reference to first principles is not a recipe for stasis. This is the paradox underlying all forms and expressions of art: they are both 'new' and derive their existence from antiquity, from tradition. Proper neo-classicism recognizes this union as the source of all creativity. Principles, such as verbal precision and respect for structural integrity, underlie every new engagement with the shifting materials of time, language development and increasing variety. Fluidity, like the eternal processes of Nature, is 'methodized' within art. So, Pope's own mastery of structure, syntax, couplet form, rhetorical and stylistic devices, and his constant respect for the roots, significance and development of words are the means by which he methodizes the shifting world that he observes around him. This is his intellectual and artistic life.

Lines 152–57

> Great wits sometimes may gloriously offend,
> And rise to faults true critics dare not mend;
> From vulgar bounds with brave disorder part
> And snatch a grace beyond the reach of art,
> Which without passing through the judgment, gains
> The heart, and all its end at once attains.

The oft-quoted fourth line here should itself be sufficient to show that Pope is offering no pallid version of what the term 'neo-classicism' is too often taken to imply. This is not a poem setting out static, absolute 'rules'. Rather, it is about how art may be created by means of imaginative energy, animating spirits. 'Snatch' is the *mot juste* here: its verbal energy is directed at those 'nameless graces' of expression that lie beyond the normal reach of the trained artist. Dull forms of 'neo-classicism' do not snatch, as well-bred people should not. Pope's startling couplet inverts the norms: the boundaries of expected behaviour are 'vulgar' in its original, non-derogatory sense of 'common'. Daring lies in the near-oxymoron of 'brave disorder', where 'brave' may be glossed as 'intrepid'. 'Gloriously offend' occupies similar territory; and underlying the entire passage is the dizzying physical image of 'rise to faults'. Pope may well have had Milton in mind when writing here. *Paradise Lost* (the previous century's great epic, from 1667) plays on the resonant implications of the words 'fall' and 'fault'. In book 9, Adam describes how the serpent's prophecy had been a lie clothed in partial truth: 'true in our Fall, / False in our promised rising' (lines 1069–70). In book 3, God is explicit, even to the extent of some slight tetchiness, when linking Adam and Eve's 'Fall' to all fault: 'So will fall/He and his faithless progeny: whose fault?' (lines 95–96; see Ricks 1963, p. 9).

Herein lies a warning. Only 'great wits' can judge when and how it is appropriate to breach the norms. Pope's line 'And snatch a grace beyond the reach of art' follows on from a more explicit message:

> Music resembles poetry, in each
> Are nameless graces which no methods teach,
> And which a master-hand alone can reach.

lines 143–45

Pope combines in the word 'grace' a sense of bestowed blessing with all the human aesthetic force of elegant writing. Triplets are relatively rare in Pope's writings, much more so than in Dryden's. Here, he appropriately makes an exception to his customary couplet mode to express such a venture: the third line itself 'reaches' out towards exceptional events. These are the province of 'a master hand alone': intrepid actions, which only those who have mastered the fundamental arts of composition can dare. Yet such do exist, and the true critic should recognize and celebrate this.

These poetic achievements are events that, once properly corroborated, take their place within the body of accepted experience. They extend knowledge, rather than challenging the basis of knowledge. Pope writes:

> If, where the rules not far enough extend,
> (Since rules were made but to promote their end)
> Some lucky licence answers to the full
> The intent proposed, that licence is a rule.

lines 146–49

Just as empiricist epistemology embraces the role of new discoveries, and sees knowledge as constantly open to revision when properly responding to scientific principles, so art and criticism can and should rise to the power of fresh imaginative sallies. Some new planet may, if we are well trained and fortunate, swim into our ken.

Lines 223–32

Samuel Johnson in his life of Pope celebrated *An Essay on Criticism* as a work which, 'if he had written nothing else, would have placed him among the first critics and the first poets (Archer-Hind 1925, II, p. 218). It has puzzled some readers that Johnson went on to pick out, and comment at some length on, Pope's Alps simile for the experience of a student's progress in knowledge. At first, we see only 'short views' of what is immediately before us; we cannot see 'the lengths behind'.

> But, more advanced, behold with strange surprise
> New distant scenes of endless science rise!
> So pleased at first the towering Alps we try,
> Mount o'er the vales, and seem to tread the sky,
> The eternal snows appear already past,
> And the first clouds and mountains seem the last:
> But, those attained, we tremble to survey
> The growing labours of the lengthened way,
> The increasing prospect tires our wandering eyes,
> Hills peep o'er hills, and Alps on Alps arise!

Johnson praises the simile as having 'no useless parts' and yet affording 'a striking picture by itself'. It 'makes the foregoing position better understood, and enables it to take faster hold on the attention; it assists the apprehension and elevates the fancy' (Archer-Hind 1925, II, pp. 218–19). It fulfils, that is to say, Johnson's recipe for a 'perfect simile', one that both illustrates and ennobles the subject, showing it 'to the understanding in a clearer view' and 'to the fancy with greater dignity' (Ibid., p. 218). It clarifies by visualizing sharply the idea being presented: that each discovery reveals beyond it an even steeper challenge. It dignifies the idea by referencing it to the grandest of the works of Nature. It is, indeed, 'Nature methodized'.

With equal precision, David B. Morris directs us to how Pope's Alps lines represent and ennoble the heart of his endeavour. The critical method Pope is so illuminating is cognate with the artistic method. The act of reading and the act of criticism lie in our constantly evolving skills of judgment. 'Judgment' is the poem's key term. Variations of the word (noun, verb etc.) occur no fewer than twenty-four times, six within the first thirty-five lines. Judgment is an art, a skill, like any other; and, like any other, it is constantly confronted with new challenges, new peaks to scale. It is a process, not a static application of a slide-rule. It exists, like art, in 'the fluctuating realm of time and change' (Morris 1984, pp. 55–56). It is, therefore, an aspect of what lies at the very core of Enlightenment epistemology. It is, Morris adds, 'a method of reasoning appropriate to a science of uncertainties'. We do not know what will open up beyond that with which we are presently engaged. That is the challenge, but also the excitement, of criticism.

We have now entered what Pope himself in his introductory analysis of the contents of the poem (added later, in 1736) designates as part two of a tripartite structure: lines 1–200, 201–559, and 560–744. The observations on Nature with which we have been principally concerned so far are the necessary spring from which flow the later sections. Now Pope provides us with the consequences for the practice of criticism.

Lines 243–52

> In wit, as nature, what affects our hearts
> Is not the exactness of peculiar parts;
> 'Tis not a lip, or eye, we beauty call,
> But the joint force and full result of all.
> Thus when we view some well-proportioned dome,
> (The world's just wonder, and even thine, O Rome!)
> No single parts unequally surprise,
> All comes united to the admiring eyes;
> No monstrous height, or breadth, or length appear;
> The whole at once is bold, and regular.

Just as complete works of art should harmonize with the world around them, so each component of a work of art should combine with its fellow parts. Johnson proposes that every word should contribute seamlessly to make up a perfect simile. Nothing should be superfluous. The degree to which a writer's conception is realised in the work of literature is a reflection of the degree to which her or his expression is integrated. The core principle is linguistic and intellectual harmony: the 'propriety' of the work, its fitness to the purpose of communication. As Pope will put it later in his *Epistle to Burlington*, 'Parts answering parts shall slide into a whole' (line 66). The very line in which this assertion is made proceeds effortlessly, 'slides' with a sense of natural ease, towards its final word, 'whole'.

In this *Essay on Criticism* passage, the same argument is made more extensively. The word 'parts' occurs twice, but not in the balanced and tight integrity of a single phrase along the lines of 'parts answering parts'. Rather, Pope separates them so that each appears once in the two sentences (lines 244 and 249). 'Wit' is a simple word with a complex linguistic and significant history. Its source lies in synonyms and reflections of words meaning 'to know; knowledge'. Works of wit are thus expressions of the general knowledge of humankind. In the first sentence, human beauty is his brief analogy for the operation of wit. In the second sentence he switches to architecture for his comparison. In both sentences, the phrasing of 'parts' is made semantically similar through a repeated pattern of negative/adjective/noun: 'not ... peculiar [particular] parts'; 'No single parts'.

In each sentence, Pope's wording is made appropriate to his meaning. He breaks the line 'Tis not a lip, or eye, we beauty call' into three parts to form a four/two/four syllabic structure. The first comma separates two facial details from each other; the second separates both from the abstract noun 'beauty', which denotes totality. By contrast, its rhyming line 'But the joint force and full result of all' contains no divisive punctuation. Instead, it 'forcefully' combines rhythmically strong adjective/noun phrases before coming to rest at 'all': striding rather than sliding to a whole. The longer second sentence locates its version of the 'single'/'all' antithesis in the two lines of its middle couplet, between a euphonious presentation of its image ('when we ... well-proportioned ... world's ... wonder') and a final couplet which gathers the three dimensions (height/breadth/length) into a conclusive 'whole' uniting energy ('bold') with harmony ('regular'). Contrarieties are located within an entity concise and yet extensive enough to contain them. The two images together combine nature (facial, human beauty) and art (the dome of St Peter's), the sphere of human activity.

Lines 289–300

> Some to *conceit* alone their taste confine,
> And glittering thoughts struck out at every line;
> Pleased with a work where nothing's just or fit;
> One glaring chaos and wild heap of wit.
> Poets like painters, thus, unskilled to trace

> The naked nature and the living grace,
> With gold and jewels cover every part,
> And hide with ornaments their want of art.
> True wit is nature to advantage dressed,
> What oft was thought, but ne'er so well expressed;
> Something, whose truth convinced at sight we find,
> That gives us back the image of our mind.

The second part of *An Essay on Criticism* (lines 201–560) lists the kinds of details which critics with poor judgment pick out. Here Pope properly criticizes those who go to a poem looking only ('alone') for striking *conceits*: elaborate or fanciful images and figures of speech that aim to surprise and engage the reader's attention by means of their ingenuity. Such critics admire poems for their showiness, their 'glittering thoughts', which try to blind the reader by their 'glaring' self-consciousness. Poets who write like this are like painters who, lacking the skill to depict truthfully nature as it really is ('naked nature'), attempt to cover up their deficiencies with shiny jewel-like ornamentation. Perhaps Pope has at the back of his mind the fallen Adam and Eve in *Paradise Lost*, who, now ashamed of their naked innocence, try to cover themselves up with leaves.

Throughout, Pope defines the alternative to such selectivity or partiality. A 'work where nothing's just or fit' concisely defines the ideal qualities: rightness—truth to nature—and appropriateness—the harmonious relationship between parts and the whole. The positive words 'wit' and 'art' are placed at key points in the unfolding argument: simultaneously at the ends of lines, couplets, quartets, and sentences (see how 'wit' chimes with 'fit' in lines 291–92; and how 'art' concludes the second quartet of lines). Line 297 then begins the third quartet by picking up 'wit' and transforming it from its discordant perversion 'wild heap of wit' ('heap' here guides 'wild' to its sense of 'disorderly') to 'True wit'.

These four lines, 297–300, constitute a central statement of the nature of art, and so the foundation of positive criticism. They have frequently been misread. They are not advocating anything as simple and restricted as 'dressing up' commonplaces to make them look good. The word 'dressed' derives from the Old French verb *dresser*, meaning 'to arrange', 'to order'. In common usage, the verb has tended to move towards a more simple sense of merely putting on clothes or ornaments. But its foundational significance is more complex. The *Oxford English Dictionary* defines 'dress' (v. 5) as to 'make ready or prepare for any purpose; to order, arrange, draw up', as dressed crab is food carefully prepared for presentation at table. Pope is continuing to develop his original nature/art distinction: the former is the source of everything; the latter is the sphere of human activity and creativity, whose aim is to reflect in forms of expression (painting, poetry etc.) the essential principles of nature. Dressing nature to advantage is bringing out the order, the energy, and the beauty of nature. Only a good knowledge ('wit') of nature can provide the basis for such an artistic activity. Good knowledge can only derive from often repeated experience of nature and frequent reflection on that experience: 'what oft was thought'. The really fine artist will look for the best and most accurate language: 'ne'er so well expressed'. When such a union of deep reflection, multiple experience and a high level of artistry is achieved, it strikes the reader (the critic) with immediate conviction: 'truth convinced at sight we find'. The poetry and the reader are thus brought into an intensely powerful imaginative harmony: poetry 'gives us back the image of our mind'. Compare what Samuel Johnson says about Thomas Gray's *Elegy Written in a Country Churchyard* (1751): it 'abounds with images which find a mirror in every mind, and with sentiments to which every bosom returns an echo'. He then adds that four stanzas of the poem 'are to me original: I have never seen the notions in any other place; yet he that reads them here, persuades himself that he has always felt them' (Archer-Hind 1925, II, p. 392). The poet has seen further into nature than the reader has. The truth he has seen is one that strikes the reader as both fresh and true. The critic acknowledges the dynamic quality of this artistic engagement in terms which are a tribute to humility, truth, and imagination: great art and great criticism.

Lines 729–34

> Such late was Walsh—the Muse's judge and friend,
> Who justly knew to blame or to commend;
> To failings mild, but zealous for desert;
> The clearest head, and the sincerest heart.
> This humble praise, lamented shade! receive,
> This praise at least a grateful Muse may give.

Talking of humility, this is the note Pope strikes in the concluding paragraph of *An Essay on Criticism*. William Walsh, a politician, poet and critic twenty-five years his senior, befriended and supported Pope when he was beginning his writing career (see Chapter 1). Walsh was a member of the Whig Kit Cat Club, and sufficiently well known to be included in the anthology of poets to which Johnson's *Lives* were written as prefaces; though, in truth, Johnson's life of Walsh is briefer than most, and is largely given over to Pope's gratitude to and respect for him. In August 1707, the nineteen-year-old Pope undertook the lengthy journey from Binfield to Abberley Lodge in Worcestershire, the Walsh family home. He stayed there several weeks, and then returned in September for what would prove to be a final opportunity (Walsh died in 1708) to converse at length and benefit from the older man's knowledge and advice (See Mack 1985, p. 116).

Pope's eulogy of Walsh at the close of *An Essay on Criticism* may be seen as fit tribute to a genuine counsellor and mentor. The lines possess the economy, clarity, and elegance of a heartfelt and truthful epitaph. This is not the time for self-indulgence. Rather, Pope exemplifies the straightforward virtue of true gratitude to one whose advice, we gather, was the gift of an honourable and thoughtful man and teacher. Consider the exact placing of 'justly' in line 730, given quiet prominence before the verb it qualifies; the simple balance of 'to blame or to commend'; the extension of these antitheses into the following line's chiastic form, where 'mild' softens any potential for animosity implicit in 'blame' and 'failings', and 'zealous' corrects any tendency to deem directness in criticism a sign of coolness; and the limpid balance combined with utmost praise in 'The clearest head, and the sincerest heart'. This is tactful writing, not in any negative or even neutral sense, but in its adoption of the qualities of the man whom it defines.

At the same time, Pope's lines demonstrate phonetic artistry, which shapes them into a duly graceful testimony. Repeated, but not excessively prominent, /d/ and /t/ plosive consonants are softened by voiced /z/ sounds ('failings mild', 'zealous for desert'), which themselves culminate in the final couplet's concise version of a peroration's forceful repetition: 'This humble praise ... This praise ... a grateful Muse'. Note also the decorous manner in which a personal tribute is channelled through the voice of a generalized and personified Muse. Pope does not simply assert his gratitude; he demonstrates that he has learnt decorum, and learnt it well.

But why does Pope conclude in this deferential and serene manner a long poem which has aspired to more ambitious and far-reaching aims? The answer is that the second and third sections of the poem are deeply concerned to connect human judgment with a moral dimension in which friendship, candour, and loyalty are key defining qualities. This has immense consequences for the way in which Pope will shape his whole career, in which ethics lie philosophically central. The second section opens with a paragraph (lines 201–14) locating pride (the converse of humility) as the key cause of poor judgment. The third section begins by asserting that critics should observe a moral propriety: 'tis but half a judge's task, to know. / 'Tis not enough, taste, judgment, learning, join; / In all you speak, let truth and candour shine' (lines 561–63). Pope proceeds to map out a history of criticism from classical times to the present; and, in this roll-call of the greats, friendship is a surprisingly dominant quality. Horace, for example, 'Will, like a friend, familiarly convey / The truest notions in the easiest way' (lines 655–56). So, when Pope comes right up to date with his own experience, it is as 'the Muse's judge and friend' that he praises his mentor. Later, it will be Henry St John, Viscount Bolingbroke, who takes over the role of Pope's 'guide, philosopher and friend'. For a poet whose reputation in later years would become more and more indelibly associated with the art of satire, friendship was actually his recurrent theme and aim—however overtaken at times by opposite forces: 'Fools rush into my head, and so I write'. In *An Essay on Criticism* as a whole entity—and to see objects steadily and see them whole is its recurrent requirement—a good writer is one who holds everything together, is inclusive, and welcoming.

4. Windsor Forest

Examples: Lines 105, 111–18, 23–24, 327–28

Of all Pope's early poems, *Windsor Forest* (1713) most deliberately pursues the Virgilian sequence of *Pastorals*—artfully conventional nature poems—leading to *Georgics*—complex poems about labour in the contemporary countryside elevated by mythical and historical references. Virgil's *Georgics* concludes with a recollection of his youthful dallying with the arts of peaceful rural life, a time when shepherds sang under the shades of the spreading beech tree. Virgil here quotes the opening line of his first eclogue, 'Tityre, tu patulae recubans sub tegmine fagi' [Tityrus, you lie under the shade of a spreading beech]. Pope imitates Virgil's textual trick by making the final line in *Windsor Forest*, 'First in these fields I sung the sylvan strains', a quotation similar to his opening line of 'Spring': 'First in these fields I try the sylvan strains'.

Windsor Forest, then, from time to time pauses to pick up on other early poems. Its 'happy the man' passage (lines 235–58) defines the tasks of ideal retirement as including, among the 'duties of the wise and good', to 'observe a mean, be to himself a friend, / To follow nature, and regard his end' (lines 250–52). The idea of following nature is straight out of *An Essay on Criticism* (see line 68), and friendship is a recurrent theme of the third part of that poem, where Pope explores the nature of the true critic and the history of criticism. The exact chronology of these early poems is actually hard to determine, and Pope's own clarifications only muddy the waters. Openness and secrecy often jostled for priority in Pope's commentary on his writings, as in his life. *Windsor Forest* was published in 1713, and the latter part, in which the Treaty of Utrecht is celebrated, is usually taken to date from some time in 1712 despite Pope's own note giving 1710 as the date for that later section, lines 291 onwards.

When exactly the earlier sections were written remains obscure, and, in any case, Pope was an assiduous reviser of his work. So, it is a somewhat fruitless task to attempt a precise chronology. It may well be that, to some extent at least, these early works emerged from entwined plans and shared causes. Poets—like critics and readers—are allowed to be at work on several schemes at the same time, despite literary historians' fondness for clear chronology. Echoes across works may even have been planned from the outset, as the philosophical implications of Nature overlap with nature as literal environment.

Line 105

Thus (if small things we may with great compare)

Pope's reflections from work to work begin with small details. They invite readers to take a momentary pause in reading one poem to recall another. This line translates *Georgics*, book 4, line 176. It appears in the midst of a minute description of the natural activities and work of bees as an ingenious and complex model of an organised society: 'Non aliter, si parva licet componere magnis' [not otherwise, if it is permitted to compare small things with great]. Pope's borrowing introduces an analogy between a hunter seizing his prey and the military conquest of a town. His invocation of Virgil brings the authority of the classical master to bear on a disturbing comparison between the human world and that of our fellow animals. Pope's rural sports passage, which follows on and provides another version of the seasonal structure he employed in his *Pastorals*, permits running parallels between war and hunting, the past and present, and Normans and Stuarts. At a wider level, the idea of comparing 'small' with 'great'—and often thereby opening up potential confusion between them—is taken up across poems. It is the source of the principal factor enabling Pope's mock-heroic poetry. For example, in canto 2 of *The Rape of the Lock*, Belinda's guardian sylph Ariel ponders what 'dire disaster' may threaten her on this day: 'Whether the nymph shall break Diana's law, / Or some frail china jar receive a flaw' (lines 103–06). At first sight, this reads as bathos, the second line's triviality a descent from the first's seriousness. Will she lose her chastity—a moral, physical and psychological action, even more so if we recognize the simmering potential danger implicit in the 'rape' of the poem's title (see Chapter 5)—or will an ornament be slightly damaged? But if the two lines are taken together, as their composition of a rhyming couplet virtually necessitates, are we to take the outcome to be comparison rather than contrast? In the decorative and glittering world of Hampton Court, human beings flirt with metamorphosis into exotic and valuable commodities, and a 'flaw' may be both a physical rent and a moral failing. The couplet's second line may be read as a metaphorical expression of its first as easily as a contrast to it.

Windsor Forest's autumnal hunting expedition is set alongside the capture of 'some thoughtless town' by British troops. Is the entrapment of a game-bird a relatively trivial incident when set against, say, the seizing of Gibraltar in the War of Spanish Succession? Are not the conflicts of the Marlborough campaigns on an altogether greater level, in size and significance? Or are they really, as Pope's line proposes, events that, however different in scale, invite comparison as being expressions of a similar human trait: an impulse to violence?

Lines 111–18

> See! from the brake the whirring pheasant springs,
> And mounts exulting on triumphant wings:
> Short is his joy; he feels the fiery wound,
> Flutters in blood, and panting beats the ground.
> Ah! what avail his glossy, varying dyes,
> His purple crest, and scarlet-circled eyes,
> The vivid green his shining plumes unfold,
> His painted wings, and breast that flames with gold?

Here is destruction in action. The verse-paragraph sharply sets up the hunter's killing of a pheasant as both an example and an emblem of the human world's arbitrary and savage attack on what nature has designed as beautiful and full of life. The poem intensely and precisely describes its object for its own sake, but it also implies through it a wider 'general truth' (Brower 1963, p. 54). As he often does, Pope divides his eight lines into two quartets, each opening with a monosyllabic exclamation, the first excitedly demanding that we bear witness, the second, in contrast, lamenting for loss.

He ensures that his emblematic image packs a strong punch by filling the lines with reiterative and emphatic forms of language. In the first couplet, the verbs are dynamic and vigorous: 'springs', 'mounts'. The participial qualifiers are full of motion: 'whirring' denotes the sound of the bird's rapidly beating wings, and 'exulting' conveys vehement joy combined with energetic action (the Latin root of the word is 'saltare', 'to leap'). The trisyllabic adjective 'triumphant' encapsulates that glorious moment, which is at once demolished by a cruel stress on 'Short' and this couplet's monosyllabic economy. It then builds up a sequence of cumulatively forceful alliterative words: 'feels', 'fiery', 'Flutters', 'blood', 'beats'. Within four lines, the pheasant's leap for joy ends by beating the ground.

The second quartet loads its description with vibrant colour, as if a pre-run for Keats's intense delineation of the serpent in the first part of his *Lamia* (1820; lines 47–56): 'glossy', 'purple', 'scarlet', 'vivid green', 'shining', 'flames with gold'. These are all designed to intensify effect through heightening of language: the greater the beauty of life, the more distressing and shameful it is for that life to be wantonly destroyed. The rhetorical question ('Ah! what avail ...') picks up a celebrated equivalent, a dying ox in Virgil's third *Georgic*: 'quid labor aut benefacta iuvant?' (line 525) [what do his toil or good deeds avail him?]. There, the ox dies in the act of labouring in the fields for human benefit; here, still worse, the pheasant is an arbitrary victim of mere human sport.

However, *Windsor Forest* is about more than killing. It opens with a long paragraph devoted to a rhapsodic description of the varied landscape of Windsor Forest itself, which is—idealistically, some might say outrageously—likened to the paradisal 'groves of Eden' (line 7). Harmony is now the keynote. For example, the following couplet presents a concise account of a prospect from the forest to far hills:

Lines 23–24

> Here in full light the russet plains extend:
> There wrapped in clouds the blueish hills ascend.

Pope gives us a representation and poetic mirror of a landscape where opposites are gracefully and elegantly reconciled, visually and linguistically. Each term in the first line has its syntactic equivalent in the second: 'Here'/'There'; 'in full light'/'wrapped in clouds'; 'the russet plains'/'the blueish hills'; 'extend'/'ascend'. So exact is the equivalence that each stage of the lines' progress follows syllable for syllable. The rhyme couples each opposite—successively foreground/background; light/shade; earth-coloured horizontals/sky-coloured verticals; concluding verbs expressing stretching forward and upward—into an interlocking whole. Nature in this vision is a contemporary version of prelapsarian idealism. The world is not yet broken, or, rather, is restored to a long-lost state. Such present peace is the state of contemporary Britain, lines 41–42 declare:

> Rich Industry sits smiling on the plains,
> And peace and plenty tell, a STUART reigns.

In an earlier period of Norman rule, England was marred by all that is the opposite of the present state: discord, violence, and oppression. The next fifty lines of *Windsor Forest* give extended and judgemental expression to the savagery of these years of barbaric rule, before order is restored and 'Fair Liberty, Britannia's Goddess rears / Her cheerful head, and leads the golden years' (lines 91–92). *Windsor Forest* is a poem of stark contrasts, of which the historical is the most politically charged.

Lines 327–28

Much later, the poem returns to a clear and unambiguous assertion that the present, with its Stuart reign, has restored absolute harmony:

> At length great ANNA said—'Let Discord cease!'
> She said, the world obeyed, and all was peace!

Couplets 41–42 and 327–28, separated by nearly three hundred lines, thus constitute a statement and re-statement of the same polemical claim: that 'peace' is the current state because, and only because, Queen Anne is the active voice ('great ANNA said') of Stuart rule. In political terms, Pope is referring to the Treaty of Utrecht, signed on 11 April 1713, which ended the many years of European wars involving British participation through the Duke of Marlborough and his Whig supporters. Queen Anne's quasi-divine status is clearly present in the way in which Pope expresses her command that discord cease in an echo—dare one say, even close to a parody?—of the creative fiat in Genesis, chapter 1.

As we noted in this book's Introduction, the vividly contemporary world of *The Rape of the Lock*, where the heroine, Belinda, forms her resolution at the card table, presents an unambiguous parody: 'The skilful nymph reviews her force with care: / "Let spades be trumps!" she said, and trumps they were' (canto 3, lines 45–46. See also Chapter 5). From one perspective, hunting and card games are smaller, and so less significant, events than the battles to which they are compared. From another perspective, they embody similar human traits: violence, a compulsion to destruction. If the latter is true, then Queen Anne's 'Let Discord cease!' and Belinda's 'Let spades be trumps!' may be triumphant exclamations, but prove to be only partial or temporary resolutions. Discord lives on in *Windsor Forest*'s hunting scenes, and in the 'rape' of Belinda's lock of hair.

5. The Rape of the Lock

Examples: Canto 1, lines 1–3, 7–8; Canto 3, lines 45–46, 105–12; Canto 2, lines 1–18; Canto 5, lines 9–34; Canto 3, lines 171–8; Canto 5, lines 123–32

The Rape of the Lock began life as an occasional poem. The occasion that prompted its composition was a suggestion made to Pope by his lifelong friend, John Caryll (see Erskine-Hill 1975, pp. 42–102). A quarrel had broken out between the Petre and Fermor families following Robert, Lord Petre's cutting off a lock of hair from the head of Arabella Fermor. Caryll proposed that a comic poem, 'to make a jest of it', might 'laugh them together again' (Spence, I, 1966, p. 44). Pope ran off a two-canto poem of 334 lines, and sent it to Caryll in September 1711. This was, most probably, the version published by the bookseller Bernard Lintot in a miscellany on 20 May 1712.

Pope claimed that the poem 'was well received and had its effect' (Ibid.), though we really only have his word for this. The poem did not go unremarked, however, as Joseph Addison noted it in *The Spectator* (no. 523, 30 October 1712) as a sign of 'rising genius among my countrymen'. Something prompted Pope to further work, perhaps a recognition that the poem had the makings of a longer, fully 'mock-heroic', version. He worked on a revision for a year or so, completing it in December 1713. This new five-canto poem of 794 lines, accompanied by six plates by Louis Du Guernier (see Halsband 1980), was published on 2 March 1714 and proved at once to be a great success. Many of the most admired sections first appeared in this extended version: the whole machinery of Ariel and his fellow sylphs, whose task is to protect and look after Belinda; Belinda's dressing-table scene; her journey down the Thames; the game of ombre; the cave of spleen episode.

Yet still, it seems, Pope was not satisfied. When *The Rape of the Lock* appeared in the 1717 collection of his *Works*, it included an additional passage early in canto 5. This is Clarissa's speech, based on that of Sarpedon to Glaucus in Homer's *Iliad* (see note on terminology later in this chapter and in Chapter 9).

The story the poem tells may be briefly summarized. Belinda, a fashionable young lady, is warned in her sleep by Ariel, her guardian 'sylph', of some dire event that will take place that day. She wakes and, in the finale of the first canto, prepares herself at her dressing-table for the day ahead. Canto 2 begins with Belinda sailing down the Thames, sylphs hovering around the sails. A Baron, desirous of her twin locks of hair, implores the powers of love for success. In canto 3, Belinda, having arrived at Hampton Court Palace, engages in ombre (a card-game) with the Baron and a third player. Belinda triumphantly wins the game. Coffee inspires the Baron to a new stratagem. As Belinda bends her head over her coffee, he cuts off one lock of hair with a pair of scissors. In canto 4, Umbriel, another spirit, descends to the cave of spleen and brings back a bag of sighs, sobs, and passions, which he opens over Belinda. An enraged Belinda laments the loss of her 'favourite curl'. The fifth and final canto begins with Clarissa's speech. This is ignored by the belles and beaux, who instead engage in a mock-battle. The poem ends with the lock of hair being metamorphosed into a star.

The narrative structure of the five cantos is chiastic. The outer cantos present reverse images of each other. The private order of Belinda's dressing in canto 1 is answered by the public disorder of canto 5's battle of the sexes. Each of these cantos has a lengthy speech at its beginning: Ariel on vanity and Clarissa on good sense. The description of the upper world inhabited by sylphs in canto 2 is matched by the underworld of gnomes in canto 4. In canto 2, beauty is powerful; in canto 4 its vulnerability is revealed. At the poem's heart, the third canto sets Belinda's triumphant victory at ombre against the loss of her lock of hair.

Canto 1, lines 1–3

Pope begins *The Rape of the Lock* with a couplet which cannot make up its mind or, perhaps more accurately, a couplet about which we cannot make up our minds. It seems to change shape depending on the angle from which we look at it. When it first saw the light of day, in the two-canto 1712 version, it ran thus:

> What dire offence from amorous causes springs,
> What mighty quarrels rise from trivial things,
> I sing

To a considerable extent, this carries the swagger of an epic opening. The two lines of the couplet march in step, locked together by the exclamatory anaphora ('What ...'), neither having time for a caesura. If they do allow an instant to take breath, it is before the parallel prepositional phrases ('from ...'), the change from a four/six syllabic form in line 1 to a six/four form in line 2 serving to enclose the couplet in a rhythmically satisfying four/six/six/four structure. The rhyme, of course, does the rest; save only that the final punctuation invites a pause before the unmistakably epic formula 'I sing', which carries on euphoniously from the rhymes. This deferral of the main verb until after the announcement of what is to be sung neatly occupies middle ground between the economical opening of Virgil's *Aeneid* ('arma virumque cano' [arms and the man I sing]) and the more expansive blank verse rhetoric of Milton's *Paradise Lost*, where the grand subject-matter fills out five lines before the poem releases its invocation ('Sing, heavenly muse').

The rhythmic majesty of the couplet is, at first, matched by equivalently assertive vocabulary. 'Dire' has at its etymological core a particularly rigorous meaning. The Latin adjective 'dirus' signifies something fearful, something awful in the proper sense of invoking awe; applied to the language of augury it meant ominous, ill-omened. As a plural noun, *dira* or *dirae*, the word was used as an appellation of the Furies, those who brought with them portents of disaster. Such connotations were maintained well into the eighteenth century. Samuel Johnson's *Dictionary* (1755) defined 'dire' as 'Dreadful, dismal, mournful, horrible, terrible, evil in a great degree'. These are 'mighty' signals, as Pope's second line's parallel adjective describes the outcome. The verbs in both lines are appropriately coupled in their forcefulness, and in their firm foundation in causality. The 'dire offence' and the 'mighty quarrels' erupt energetically from their sources.

And yet. Is there something a shade inadequate about the word 'quarrels'? A shade juvenile or, at least, immature? Would, say, 'strife' seem more in keeping with the level of high seriousness conveyed by the other words? Or, given that we need a disyllable, 'contests'? Did such a thought occur to Pope himself when he came, in 1714, to raise his two-canto structure to a fuller, more crowded, five-canto narrative? Sure enough, in that rendition, we find that 'mighty quarrels' has become 'mighty contests'. Otherwise, the couplet remains the same.

And yet, what about the phrase 'amorous causes'? Does that really maintain the ominous level of 'dire'? It was in 1713, while Pope was busily upgrading the poem, that he committed himself to producing a verse translation of the whole of the *Iliad*. Put Homer's militaristic, not to say relentlessly violent, epic alongside *The Rape of the Lock*, and what ensues? Pope's version opens: 'Achilles' wrath, to Greece the direful spring / Of woes unnumbered, heavenly goddess, sing!'

The overlap in vocabulary is striking: the phrase 'direful spring' brings together the 'dire' and 'springs' of *The Rape of the Lock*, simply changing the grammatical forms. 'Wrath' maintains a level of high seriousness: more biblical than, say, 'anger'. 'Woes unnumbered' draws attention to consequences rather than causes through a Miltonic inversion of adjective and noun, and an impressive juxtaposition of monosyllabic and trisyllabic pitched at a solemn level. Pope repeats the word 'wrath' in the third line, and the seventh line expresses the poem's initial contest in the clause 'Since great Achilles and Atrides [that is, the Greek commander Agamemnon] strove'. The fifth couplet again uses repetition with grammatical variation for purposes of thunderous emphasis: 'Declare, O Muse! in what ill-fated hour / Sprung the fierce strife'. This is no mere 'quarrel', and there is no reference to anything like an 'amorous cause'. Instead, the range of reference is consistently masculine and aggressive.

And yet, the actual objects of the violent contest are revealed, beginning in the eighth couplet of Pope's translation, to be female prizes of war. As in the Homeric original, the name of the first is suppressed in favour of the 'captive daughter' of Chryses, so maintaining a wholly male emphasis. Agamemnon, as the narrative proceeds, refuses to release Chryseis (her proper name) to her father, and, when Achilles argues for her release, threatens to seize Achilles' own prize, Briseis. These great generals, then, have their female captives. When Agamemnon, obliged to part with 'his' Chryseis, does indeed take Briseis from a furious Achilles, the latter retires from the field. All this, the action of the *Iliad*'s first book, takes place within a wider context: the convergence of Greek fleets and armies on plains before the city of Troy. Their aim is to force the release of Helen, wife of the Greek Menelaus, who has been seized by the Trojan Paris. Are these 'amorous causes'? In the context of mainstream epic and its masculine codes, would this be an understatement or a euphemism?

It is time to return to *The Rape of the Lock* and to complete the couplet. For, if 'amorous causes' is a questionable phrase, its equivalent in the second line, 'trivial things', opens up complete disparity. It is quite a descent from 'mighty' to 'trivial'; and 'things' is as hopelessly vague as 'causes' is logically precise. The vocabulary talks of rising, whereas Pope's placing of 'from trivial things' after the verb 'rise' weakens the grand rhythmic and syntactic parallel. Contrast, say, 'What mighty wars from trivial things arise.' The effect is to shake the structural relationship between the lines by introducing a chiasmus: 'from amorous causes springs'/'rise from trivial things'. It is of the nature of chiasmus to ask the reader how the syntax constructs the meaning. Here, the first line uses an 'ab' structure and the second a 'ba'. Does the rhetorical device expose contradiction (ab *versus* ba), or does the ab/ba pattern satisfyingly bring the syntax back to where it began?

The Rape of the Lock is subtitled 'Heroi-Comical', in imitation of its principal model, Nicolas Boileau's *Le Lutrin* ('The Lectern': 'poème héroi-comique', 1674–83). Boileau's six-book satire casts a comic light on ecclesiastical politics by applying a high and serious style to a trivial dispute in order to expose the absurdity and vanity of its participants. The genre works by simultaneously belittling and inflating. The style looks down on the content; the content is puffed up by the style. But, as the opening couplet of *The Rape of the Lock* demonstrates, Pope adds a subtler and more nuanced treatment to his vocabulary and syntax by introducing variations that further destabilize the narrative and the social and personal attitudes being displayed. Readers are frequently challenged by the shifting sands of Pope's style, seldom quite sure of their foothold. We shall now look at some examples of Pope's questioning procedures.

Canto 1, lines 7–8

Having assured us that 'Slight is the subject' (line 5), an assertion that echoes the bathetic phrase 'trivial things' in the opening couplet, Pope completes his introduction by giving us a foretaste of the events the poem will unfold. So,

> Say what strange motive, Goddess! could compel
> A well-bred lord to assault a gentle belle?

Strange indeed it must be, the exclamatory rhetoric insists. After all, good breeding guarantees good behaviour, does it not? As Oscar Wilde's Lady Bracknell declares, 'Untruthful! My nephew Algernon? Impossible! He is an Oxonian.' (*The Importance of Being Earnest*, 1895) But there it is, in the middle of the line: 'assault'. Pope is, of course, playing with the tone of voice, attributing to it a quality of mock-surprise that only serves to highlight the reality of male actions. 'Trivial thing'? Well, actually, that phrase itself has been undermined from the very outset. The poem's title announces its subject in stark terms. And it is no use trying to hide behind etymology. The Latin 'rapere' did indeed cover a range of nuances around the central idea of 'seizing', but sexual violence was certainly included; and, in English usage, the sexual sense went along with other forms of aggression from the start.

The actual event the poem narrates is the Baron's cutting off a lock of hair. As such, it is a belittlement of the seriousness of 'assault' and 'rape'. But, conversely, the vocabulary used conveys the highest degree of moral condemnation and physical actuality. This simultaneous lowering and heightening is mock-heroic's destabilization of perspective. We are asked, indeed obliged, to consider how easily or uneasily the deed itself—a deliberate act of violation of a female body—sits alongside that instability.

Canto 3, lines 45–46

> The skilful nymph reviews her force with care:
> 'Let spades be trumps!' she said, and trumps they were.

The chief set-piece in the third canto is the game played by Belinda and 'two adventurous knights' (line 26), one of whom is the Baron. Each player is dealt nine cards, and the winner is the one who takes the most tricks. The ombre (*hombre* is Spanish for 'man') is the player who has the option of naming the trump suit—in this round, it is Belinda. She wins the first four tricks, then the Baron wins the next four. The decisive ninth trick is triumphantly won by Belinda with her king of hearts.

The running mock-heroic joke is that a banal game of cards is described as if it were an actual battle joined by real kings, queens, knaves, and their troops. Each action is therefore elevated to a level of significance out of kilter with the trivial reality. Pope fills his lines with as many such high-flown fancies as he can. So here Belinda's hand of cards is a 'force'; her choice about which suit to declare as trumps requires skill and studious attention; that decision is announced as if it were a divine fiat, such as that in Genesis 1. 3 ('And God said, Let there be light'); and the effect of her exclamation is expressed as a sublimely concise demonstration of her supreme power ('and there was light').

All this is playfully absurd. It is of a piece with the original purpose of the poem: to 'make a jest' of the trivial event which set off a real quarrel between the Petre and Fermor families. The mock war that is a game of cards resembles a ridiculous enactment of a battle of the sexes (both Belinda's opponents, the baron and the anonymous third party, are men) which in canto 5 will degenerate into a farcical combat between belles and beaux.

And yet Pope's vivid and imaginative rendering of the trivial minutiae of the ludicrously inflated events invests them all with vivacity and sheer delight. The cumulative result is a comic mini-epic of its own. Yes, the poem is a satirical portrait of a society taking itself too seriously, of human beings imagining themselves to be hugely more significant than they are. But the poem also enters into the spirit of those people and the world they inhabit with a gusto that carries the reader along with its energy and untiring display. Take, for example, the brewing and consumption of coffee, which follows the game of ombre.

Canto 3, lines 105–12

> For lo! the board with cups and spoons is crowned,
> The berries crackle, and the mill turns round;
> On shining altars of Japan they raise
> The silver lamp; the fiery spirits blaze:
> From silver spouts the grateful liquors glide,

> While China's earth receives the smoking tide:
> At once they gratify their scent and taste,
> And frequent cups prolong the rich repast.

Poetic style here presents a veritable cornucopia of elevation. Periphrasis (or circumlocution) expands the event, while linguistic register raises it and felicitous phrasing renders it as smooth as the drink itself. Lacquered tables take on the air of exotic locations and religious rites. Flames are invigorated with animation and vitality. Attractiveness and costliness are given impetus by verbal and positional repetition: 'The silver lamp' / 'From silver spouts'. Scale is heightened by hyperbolic vocabulary: 'blaze', 'tide'. The close verbal relationship of 'grateful' and 'gratify' (both words derive from the Latin adjective 'gratus', meaning 'causing pleasure') echoes the blended sensory delights of scent and taste. Everything takes on the grandeur and impressiveness of a ritual; and everything flows with graceful ease. The line 'From silver spouts the grateful liquors glide', with especial appropriateness, glides across the page with a steady euphonious flow. The whole event is a miracle of 'taste', in every sense.

This all reflects the social situation in which the event takes place. Hampton Court Palace stands by the 'silver Thames' (canto 2, line 4) and possesses the prestige and power of a royal residence: 'Here thou, great Anna! whom three realms obey' (canto 3, line 7). Coffee-taking was still, in the early eighteenth century, an experience imbued with the savour of the remote and the valuable. The word coffee derives from Turkish. The drink is made by literal infusion, which acts as a metaphor for one culture being instilled into another. Pope's stylistic 'elevation' is thus generous testimony to the excitement of a wonderful alternative to common native practices. It is all gratifyingly extravagant and so deserves, indeed demands, a dignified manner. The hyperbole may expose pretentiousness and conspicuous consumption, but it also produces a delicious surface, a flow of language luxurious to the tongue. The verse is suffused with the associated pleasures of the event. If to its share some human errors fall, take but the cup, and, to quote from Pope's expansive description of the launching of Belinda on her voyage down the Thames to Hampton Court, 'you'll forget 'em all'. Here is that passage, with its colloquial ending.

Canto 2, lines 1–18

Not with more glories, in the ethereal plain,
The sun first rises o'er the purpled main,
Than, issuing forth, the rival of his beams
Launched on the bosom of the silver Thames.
Fair nymphs, and well-dressed youths around her shone,
But every eye was fixed on her alone.
On her white breast a sparkling cross she wore,
Which Jews might kiss, and infidels adore.
Her lively looks a sprightly mind disclose,
Quick as her eyes, and as unfixed as those:
Favours to none, to all she smiles extends;
Oft she rejects, but never once offends.
Bright as the sun, her eyes the gazers strike,
And, like the sun, they shine on all alike.
Yet graceful ease, and sweetness void of pride
Might hide her faults, if belles had faults to hide:
If to her share some female errors fall,
Look on her face, and you'll forget 'em all.

In a critique of what he saw as the monotony of Pope's versification, the nineteenth-century poet and essayist James Leigh Hunt cited this description of Belinda as an example of repetitive seesaw rhythm (Jones, Edmund D. 1916, p. 339).

Geoffrey Tillotson (1958, pp. 182–85) and Winifred Nowottny (1962, pp. 7–8) both defended Pope. The former noted that Leigh Hunt misrepresented the passage by ignoring some variations in punctuation. Nowottny added that such a (relatively)uniform passage runs contrary to Pope's customary attention to varied and astute versification, that the lines preceding and following do not share such sameness, and that the lines being criticized form a block that constitutes a single unit of meaning, a description of Belinda's person and demeanour. She further observed that the passage is narrating how 'beneath the outward animation of Belinda's looks there lies a level imperviousness, the even-handed indifference of the enthroned beauty to her rout of admirers'. So, the rhythmic repetition, which contrasts strongly with a high degree of linguistic vitality and variation in the lines, creates a sense of Belinda's bright vivacity—her inherent character—being contained and constricted by the frame within which it is placed. The seventh couplet, indeed, precisely and explicitly defines this very point:

> Bright as the sun, her eyes the gazers strike,
> And, like the sun, they shine on all alike.

Pope appears to go out of his way to choose the commonest possible simile ('banal', Nowottny calls it (p. 8)) and it simply shines, not even making the effort to beam, blaze, or glow. Having chosen a familiar image, Pope then ensures that his verb drains it of whatever energy it has. One might add that Pope even repeats the same simile in the same place in each line: 'Bright as the sun', 'And, like the sun'. Also, the rhymes are conspicuously contrary in force: 'strike', 'alike'. Vigour meets utter blandness. Her admirers are hit by Belinda's shining eyes, with the odd result of being 'struck' into the most passive of observers, 'gazers'. Belinda has the power to reduce everyone to ciphers.

Pope's description recalls one of Shakespeare's famous set-pieces, Enobarbus's account of Cleopatra's first appearance to Antony, sailing down the Nile (*Antony and Cleopatra*, II, ii): 'The barge she sat in, like a burnished throne, / Burned on the water'. Pope's noun 'gazers' adapts Enobarbus's verb, which concludes the voyage with its most extravagant conceit: Antony 'did sit alone, / Whistling to the air; which, but for vacancy, / Had gone to gaze on Cleopatra too, / And made a gap in nature.' Had it been allowed to by the laws of nature that prevent a vacuum, even the air would have left the shore and gone to join all the other gawping admirers of this ostentatious arrival. But there is one crucial difference between Shakespeare's purple passage and Pope's variation on it. Enobarbus draws out his description in order to make a point. To Maecenas' remark that Antony must now leave Cleopatra for good, Enobarbus famously retorts, 'Never! He will not. / Age cannot wither her, nor custom stale / Her infinite variety.' Cleopatra's dramatic, highly staged appearance is one aspect of her ability to contrive a self-image successfully designed to exercise complete mastery of her control of others. Her beauty is political. It is central to her statecraft, her manipulation of authority within an intensely patriarchal society, that of the Roman state and its empire. By contrast, Belinda—our modern Cleopatra—sails down the Thames towards a reversal of Cleopatra's power. Her brief moment of triumph is played out on a pathetically tiny battlefield, a card table. Her real defeat follows when the poem's central and metonymic act takes place: the Baron's cutting off of her lock of hair. There, Belinda's beauty is a sign of her weakness. She lacks the power to withstand, or even sense the danger of, male violence towards her female appearance. She lacks the astuteness that might ensure her victory in the battle of the sexes. Her voyage down the Thames demonstrates how her potential for vital energy is constrained by her lack of self-awareness and recognition of the unshakeable realities which encase all human, especially all female, actions. Clarissa's speech in canto 5, Pope's last addition to his poem, spells out those inevitable facts, the ineluctable limits on human freedom.

Canto 5, lines 9–34

'Say why are beauties praised and honoured most,
The wise man's passion, and the vain man's toast?
Why decked with all that land and sea afford,
Why angels called, and angel-like adored?
Why round our coaches crowd the white-gloved beaux,
Why bows the side-box from its inmost rows?
How vain are all these glories, all our pains,
Unless good sense preserve what beauty gains:
That men may say, when we the front-box grace,
Behold the first in virtue as in face!
Oh! if to dance all night, and dress all day,
Charmed the smallpox, or chased old age away;
Who would not scorn what housewife's cares produce,
Or who would learn one earthly thing of use?
To patch, nay ogle, might become a saint,
Nor could it sure be such a sin to paint.
But since, alas! Frail beauty must decay,
Curled or uncurled, since locks will turn to grey;
Since painted, or not painted, all shall fade,
And she who scorns a man, must die a maid;
What then remains but well our power to use,
And keep good-humour still whate'er we lose?
And trust me, dear! good-humour can prevail,
When airs, and flights, and screams, and scolding fail.
Beauties in vain their pretty eyes may roll;
Charms strike the sight, but merit wins the soul.'

Clarissa sets out her argument in twenty-six lines, the same length as Pope's translation of Sarpedon's speech to Glaucus in *The Iliad* (see Chapter 9). The structure is clear, measured, and rational, whereas it is surrounded by demonstrations of human irrationality culminating in the ludicrous battle of the belles and beaux that follows despite Clarissa's intervention. Four sections are readily identified (a–d).

(a) lines 9–14 (i. e. six lines)

Why do men so worship and adore beautiful women?

Male obeisance is rendered absurd by its excessive abasement, an affliction common to all men, from the 'wise' to the 'vain'. 'Vain' here carries its etymological sense of 'empty' (Latin 'vanus') as well as its general modern significance as a moral term. 'Wise' and 'vain' are thus antithetical: however full of knowledge or empty of sense men are, they all succumb. The extravagant absurdities of male behaviour fill the whole world. They scour the planet by land and sea in pursuit of all the precious resources they can find to adorn the objects of their adoration. They allocate to women semi-divine status. The rapid repetition of 'angel' in line four exposes the unthinking folly of such behaviour. They also treat women as special objects of attention in social situations, in perverse contradiction of the rationale of those situations. Surrounding coaches impede movement, which is their intended function. Theatre audiences ought to be looking at the stage. The absurdity is total: it is not only the front row that bows but all rows. To idolatry, then, we can add the madness of crowds. Clarissa's increasingly incredulous repetitions of 'why' dominate the lines: five times in six lines, four of them in the prominent position of the beginning of the line. Why on earth do they do it?

(b) lines 15–18 (i. e. four lines)

All this attention and glorification is in vain unless beauty is accompanied by good sense and virtue.

More vanity, again with the double sense: Clarissa is deftly driving home her principal 'moral'. Now she adds her approved alternatives to vanity in good sense and virtue, a judicious combination of the abstract ideal of the latter with the pragmatism of the former. But how realistic is this advice? How many men, given the wry observation of their behaviour in the preceding lines, are likely to be struck as much by virtue as by beauty?

The first ten lines, then, divide into six for the absurd veneration of physical attraction, four for the accompanying moral. The order proposes the latter as a proper counter to the former, but the number of lines stack up conversely. The six/four ratio reflects one of the common rhythmic divisions of iambic pentameters, so that (a) and (b) act as an extension of an individual line into syntactic sections. Clarissa is indeed in control of her speech.

(c) lines 19–24 (i. e. six lines)

> If devoting all one's time to pleasure could ward off disease and prevent aging, we would readily scorn humble diurnal tasks and ignore moral judgements of our behaviour.

The first couplet of this section ('Oh! if to dance all night, and dress all day, / Charmed the smallpox, or chased old age away') has been thoroughly and brilliantly analysed by A. D. Nuttall (1984, pp. 27–28) as a demonstration of Pope's mastery of multiple antitheses:

> If we take the smallest contrasts first, vigorously active dancing is contrasted with night (normally a time for sleeping), dressing (usually done before the day begins) is contrasted with the day, 'Charmed'... is contrasted with the disgusting smallpox, and the nimbleness of 'chased' contrasts with 'slow old Age'. Then dancing all night is contrasted with dressing all day, and the insinuating gentleness of charming away the smallpox is contrasted with the rough expulsion of old age. Finally, the entire idea of dancing all night and dressing all day (the first line) is set against certain grim consequences with which it is unable to deal in the second line.

Thus, the four half-lines contain their own antitheses; the two full lines are themselves antithetical; and the entire couplet consists of two antithetical lines, an inter-relationship pointed and heightened by the consonance of its rhyming ('day' / 'away'). Pope—and Clarissa—have managed to pack seven instances of antithesis into two lines of poetry and eighteen words.

There is, some might feel, a risk that such intensity of rhetoric might render the lines over-mechanical and reiterative. Pope is too acute and aware an artist to allow this to be the case. There are three ways in which he energizes, varies, and fills the lines with semantic vitality. Nuttall himself notes one of these: 'The terms of an antithesis may echo or contrast with one another. The poet has, so to speak, an unsymmetrical freedom within the formal symmetry of the method to vary echo with contrast or to conceal one within the other.' For example, the noun phrases 'all night' and 'all day', components of the linear antithesis of the full line 19, are in contrast; while the nouns in line 20 ('smallpox', 'old age') are more similar than different, as both bearing ill news for innocent, or naïve, youth: youth's a stuff will not endure, and disease can strike at any time. Pope writes in the knowledge that Lord Petre, whose treacherous act set the whole plot going, himself died of smallpox in 1713 at the age of twenty-three. Lady Mary Wortley Montagu, with whom Pope formed an ambiguous friendship about 1715 and fell out catastrophically in the 1720s, is famed for her importation from Constantinople of the method of inoculation against smallpox. A similar inoculation against old age has not been forthcoming, alas. Nuttall's crucial point is that antitheses can be formed of various shades of inter-relationship along a spectrum of possibilities, ranging from outright opposites to different nuances of similarity.

Pope's second procedure is metrical variety. Following on from the six/four structure of the first ten lines of the speech, the eleventh (line 19) begins with a half-line of six syllables and is completed by a half-line of four syllables: 'Oh! if to dance all night, / and dress all day'. The second line of the couplet reverses the pattern: 'Charmed the small pox, / or chased old age away'. He thereby produces a rhythmical chiasmus (six, four, four, six), a rhetorical variant on the simple antithetical patterns composing the meaning of the couplet. Further, the two lines demonstrate rhythmical fluidity in different ways. Line 19 can be spoken or read with a regular iambic beat, but the initial exclamatory 'Oh!' pulls some degree of stress towards itself ('Listen!'), and the repetition of 'all' invites another degree of stress to act in counterpoint to regular iambics. Line 20 opens with a strongly accented verb, 'Charmed' and proceeds through a disyllabic word, 'smallpox', in which both parts call for some—if not quite an equal—amount of stress; its second half then has a noun-phrase, 'old age', which again presents equal emphases. The entire couplet is an intricate and aurally stimulating dance.

The third energizing force in the couplet involves meaning and sounds. Nuttall reads the verbs 'Charmed' and 'chased' as an antithesis, describing the first as 'insinuating gentleness' and the second as 'rough expulsion'. However, the two actions are more closely bound together than his interpretation suggests. Pope hints at this through obvious alliteration and grammatical fluidity. The latter involves the adverb 'away', which concludes the line and includes the couplet's rhyme. It can be read as qualifying either just the verb 'chased' or both verbs: 'charmed the small pox / chased old age away', or 'charmed the small pox [away] / chased old age away'.

The *OED* compilers were sufficiently convinced that the latter is the correct, or at least a correct, reading to cite Pope's couplet as an illustration of the usage of the extended 'charm away' (*OED*, 'charm' v. 1c). Pope further intimates a semantic linking of the two actions by the repeated /l/ sounds in the objects of the verbs ('smallpox', 'old age'), which discreetly follow up the more emphatic 'all/all' repetition in the first line and help to bind the couplet together aurally. Also, the verbs in that first line are semantically linked: the reason that all day is spent in dressing is to prepare for the dance. This is not to contradict Nuttall's interpretation, but to add to it. Pope's couplet is resonant with multiple meanings. As William Empson observes when commenting on the slide in meaning from 'charmed' to 'charmed away', these slight variations of suggestion add vivacity to the line (1953, p. 72).

(d) lines 25–34 (i. e. ten lines)

> But because our beauty will, however we try to enhance and preserve it, fade with time, all we can do is to retain our good humour and trust to merit rather than appearance.

Clarissa's emphatic opening conjunction, 'But', indicates the turn in her argument towards its principal conclusion. All dreams of eternal youth become insubstantial when we are obliged to confront waking reality. Her language brooks no qualification: 'frail beauty *must* decay', 'locks *will* turn to grey', 'all *shall* fade', '*must* die'. Her moral is sustained by emphatic repetition, both within these concluding lines ('good-humour' in lines 30 and 31) and in picking up on the earlier 'vain' (lines 10, 15, and 33), 'beauties' (lines 9 and 33) and 'charm' (lines 20 and 34). The entire speech is thus carefully held together.

The rational clarity of its structure produces a clear weighting towards its real point, its 'moral'. These ten lines are set against six lines of wishful thinking (section (c)). The longest sub-section is the speech's conclusion. Clarissa's moral proposes an appropriate and dignified response to the grim but unavoidable fact: the inevitability of time's destructive power. Clarissa's speech here alters the shape and tone of Sarpedon's. But the divergence is not that stark. The premise, after all, is the same—we are all mortal—so that both speeches share an elegiac basis; and one could say that each is, in its way, a logical or at least understandable reaction.

Finally, though, Clarissa's speech is ethically distant from Sarpedon's. In the world of the *Iliad*, 'honour' is unremitting in its demands on the warrior, and it is determinedly male-centred. Something very different is required in the modern world: a new and mature morality, and one that is female-centred. Men behave absurdly, but wise women will not be fooled into falling for short-sighted and shallow solutions. Men's attribution of 'honour' to superficial beauty (line 9) will not last. Were we to change the word slightly to 'humour', an extensive shift would be effected: a muted conclusion, perhaps, but a truer one.

Note on Terminology

A note on Clarissa's speech, added by Pope in later editions, calls it a 'parody' of Sarpedon's speech to Glaucus. The 1714 edition subtitles the poem an 'heroi-comical poem'. As we have noted, this echoes the subtitle to Boileau's *Le Lutrin*, 'Poème Héroi-Comique'. Boileau's poem was the most substantial model for *The Rape of the Lock*, and the strongest influence on what became a small-scale genre of similar poems, such as Samuel Garth's *Dispensary* (1699). In his prefatory address, 'Au lecteur', to the 1674 publication of the first four *chants*, or cantos, Boileau described his poem as 'un burlesque nouveau', in which, unlike earlier burlesques where the characters of epic (such as Dido and Aeneas) were belittled by being made to speak 'comme des harengères et des crocheteurs' [like fishwives and picklocks], ordinary or even low characters would be given the language and register of figures from heroic and epic verse.

A burlesque conventionally derides 'high' art by demeaning the speech and actions of its heroes and heroines. A parody, as normally defined, is also about ridiculing its victims—individual works or authors, or whole genres—by comic imitation of their style through exaggeration or application to inappropriate subjects.

It is all a little confusing, especially as Clarissa's speech can hardly be seen as mocking Sarpedon's. It may undermine Homer's ethos by implying that the heroic code his character enunciates is out of date or no longer ethically relevant, but Clarissa's speech is at least equally dignified and serious; and, as we have seen, remarkable for its rhetorical, structural, and stylistic richness. It is about transferring the ethos of one moral code to another, one that represents updated, eighteenth-century and enlightened ethics. Such a view presumably underlies Reuben Brower's assertion that Pope, when he uses the word to refer to the genre of 'imitation', must mean 'parody 'in the sense of 'more or less faithful reproduction of a writer's style without lowering or burlesquing it' (Brower 1959, p. 284).

Such slipperiness of terminology is a useful reminder that it is usually unwise to allow it excessive powers of definition. Rather, terminology often reflects nuances of usage, and is more a useful guide than an absolute decree. *The Rape of the Lock* and *The Dunciad* are Pope's two great essays in the art of mock-heroic, or mock-epic (another commonly used term), and they do share some generic and stylistic features, such as comic or ludicrous versions of the noble material of epic. In *The Rape of the Lock*, the battle of the belles and beaux in canto 5 is such an event. But the tone and register of *The Dunciad* are notably distinct: darker, more savage, less playful. Both are comic but to different ends and with different means. In *The Rape of the Lock*, a two-way process applies: epic action is miniaturized, while the language used ranges from near-slang to dignified. Clarissa's speech may be seen—fittingly for the poem's last passage in terms of the date of its composition—as the crown in the poem's evolution from occasional light comedy to full-scale comedy of manners.

Canto 3, lines 171–78

'What time would spare, from steel receives its date,
And monuments, like men, submit to fate!

> Steel could the labour of the Gods destroy,
> And strike to dust the imperial towers of Troy;
> Steel could the works of mortal pride confound,
> And hew triumphal arches to the ground.
> What wonder then, fair nymph! thy hairs should feel
> The conquering force of unresisted steel?'

These exultant lines spoken by the Baron conclude the central canto of *The Rape of the Lock*, where Belinda has conquered in the miniature battle of the cardtable, and has then lost her 'best', her 'favourite curl' (canto 4, line 148) to the rapacious Baron, armed with a 'glittering forfex' (canto 3, line 147): a pair of scissors. That event is rendered by an intensive reiteration of the idea of fate: scissors are a 'fatal engine', Ariel's loss of power to protect Belinda sees him 'resigned to fate', and 'fate urged the shears'. An appeal to fate lies at the heart of epic. Dryden translates the opening line of Virgil's *Aeneid* as 'Arms and the man I sing, who forced by fate'. And now in these final lines of the canto 'monuments, like men, submit to fate'. This is epic's ultimate tragedy. Whatever great deeds we perform, however heroically we act, our mortality is inescapably the end.

So, too, in the world of mock-epic time acts as the inescapable path to loss, to mortality; except, of course, that it is all reduced in scale: wars to card games, swords to scissors, bodies to locks of hair. What is not reduced is the human reaction: hence the mock-epic gap between language and action. The last couplet in canto 3 represents this divergence: the loss here acknowledged is the lock of hair. Surround it, as language can, with the grand register of 'conquering force' (cf. the 'force' renewed by our skilful nymph in the form of her hand of playing cards), and the outcome is distance between words and actions, the bathos we have seen to be characteristic of mock-heroic.

Yet that last couplet comes to rest on the passage's key word, 'steel'. Indeed, 'steel' resounds through the lines with the force of swords beating on shields, its harsh 'st' sound reflecting its martial object and the events of epic where steel 'strike[s] to dust the imperial towers of Troy'. Does mock-epic inevitably bring to mind epic itself, sharing its ground and its language? Or is this to take it—and life—all too seriously? The final paragraphs of the whole poem suggest the latter by reverting to another classical paradigm, metamorphosis.

Canto 5, lines 123–32

> But trust the Muse—she saw it upward rise,
> Though marked by none but quick, poetic eyes:
> (So Rome's great founder to the heavens withdrew,
> To Proculus alone confessed in view)
> A sudden star, it shot through liquid air,
> And drew behind a radiant trail of hair.
> Not Berenice's locks first rose so bright,
> The heavens bespangling with dishevelled light.
> The sylphs behold it kindling as it flies,
> And pleased pursue its progress through the skies.

In this world of magical transformations, locks of hair are, like mythical heroes, elevated to something far grander and more beautiful than any mere earthly matters. Romulus, the supposed founder of the power of Rome, was transported to heaven and never seen again on earth save once to Julius Proculus (see Livy, *Ab Urbe Condita*, book 1). Berenice, the wife of Ptolemy III of Egypt, dedicated a lock of hair to ensure her husband's safe return from war. Her court astronomer let it be known that the hair had been metamorphosed into a constellation (*coma Berenices*). These myths, cognate with the transformative world of poetic licence, tell a very different story from those of dour martial epics. And they do so by another, far more attractive, form of elevation of language above mere reality. The 'Muse'—poetry itself—is imbued with the power of light and life. 'Poetic eyes' realize the force latent but imprisoned within Belinda sailing down the Thames. There, her 'lively looks' are 'quick as her eyes': quick in the sense of vitality, energy, rapidity, and of life itself. But, whereas Belinda's were fatally 'unfixed', poetry's eyes look on the beauty they create: a rising star, shooting through pure transparent ('liquid') air to form 'a radiant trail' in which 'bright' chimes with 'light' and 'flies' with 'skies'. This is the power of comedy, its creation of a world that is 'light and bright and sparkling', as Jane Austen characterized *Pride and Prejudice* (1813) in a letter to her sister Cassandra. At the same time, the best comedy uses 'shade ... anything that would form a contrast and bring the reader with increased delight to the playfulness and epigrammatism of the general style', as Jane Austen—playfully—went on to accuse her novel of lacking (Le Faye, letter 80, 1997, p. 203).

At the end, *The Rape of the Lock* has made up its mind. *The Rape of the Lock* is, wrote Samuel Johnson, 'universally allowed to be the most attractive of all ludicrous compositions' (Archer-Hind 1925, II, p. 220). It is so because of, not despite, its 'shades'. Its darkness is deeply disturbing. The epic world of male aggression and its direful codes of 'heroic' behaviour lurk behind the small-scale events of the poem. Like the goblins in Beethoven's fifth symphony as heard and interpreted by Helen Schlegel in chapter 5 of Forster's *Howards End* (1910), the poem's double focus—its radical generic uncertainty—keeps resounding in our ear before being swept away in the poem's finale. The goblins can always return. In the meantime, the comic Muse will prevail. Anyone for mock-heroic?

6. *Epistle to Mr Jervas*

Examples: Lines 13–14, 21–22, 39–46, 47–54

Pope's *Epistle to Mr Jervas* was first published in a 1716 edition of John Dryden's translation of Charles-Alphonse Dufresnoy's verse treatise *De Arte Graphica*. It is not the very first of his verse epistles to appear, as the *Epistle to Miss Blount, with the Works of Voiture* had been published in 1712 under the title *To a Young Lady*. However, both poems, together with the *Epistle to Miss Blount, on her Leaving the Town after the Coronation*, emerge from the same period of Pope's life. All three share a relaxed familiarity, a sense of friends engaged in amicable, civilized, and respectful interchange. We shall look more closely at the two Miss Blount poems when examining the later *Epistle to a Lady*, whose addressee is Martha Blount. The Jervas epistle serves as a good introduction to a genre which increasingly takes centre stage as Pope's writing career unfolds. The poem also belongs here because it continues topics that have emerged in the *Pastorals*, *An Essay on Criticism,* and *Windsor Forest*, notably friendship (the word 'friend' appears three times in the poem, at lines 1, 21, and 52), artistic apprenticeship, and mortality—the 'Et in Arcadia Ego' strain encountered in 'Winter'.

As a verse epistle, it takes its place within a classical and Renaissance tradition which combines, in varying degrees, elements of formality and informality. These include choice of verse form (for example, octosyllabic lines favour a more relaxed, even colloquial, mode of address than do decasyllabic lines), handling of verbal register along a spectrum of familiarity, tendency towards private confidences or public declarations, and how far a clearly defined structure is maintained.

Charles Jervas (1675–1739) was a portrait painter who had studied under Sir Godfrey Kneller. After Kneller's death in 1723—Pope wrote the epitaph for his tomb in Westminster Abbey—Jervas succeeded him as court painter. Acclaimed by Richard Steele in the fourth number of *The Tatler* (1709), Jervas probably met Pope through Whig connections. During 1713, Pope lived in Jervas's London home and took painting lessons from him. For a full examination of Pope's interest in and relationship with the visual arts, see Brownell (1978).

Lines 13–14

> Smit with the love of sister-arts we came,
> And met congenial, mingling flame with flame;

The *Epistle to Mr Jervas* testifies to a personal relationship and shared experiences resulting from mutual respect of an artist in one medium for a fellow-artist in another. The notion of poetry and painting as sister arts dates back to classical antiquity and was revived in the Renaissance. Dryden in an epistle to Sir Godfrey Kneller wrote that 'our arts are sisters' (line 89). For a full analysis of Dryden's contributions to the sister arts tradition, see Hagstrum 1958, chapter 7. The 'sister-arts' produce their mirror-image in two brothers in art, each of whose nature and enthusiasm reflects the other's. The two 'flames' are strands of a metaphorical thread which begins with 'Dryden's native fire' in the first paragraph (line 8) and continues into the third paragraph in 'Fired with ideas of fair Italy' (line 26). Each 'flame' is the dynamic result of 'love'. The two phrases containing these assertions of energy deriving from fellow-feeling begin and end the couplet: 'Smit with the love', 'mingling flame with flame'. Within them lie direct and unfussy verbs: 'we came', 'met'. Again, Pope works into his poem a significant linguistic sequence: forms of 'we' and 'our' occur eight times between lines 13 and 35. 'Congenial' combines adjectival and adverbial meanings to define Jervas and himself as kindred spirits who, working together, generate creative activity of a force consistent with 'flame'. Pope is saying that he and Jervas were both fired up by a spirit they recognized in each other. In the sister arts, two men discover brotherly affection and affinity.

Lines 21–22

> How oft review; each finding like a friend
> Something to blame, and something to commend?

As well as likeness, a strong element of integrity and individual autonomy is asserted. The paragraph that begins 'Smit with the love of sister-arts we came, / And met congenial, mingling flame with flame' ends with a staunchly honest corrective to such claims of intense fellow-feeling. This is the third and last of a series of couplets (lines 17–22) bound together by triple repetition of 'How oft' at the beginnings. The effect is cumulative and emphatic, and here adds an element of formal structure within generally relaxed communication. Pope's pattern is rigorously open-eyed and unsentimental. Where the first of the trio reads like a holiday diary ('How oft in pleasing tasks we wear the day, / While summer-suns roll unperceived away?') and the second attests to a growing creative partnership ('How oft our slowly-growing works impart, / While images reflect from art to art?'), the third couplet steps back in a gesture of objectivity and—in another sense—reflection. A modern cliché, 'critical friend', hovers over the main verb, 'review', with its connotations of full and objective judgment. And the balanced second line of the couplet represents a process of measured and equal honesty, an admirable and respectful confirmation that, after all, it is the two men's commitment to their art that takes precedence even over their strong admiration for each other as brothers in art.

Such clarity and honesty of judgment extend into the second section of the poem. Pope's warm conviction of the triumphant power and value of the arts attains its climax in the couplet 'Thence endless streams of fair ideas flow, / Strike in the sketch, or in the picture glow' (see lines 39–46, below). From this point, he modulates his tone from celebration to meditation. Pope displays an objectivity that brings a more measured, even humble, reflection on the limitations of art itself. The poem's finale, then, is an extended commentary on the wider, public rather than private, topic at the heart of the matter.

But, before we reach the epistle's solemn conclusion, the third and fourth paragraphs rhapsodically celebrate the inspiring influence of classical and Renaissance Rome and its artefacts on the imaginations of

Jervas and Pope, painter and poet. Here is the fourth, which opens with a reference to Dufresnoy's treatise.

Lines 39–46

> How finished with illustrious toil appears
> This small, well-polished gem, the work of years!
> Yet still how faint by precept is expressed
> The living image in the painter's breast?
> Thence endless streams of fair ideas flow,
> Strike in the sketch, or in the picture glow;
> Thence beauty, waking all her forms, supplies
> An angel's sweetness, or Bridgewater's eyes.

How admirable, Pope is saying, how carefully worked, how preciously prepared is Dufresnoy's poem! But, however well written, no verbal set of instructions can possibly match the sheer vitality of great visual art. Verbs and participles carry the main line of energy: 'living', 'flow', 'Strike', glow', 'waking'. The third couplet is the climax, its very form embodying Pope's warm conviction of the triumphant power and value of the painter's art. 'Thence endless streams of fair ideas flow' expansively fills out a complete line without a pause, its metaphor expressive of unstoppable continuity and its phonic move from short vowels ('Thence endless') to long ('streams ... fair ideas flow') giving physical force to pent-up energy being released. The succession of /v/ and /f/ sounds ('of fair ... flow') helps hold together that moment of relaxation. In contrast, the line's rhyming partner, 'Strike in the sketch, or in the picture glow', uses chiasmus to distinguish between the vigour of the preliminary drawing and the luminous colour of the final painting. So, the two verbs dominate: 'Strike' being given added emphasis by reversal of the regular iambic metre elsewhere retained and 'glow' attracting the element from its rhyming partner to express the liquidity of light.

However, despite all its evocation of life, and the power of art to convey a sense of life, there is one counterforce that cannot be resisted. The paragraph ecstatically ends with a focus on the semi-divine image of 'Bridgewater's eyes', a phrase which concisely (and conveniently) continues the liquid metaphor into naturally glowing light. But the woman herself—Elizabeth, Countess of Bridgewater, daughter of the famous Duke of Marlborough—has, even as Pope's epistle celebrates her name, recently succumbed to the deadly curse of smallpox. So, the poem's animated tone is equally suddenly brought to an untimely stop.

Lines 47–54

> Muse! at that name thy sacred sorrows shed,
> Those tears eternal, that embalm the dead:
> Call round her tomb each object of desire,
> Each purer frame informed with purer fire:
> Bid her be all that cheers or softens life,
> The tender sister, daughter, friend, and wife:
> Bid her be all that makes mankind adore;
> Then view this marble, and be vain no more!

Here, the first couplet's 'eternal' recalls the earlier 'endless', but those flowing streams are turned into tears. 'Embalm' then buries the departed within the unremittingly cold rhyme of 'shed'/'dead'. This, the fifth paragraph, is the poem's key transition. The 'name' Bridgewater brings the poem to its temporary halt, and death into the Arcadia of art.

Funereal images then suffuse the language. A melancholy succession of 'embalm', 'tomb', 'marble', marked by alliteration and long vowels, invites us to approach and 'read' the name on that marble tomb. It is Bridgewater, a woman whose demise demands the poet's invocation of a 'muse' of sorrows. The word 'name' is also the entire poem's final destination. It completes an epistle—an address from one living name to another, Pope to Jervas—which has celebrated the names of those distinguished artists (Raphael and company), contemporaries (Marlborough, Worsley), and poetic élite (Myra, the assumed name of the addressee of love lyrics by Pope's patron, George Granville; Pope's own 'Belinda' from *The Rape of the Lock*; and his actual muses, Teresa and Martha Blount), who people the poem with indelible bonds of art and life. Thomas R. Edwards trenchantly defines as a chief feature of Pope's poetic manner 'a balance between opposing feelings and points of view, a sustained mediation in the case of *Jervas*, between the idea that art is a consolation for time and the idea that art can preserve painfully little when held up against our personal losses' (Edwards 1963, p. 5). The poem's mostly celebratory mood thus ends in humility: 'Alas, how little from the grave we claim! / Thou but preserv'st a face, and I a name'.

7. Eloisa to Abelard

Examples: Lines 59–72, 85–98, 163–70, 263–76

Pope's longest and most turbulent essay in the Ovidian mode was first published in the 1717 *Works*. It is modelled on the *Heroides* (letters from heroines), one of which, *Sappho to Phaon*, Pope had earlier translated. *Eloisa to Abelard* could thus be seen as Pope's original contribution to, and development of, a genre he has already tested, and whose popularity among Ovid's poems from the Renaissance on was second only to that of the *Metamorphoses*. In choosing the story of Eloisa and Abelard, Pope also tuned into a narrative of long-acknowledged power. Peter Abelard was a twelfth-century French theologian who fell in love with his pupil Heloise. When their liaison was discovered, Abelard was castrated and entered monastic life, and Eloisa became a nun. Their letters were highly regarded from their Latin publication in 1616. Pope's source was a prose translation by John Hughes (1713), from a French version. His decision to take on Eloisa's voice makes this Pope's most remarkable essay in empathetic representation.

Lines 59–72

In this verse-paragraph, Eloisa reflects on how she fell in love with Abelard:

> Thou knowst how guiltless first I met thy flame,
> When love approached me under friendship's name;
> My fancy formed thee of angelic kind,
> Some emanation of the all-beauteous mind.
> Those smiling eyes, attempering every ray,
> Shone sweetly lambent with celestial day:
> Guiltless I gazed; heaven listened while you sung;

> And truths divine came mended from that tongue.
> From lips like those what precept failed to move?
> Too soon they taught me 'twas no sin to love:
> Back through the paths of pleasing sense I ran,
> Nor wished an angel whom I loved a man.
> Dim and remote the joys of saints I see,
> Nor envy them that heaven I lose for thee.

Eloisa here dramatically and viscerally narrates how, for her, Abelard began as an 'angelic' figure (line 61) but became something grander and more powerful—a man. This is the sheer audacity, indeed blasphemy, of Eloisa's testimony. Line 70 expresses her belief in the starkest and clearest terms: 'Nor wished an angel whom I loved a man'. Every word is a monosyllable except 'angel'. That word, originally a definition of Abelard's being, is now consigned to a negative by the first word in the line, 'Nor'; it is replaced by a transparent, frank, and simple statement of the new truth: 'whom I loved a man'. This clause balances the first in syllabic count and rhythmic emphasis: 'wíshed', 'ángel'/'lóved', 'mán'. The slide from 'angel' to 'man' is also phonically eased by the internal half-rhyme of 'an-gel' and 'man'. The change is effected by simply altering the pronunciation of a single vowel. As the Virgilian tag has it, 'facilis descensus averno' [easy is the descent to hell] (*Aeneid*, book 6, line 126), except that loss of heaven (line 72) is gain of love: hell has been displaced.

The middle couplet of the seven lies at the core not only of the paragraph but of the psychological truth behind Eloisa's innocent confession:

> Guiltless I gazed; heaven listened while you sung;
> And truths divine came mended from that tongue.

Abelard's beauty and power were simply greater than those of heaven. Grace and authority now live in a human voice, in human art. The rhyming of 'sung' and 'tongue' is the most daring element in Eloisa's profession, all the more so for the emphatic trochee (reversed iamb) with which the couplet begins: 'Gúiltless'. The subdued physical intimacy of 'tongue' is then exposed by the sensuous 'lips' that follow immediately (line 67). 'Flames' and 'lips' are two of the physically potent words that resound throughout *Eloisa to Abelard*. 'Tears', as we shall see, is another. This is a poem of extremes, obsessive in its repetitiveness. The process conveyed in Eloisa's narrative is that of a reverse metamorphosis. Man is not transformed into another part of creation, as in the pattern of Ovid's *Metamorphoses*, but re-emerges as a man from his previous semi-divine appearance. The imagined world of the saints recedes into a 'dim and remote' past (line 71), just as Abelard's true humanity is revealed once Eloisa's original formation of her 'fancy' (line 61) is shown to have been false.

Pope's theological audacity is matched by his linguistic inventiveness. The *Oxford English Dictionary* cites lines 63 and 64 as examples of the use of 'attemper' to mean 'modify the temperature of', and of 'lambent' to mean 'emitting, or suffused with, a soft clear light' ('attemper' v. sense 2). 'Lambent' derives from the Latin verb 'lambere', meaning a flame licking, or playing lightly on, a surface without harming it. Pope's line is the *OED*'s first citation of this sense being applied to light radiating from a pair of eyes ('lambent' a. sense 1 c). He prepares us for this semantic originality by emphatically placing 'flame' as a rhyme-word in the paragraph's opening couplet. Abelard is the flame which alerts Eloisa's 'pleasing sense'. His 'smiling eyes' moderate the rays of the sun from which the life-force of creation emanates, rendering them 'sweetly lambent with celestial day'.

Lines 85–98

> Should at my feet the world's great master fall,
> Himself, his throne, his world, I'd scorn 'em all:
> Not Caesar's empress would I deign to prove;
> No, make me mistress to the man I love;
> If there be yet another name more free,
> More fond than mistress, make me that to thee!
> Oh happy state! when souls each other draw,
> When love is liberty, and nature, law:
> All then is full, possessing, and possessed,
> No craving void left aching in the breast:
> Even thought meets thought, ere from the lips it part,
> And each warm wish springs mutual from the heart.
> This sure is bliss (if bliss on earth there be)
> And once the lot of Abelard and me.

These lines represent the high-point of Eloisa's ecstatic hymn to human love.

Love is empowerment. The first two couplets drive home this message with all the force that contempt for conventional manifestations of power can summon. Think of the most dominant forms that temporal authority can take—'the world's great master', 'Caesar'. Think of the symbolic shapes of that power—'throne', 'world'. Think of worldly power as made female-specific—'empress': Caesar's fellow commander, and even, perhaps, commander of him. All are shoved aside in a demeaning *aphaeresis* (suppression of a letter or syllable at the beginning of a word): 'I'd scorn 'em all'. They are simply not worth the bother of a pretence of respect. The 'Not'/'No' emphatic starts to the following lines press home the message.

Love is freedom. An earlier pair of couplets (lines 73–76) declared 'How oft, when pressed to marriage, have I said, / Curse on all laws but those which love has made? / Love, free as air, at sight of human ties, / Spreads his light wings, and in a moment flies.' The present passage follows up this audacious affirmation with a blunt use and repetition of the word 'mistress'. The term here draws fully and unashamedly on its dual sense of a woman with authority over others and a woman who illicitly or unconventionally takes the place of a wife. The stakes are then further raised in lines 89–90: 'If there be yet another name more free, / More fond than mistress, make me that to thee!' The parallel phrases at the heart of the couplet, 'more free, / More fond', are particularly felicitous. The status of mistress is thereby endowed with the strongest possible affection. Sexual freedom is coterminous with the highest possible love. Why is this? Line 92, defining this 'happy state', supplies the answer: 'When love is liberty, and nature, law'. Social bonds, the ties represented in legal process, are inferior to those of 'nature'. Law encases, encumbers, limits; nature frees, lightens, releases. 'Love is liberty' is an aphorism that resounds with truly revolutionary fervour.

Love is mutuality. The effect of such freedom is equality. As neither partner is bound by external, artificial constraints, neither partner can be less or more free than the other. Freedom becomes an absolute, not a condition relative to circumstances or extrinsic pressures. This is a state in which 'souls each other draw' (line 91). 'All then is full, possessing, and possessed' (line 93) embodies in its structure this idea that love so freed becomes entirely defined by love itself: there is no room for further, peripheral matter. The first four words, 'All then is full', make up the simplest and yet most complete statement of the relationship, with 'all' and 'full' harmonizing appropriately. The metrical weight of the line is thrown onto the longer second half, which is filled out by the heavy active and passive forms of the same word, 'possessing' and 'possessed'. The opposite would be the devastating and elemental emptiness of a 'void'. Complete absorption of the two partners is the result, as Eloisa goes on to assert: 'And if I lose thy love, I lose my all' (line 118).

Lines 163–70

The poem now must change its notes to tragic. For loss of Abelard is indeed what has happened—Abelard as presence and sexual partner.

> But o'er the twilight groves and dusky caves,
> Long-sounding isles, and intermingled graves,
> Black Melancholy sits, and round her throws
> A death-like silence, and a dread repose:
> Her gloomy presence saddens all the scene,
> Shades every flower, and darkens every green,
> Deepens the murmur of the falling floods,
> And breathes a browner horror on the woods.

Loss of love is deprivation of light. Darkness takes over from 'celestial day' (line 64), filling the poem as it does the world because it *is* Eloisa's world: 'twilight', 'dusky', 'Black', 'gloomy', 'Shades', 'darkens', 'browner'. The deity who now inhabits and rules is Melancholy. Her entry is prepared for us as early as the third line of the poem: 'And ever-musing melancholy reigns'. Joseph Warton, the eighteenth-century critic who wrote the first full-length study of Pope's poetry, was sensitively tuned to Pope's painterly personification. Indeed, as a young man in the 1740s, Warton had written a volume of visually aware descriptive and reflective *Odes* (1746). 'The Image of the Goddess Melancholy sitting over the convent, and, as it were, expanding her dreadful wings over its whole circuit, and diffusing her gloom all around it, is truly sublime, and strongly conceived' (Warton 1806, I, p. 315; in Barnard, p. 405). Quoting Warton, Jean Hagstrum in *The Sister Arts*, his classic study of literary pictorialism in seventeenth- and eighteenth-century English poetry, notes how, in *Eloisa to Abelard*, Pope follows Ovid's *Heroides* in 'creating sympathetic landscape as a kind of visual accompaniment to the emotions'. Hagstrum goes on to observe that the potency of the goddess lies primarily in her role as an agent: 'She is not acted upon; she acts. She does not merely share the surrounding gloom; she creates it' (1958, pp. 218–20). Pope's succession of varied verbs translates agency into literary form: 'throws', 'saddens', 'Shades', 'darkens', 'Deepens', 'breathes'.

Pope has visited this territory before, in 'Winter', the fourth of his *Pastorals*. Thyrsis's lament for the loss of Daphne is replete with the language of melancholy that Eloisa now picks up:

> See gloomy clouds obscure the cheerful day (line 30)
>
> In hollow caves sweet Echo silent lies,
> Silent, or only to her name replies (lines 41–42)
>
> The balmy zephyrs, silent since her death (line 49)
>
> The trembling trees, in every plain and wood,
> Her fate remurmur to the silver flood (lines 63–64)
>
> The winds and trees and floods her death deplore (line 67)

Pastoral and pastoral elegy are intimately related: 'Et in Arcadia ego'— 'And I, death, am also in Arcady'. Line 166 from our present extract most forcefully imposes on the scene, and so on Eloisa's emotional experience, this intrusion of death into love's world, of elegy into the elegiac epistle: 'A death-like silence, and a dread repose'. Silence, as in 'Winter', is sensory deprivation, not the devotional solemnity due to the setting of a convent. 'Death' and 'dread' make the strongest phonetic connection in the line, combining plosive alliteration with repetition of the same short, uncompromising vowel. However, the line and the couplet come to a close on the softer sounds of 'repose' where the weight is on the long vowel and voiced /z/. The sequence of verbs that follows maintains this blending. For example, the final couplet's verbal parallel of 'Deepens' and 'breathes' chimes its long vowels and brings each word to a voiced ending. A veil is, as it were, spread over the harsh reality, as it so often is in pastoral elegy. The real agency and energy of the poem and of Eloisa's feelings are elsewhere.

Lines 263–76

> What scenes appear where'er I turn my view?
> The dear ideas, where I fly, pursue,
> Rise in the grove, before the altar rise,
> Stain all my soul, and wanton in my eyes.
> I waste the matin lamp in sighs for thee,
> Thy image steals between my God and me,
> Thy voice I seem in every hymn to hear,
> With every bead I drop too soft a tear.
> When from the censer clouds of fragrance roll,
> And swelling organs lift the rising soul,
> One thought of thee puts all the pomp to flight,
> Priests, tapers, temples, swim before my sight:
> In seas of flame my plunging soul is drowned,
> While altars blaze, and angels tremble round.

Another seven-couplet paragraph matches the first example we examined. Like that early passage, its dramatic effect is to shift the weight of Eloisa's emotion from the divine to the human. Within the convent, at the very holiest of its devotional places—its chapel, its altar—images of Abelard disrupt and disturb Eloisa's vain attempts to commit herself to rituals of worship, to channels of authorized veneration. The fourteen-line structure again allows Pope to locate at its heart the most direct and stark expression of the writer's helpless compulsion: 'Thy voice I seem in every hymn to hear, / With every bead I drop too soft a tear.' The constituent elements of divine worship ('every hymn', 'every bead') are enclosed within vivid and highly personal experience. The first-person pronoun governs each line, and the true object and expression of Eloisa's feelings begin and end the couplet: the 'voice' of Abelard, whose 'tongue' earlier was stronger than the word of God (line 66), and the tears she sheds, which punctuate the poem with the obsessive, incremental force we have earlier noted as a dominant feature of the poem's rhetoric.

The poem is marked by a violent clash of strong opposites, the elements of fire and water. Those recurrent tears are one expression of the latter, enhanced by semantically related images such as sighs. The 'flame' we encountered earlier, also carried in semantically related words such as 'fire' and 'blaze' (for example, the startling line 182:

'Love finds an altar for forbidden fires'), expresses the former. In the present paragraph, both converge in the final couplet: 'In seas of flame my plunging soul is drowned, / While altars blaze and angels tremble round.' As with the most powerful paradoxes, both elements emerge from the union with enhanced energy. Appurtenances of religion—priests, tapers, temples—are lost in the hallucinatory experience of the preceding line ('swim before my sight'). Water swells into 'seas' which drown Eloisa's theologically immortal part, her soul, a metaphor for overwhelming flames that encompass her and the altar before which she kneels.

Eloisa to Abelard is one long cry of painful and ecstatic conflict, sustained by the paradoxes typified by 'seas of flame'. Ovid is, of all classical poets, the one most bound to 'multiple levels of awareness', to perceptions of 'identity and the divided self' (Green, ed. 1982, p. 59). Has any of Ovid's English imitators expressed these divisions more forcefully, more dangerously, than Pope in this poem? Has any English poet voiced more violently a fusion of two selves: Eloisa the wife of Abelard and Eloisa the nun; Eloisa and Abelard, female and male, first- and second-person pronouns? 'Thee' and 'thy' resonate through the paragraph (lines 267, 268, 269, and 273), while the intense subjectivity of 'I' and 'my' counterpoints even more incessantly (lines 263, 264, 266, 267, 268, 269, 270, 274, and 275). For 'I'—Eloisa—and 'thou'—Abelard—are, at one and the same time, eternally separated and bound together on a wheel of fire.

8. *Elegy to the Memory of an Unfortunate Lady*

Examples: Lines 55–68, 75–82

The *Elegy to the Memory of an Unfortunate Lady* was first published in Pope's collected *Works* of 1717, under the title of *Verses to the Memory of an Unfortunate Lady*. It is fair to say that it has, from that first publication to the present day, proved to have been among the most disconcerting of his poems. When reading many critics and commentators, one detects varying degrees of discomfort and uncertainty of response. Some, even if they do not openly declare it, are unhappy about its subject: a woman's suicide. Others have been more concerned with attempting to trace—fruitlessly—the identity of the woman than with honestly reading the poem. The generally held view nowadays that no specific individual is meant has not, on the whole, been accompanied by a rigorous revaluation. Hence, its status within Pope's *oeuvre* has remained marginal, and its considerable emotional power insufficiently recognized.

Lines 55–68

The first half of the poem narrates the situation leading to the lady's suicide, but it does so in such an indirect and imprecise manner that many readers have been left frustrated and, therefore, unsympathetic. A consequence is that Pope's art in building from discretion of reference towards precision of emotion has been underestimated. From line 47, Pope's attention switches fully to the lady's present predicament: a dead woman who has lacked, and still does lack, her proper rites and the due attention of those once dear to her. Instead, her fate has been consigned to 'foreign hands'—the phrase is emphatically repeated at the beginning of lines 51, 52, and 53—and to 'strangers' (line 54). To this desolating circumstance, the poem responds with indignant rhetoric:

> What though no friends in sable weeds appear,
> Grieve for an hour, perhaps, then mourn a year,
> And bear about the mockery of woe
> To midnight dances, and the public show?
> What though no weeping loves thy ashes grace,
> Nor polished marble emulate thy face?
> What though no sacred earth allow thee room,
> Nor hallowed dirge be muttered o'er thy tomb?
>
> lines 55–62

The trio of 'What though?' openings reflects the preceding trio of 'foreign hands', answering it with bitterness rising to outrage. The lady has been deprived of 'friendly' mourners. Yes, but what commonly constitutes such mourning? Is it short-lived grief and the 'trappings and the suits of woe', as a reproachful Hamlet puts it to a court and to a mother celebrating a new marriage undertaken with unseemly haste (William Shakespeare, *Hamlet*, II. 2)? Hamlet's sardonic notes may be heard in the 'mockery' of 'midnight dances and the public show'. She has been deprived of a tomb. Yes, but what genuine feeling is symbolized in graven 'weepers' or a shiny image? Most daringly of all, what price the rites of a funeral dirge and 'sacred earth'? The poem's tone here rises to a challenging, even outrageous, level of sarcasm: the grudging 'allow thee room' is, one might say, close to the bone.

All this sets up the poem's emotionally charged and committed rejoinder:

> Yet shall thy grave with rising flowers be dressed,
> And the green turf lie lightly on thy breast:
> There shall the morn her earliest tears bestow,
> There the first roses of the year shall blow;
> While angels with their silver wings o'ershade
> The ground, now sacred by thy relics made.
>
> lines 63–68

This response, with its total change of mood, is morally greater than the appurtenances of conventional religious rituals because it is authentic, the grace of nature adorned by the elegance of art. Pastoral here rises to the level of elegy. Nature supplies the simple but delicate respect due to the victim of human impropriety and malignance. Nature itself will produce the flowers with which the lady's grave may properly be 'dressed'. The 'first roses of the year' will delicately acknowledge her youth, her untimely death in the morning of her life. Early dews will be the natural tears denied by human agency. In place of the artificiality of stately monument, 'green turf' will be her respectful and sensitive covering. Lying behind this line is the Roman epitaphic inscription 'sit tibi terra levis' (sttl), elaborated in Martial's epigram book 5, 34: 'mollia non rigidus caespes tegat ossa nec illi, / terra, gravis fueris: non fuit illa tibi' [may no hard turf cover her gentle bones; nor, earth, lie heavily on her: she was no heavy weight on thee]. Ben Jonson's tender epitaph *On My First Daughter* (1616) memorably translates these sentiments into the light octosyllabic couplet of its conclusion: 'This grave partakes the fleshly birth, / Which cover lightly, gentle earth'.

This tasteful tribute rises to its climax in its final couplet. The 'ground'—Martial's 'terra', Jonson's 'earth'—will itself be sanctified by the lady's presence. Pope's bitter reflection on the conventionally conceived 'sacred earth' (line 61) is transformed into its proper equivalent. Nature's holiness is the source of the truly angelic. All this lies in the future, in the triadic repetition of 'shall' (lines 63, 65, 66); but the last line sets it in the present: 'now'. And where is this present? In the poem itself. The lines that we read are the poetic epitaph for one meriting the angelic presence. The lady lives not only in some foreign field, but in the poem.

Lines 75–82

Pope takes a further emotional and graceful step to conclude the poem:

> Poets themselves must fall, like those they sung;
> Deaf the praised ear, and mute the tuneful tongue.
> Even he, whose soul now melts in mournful lays,
> Shall shortly want the generous tear he pays;
> Then from his closing eyes thy form shall part,
> And the last pang shall tear thee from his heart,
> Life's idle business at one gasp be o'er,
> The Muse forgot, and thou beloved no more!

The paragraph begins with the kind of structurally significant couplet characteristic of Pope's mature style. The caesuras fall at the sixth and then fourth syllables. Six-syllable half-lines thus begin and end the couplet, and these define the fate of poets: they 'must fall', leaving 'mute' their 'tuneful tongue'. The shorter half-lines are enclosed within, and these refer to their subjects whose praise they sung. Metrically and semantically, then, we have the gentler sort of chiasmus, in which the loved subject is metaphorically embraced by poets' voices. But each line as a totality is complementary in its meaning. Poets and those they sing are alike in their mortality, and in their consequent deprivation ('deaf', 'mute'). Strong opening trochees further link the lines ('Póets', 'Déaf the') to provide counterweight to the rhymes at the end.

This generalized couplet then 'melts' into the personal tones of the second: 'Even he'. At this point firm structure gives way to lyrical elegance, the rhythm merging with the mood conveyed and phonically expressed in the predominantly long vowels and liquid consonants ('soul', 'melts', 'mournful', 'lays'). These melancholy tones, however, make way in their turn for the painful third couplet. Intensely personal feeling is rendered by the familiar form of address ('thy', 'thee') and the violent verb, 'tear', which, cruelly and almost mockingly, re-voices the 'generous tear', turning sympathetic weeping to anguish. This is the ultimate act of enforced loss of memory: 'thou beloved no more' brings the language of intimacy ('thou') up against resonant emptiness. The bleakness of this finale is deeply personal and comes close to a refutation of the poem's title. Memory is lost at the very moment the poet joins the lady in death.

However, the poem itself still remains, and we need to balance the desolation of its final paragraph with the beauty and transfiguration of the lines examined above. Pope has already demonstrated, in his translation of Ovid's *Sappho to Phaon*, his knowledge of classical elegiacs. His epistolary *Eloisa to Abelard*, which also was published for the first time in the 1717 *Works* and shows every sign of having been written at a time near to the *Unfortunate Lady*, is an imaginative *tour de force* deriving from the same source as *Sappho to Phaon*: that is, Ovid's *Heroides*, letters written by heroines to their lovers.

The change in title of our present poem, from *Verses* to *Elegy*, points in the same direction. Pope is using the tradition of classical elegy to give voice both to female speakers and to a profoundly personal sympathy with female victims of desertion or the intensity of their own emotions. In classical elegy, the absence of a theological solution to the stark reality of human mortality means that resolution can be achieved only in a form which expresses and sets in equipoise both particular grief and universal resignation. Classical elegy is, in this way, profoundly humanist and vitally poetic. (See Williamson 1993, pp. 39–72 [esp. pp. 54–55].) Pope's conclusion to his *Elegy to the Memory of an Unfortunate Lady* writes of the poet's 'closing eyes' from which the lady's form 'shall part'. As Roger Lonsdale notes in his edition of *The Poems of Thomas Gray, William Collins, Oliver Goldsmith* (1969, p. 133n), English poetry's outstanding elegy, Thomas Gray's *Elegy Written in a Country Churchyard* (1751), picks this phrase up in a stanza at the core of its meaning:

> On some fond breast the parting soul relies,
> Some pious drops the closing eye requires;
> Even from the tomb the voice of nature cries,
> Even in our ashes live their wonted fires.
>
> lines 89–92

Pope's *Elegy* is his own sympathetic poetic response to, and expression of, that human requirement, which is given its supreme form in Gray's great poem.

9. Homer, *The Iliad*

Examples: Book 12, lines 371–96; Book 8, lines 371–74

Pope's translation of Homer's *Iliad* was printed by Bernard Lintot in instalments from 1715 to 1720. Pope organized a private subscription for its publication, attracting 575 names. It proved to be a reputational and financial success, establishing him as the foremost poet of his age and going much of the way to ensure his independence of means. Homer's *Odyssey* followed in 1725–26, with even more subscribers, though this time Pope himself translated only twelve books, the other twelve being quietly allotted to two assistants, William Broome and Elijah Fenton. The result was still a considerable sum in profits.

A fully representative account of the Homer translations would require a book of its own, and lies outside the remit of the present study. However, some indication of their quality will, I hope, provide at least an introductory sketch of Pope's achievement in what was his principal task over a decade. We shall therefore examine two examples from the *Iliad*, which represent two of the most important elements of Homer's epic.

The first, Sarpedon's speech to Glaucus on the battlefield in book 12, is of particular interest for two reasons. Pope had originally translated it, as part of a longer *Episode of Sarpedon*, in Jacob Tonson's 1709 *Miscellanies* (the collection in which his *Pastorals* also appeared) and incorporated it, with a few small changes, in the final complete *Iliad*. Secondly, it was the model for Clarissa's speech in *The Rape of the Lock*, which, as we have seen, Pope added to that poem in the 1717 *Works*.

Homer's *Iliad* is 'relentlessly martial in tone and detail' (Kirk 1985, p. 374). It derives from and enunciates a heroic code: status within a martial society is dependent on maintenance of specific (male) qualities by which, and by which alone, 'honour' is achieved. That status demands endurance of—indeed, pursuit of—every possible trial of those qualities. The greater the crisis, the more necessary a response. A man in a leadership position must—as a matter of duty, of self-esteem, and of social reputation—demonstrate that he can yet again rise to meet the new challenge.

The Iliad's 'style as a whole, together with the treatment of situations and characters, remains severe and dignified, as might be considered appropriate to a heroic age and a heroic standard of values' (Kirk 1985, p. 74). Nowhere is such a style exemplified more powerfully than in the Trojan Sarpedon's exhortatory oration to Glaucus. His speech is positioned at the mid-point of the poem, and constitutes the epic's classic definition of its code. The principal question at the heart of that code is 'What is a man's life worth?' (Jones, 2003, p. xiv). Pope's decision to translate this speech so early in his career is, as much as his *Pastorals*, a submission for recognition as the newly emergent voice in English poetics. Both are direct challenges to existing acknowledged excellence. In the case of Sarpedon's speech, that ground was held by Sir John Denham, whose *Cooper's Hill* (1642) also reigned supreme over the topographical/reflective poem. Pope's *Windsor Forest* (1713; see Chapter 4) would soon respectfully match and surpass that model as well. After three lines of introduction ('Thus to Glaucus spake / Divine Sarpedon, since he did not find / Others as great in place as great in mind.'), Denham's version of the speech occupies twenty-six lines:

> Above the rest why is our pomp, our power,
> Our flocks, our herds, and our possessions more?
> Why all the tributes land and sea affords,
> Heaped in great chargers, load our sumptuous boards?
> Our cheerful guests carouse the sparkling tears
> Of the rich grape, whilst music charms their ears.
> Why, as we pass, do those on Xanthus' shore
> As gods behold us, and as gods adore?
> But that, as well in danger as degree,
> We stand the first; that when our Licians see
> Our brave examples, they admiring say,
> Behold our gallant leaders! These are they
> Deserve the greatness, and unenvied stand,
> Since what they act transcends what they command.
> Could the declining of this fate (oh, friend!)
> Our date to immortality extend?

> Or if death sought not them who seek not death
> Would I advance? Or should my vainer breath
> With such a glorious folly these inspire?
> But since with Fortune Nature doth conspire,
> Since age, disease, or some less noble end,
> Though not less certain, doth our days attend;
> Since 'tis decreed, and to this period lead
> A thousand ways, the noblest path we'll tread,
> And bravely on till they, or we, or all,
> A common sacrifice to honour fall.

Denham's distinguished translation is marked by division of its argument into four clear stages, which follow Homer's original structure scrupulously while allowing the verse to breathe outwards to the measure of the heroic couplet mode that Denham, among others, did so much to normalize as the standard form for the age.

Lines 1–8 ('Above the rest ... as gods adore') define the status quo, that is the dominant positions presently occupied by Sarpedon and Glaucus in their realms; positions that are—here Denham follows Homer precisely—tantamount to apotheosis. This is the premise of which Sarpedon rhetorically demands the cause with a trio of 'why's (lines 1, 3, and 7). These directly follow Homer's original.

Lines 9–14 ('But that ... what they command') supply the answer to these rhetorical questions through an introductory 'But that'. Their status is the result of their deserts (line 13), realized by their continuing demonstration of merit through action (line 14). Denham's introduction of the sonorous idea of 'transcendence' is his inspired strengthening of the Homeric original.

Lines 15–19 ('Could the declining ... these inspire') switch the rhetoric to the subjunctive mode. 'Were it possible, my friend, that our renunciation of this status could perpetually defer our mortal end, would I propose that we should now advance to the front ranks of combat?'

Lines 20–26 ('But since ... honour fall) respond with another 'But' (line 20, echoing line 9). Another trio—the three 'since's (lines 20, 21, and 23) matching the 'why's in the opening section, but transforming them from questions to statements of causes derived from unquestionable facts—picks up the earlier statement of principle at the heart of the speech: 'Since what they act transcends what they command'. Just as our status has been earned by unwavering commitment to great action,

Sarpedon is saying, so the unyielding reality of our mortality demands that we choose the noblest mode of advancement towards death.

Pope had earlier praised Denham's 'strength'—his emphatic and concise style—in *An Essay on Criticism* (line 361). Here, the forceful propulsion and integration of his argument constitute a self-definition of the language required for a vigorous statement of the martial mode. Heroic couplets, we may say, embody the heroic code. They are the appropriate dress for a celebration of valour.

Pope's equivalent act of bravery is to march onto Denham's ground. It is no coincidence that his version of Sarpedon's speech is also of twenty-six lines.

Book 12, lines 371–96

'Why boast we, Glaucus! our extended reign,
Where Xanthus' streams enrich the Lycian plain?
Our numerous herds that range the fruitful field,
And hills where vines their purple harvest yield,
Our foaming bowls with purer nectar crowned,
Our feasts enhanced with music's sprightly sound?
Why on those shores are we with joy surveyed,
Admired as heroes, and as gods obeyed,
Unless great acts superior merit prove,
And vindicate the bounteous powers above?
'Tis ours, the dignity they give to grace;
The first in valour, as the first in place;
That when with wondering eyes our martial bands
Behold our deeds transcending our commands,
Such, they may cry, deserve the sovereign state,
Whom those that envy dare not imitate!
Could all our care elude the gloomy grave,
Which claims no less the fearful and the brave,
For lust of fame I should not vainly dare
In fighting fields, nor urge thy soul to war.
But since, alas! ignoble age must come,
Disease, and death's inexorable doom;
The life which others pay, let us bestow,
And give to fame what we to nature owe;
Brave, though we fall, and honoured if we live;
Or let us glory gain, or glory give!'

Pope clearly has learnt much from his predecessor: his implied claim to deserve equal status (let us say, his poetic equivalence of Glaucus's unspoken acceptance of Sarpedon's exhortatory challenge) entails not an evasion of, or alternative to, the example set by Denham but an inclusion of it and an extension of its literary achievement. Thus, he follows Denham in the basic structure of the speech but offers various forms of rhetorical strengthening or enhancement.

His opening 'Why' is taken direct from the triad of 'Why's in Denham's first section, and so sustains the Homeric original. But Pope restricts himself to one repetition, at line 377, and makes room, within the same number of lines as Denham (eight), for a greater degree of descriptive resonance. Denham's bare list of 'Our flocks, our herds, and our possessions' (line 2) becomes 'Our numerous herds that range the fruitful field' (line 373). The verb here adds not just variety in linguistic forms but an enriching sense of movement and extension (cf. 'extended', line 371), while the phrase 'fruitful field' acts as a poetically concentrated expression of creativity. The Trojan princes' rule is vitally productive, and Pope wants to emphasize this from the start, rather than wait, as Denham does, until his fourth line before expressing the richness of their lands ('load our sumptuous boards'). Pope's promotion of the river Xanthus from Denham's seventh line to his second, together with the added fecundity of the plural 'streams' and the verb 'enrich' (again, promoting Denham's 'rich' from his sixth line) provides further strengthening. Pope, moreover, adopts Denham's use of concise and expressive word order within lines and couplets but gradually enhances Denham's model in order to build towards the extraordinary dynamic at the climax of Sarpedon's speech. So, Pope takes Denham's 'As gods behold us, and as gods adore' (line 8) with its verbal parallelism and metrical equivalence (two stresses and five syllables in each half-line), and transmutes it into his own 'Admired as heroes, and as gods obeyed' (line 378). He retains his predecessor's parity of metre but alters the word-order to the sharper structure of a chiasmus. By so doing, he draws attention to his more discriminating variation of language than Denham's simple repetition of 'gods'. The Trojan leaders are loved as heroes (and so mortals), for which 'admired' is the *mot juste*, and are revered as gods (and so accorded immortal status), for which 'obeyed' is a verb that adds a touch of fear to veneration.

Pope then ensures that his verse is kept vibrant through modulation of syntax. For example, four lines further on, he deploys parallel rather than chiastic syntax in 'The first in valour, as the first in place' (line 382). Denham had (equally successfully) varied his verse, after the alliterative parallelism of 'as well in danger as degree', by emphatically holding the word 'first' over to a strongly concise half-line, 'We stand the first'. Both poets are alert to the power of variation. In further discreet recognition of his predecessor, Pope incorporates a stroke of genius. Denham's line 'Since what they act transcends what they command' becomes, with minimal variation, 'Behold our deeds transcending our commands'. Even the verb is taken from Denham's 'Behold our gallant leaders' with only a shift from imperative to simple present.

It is in the concluding six lines that Pope attains the peak of his semantic and structural enhancement. He retained these lines in his complete *Iliad* without any changes from his first (1709) version of them:

> But since, alas, ignoble age must come,
> Disease, and death's inexorable doom;
> The life which others pay, let us bestow,
> And give to fame what we to nature owe;
> Brave, though we fall; and honoured if we live;
> Or let us glory gain, or glory give!

Sarpedon's appeal is founded on a view that we in our lives face alternatives: to submit passively to the inevitable or to act with spirit to wrest fortune into our own hands. An extended paraphrase of the final two couplets will demonstrate how economically Pope manages both to contain the thought and to give it full value through resonant implications: 'Other people (reluctantly) surrender their life as a duty when required to do so. Let us (freely) present it as a gift. Nature demands that each of us resign his life to it (as the source and end of existence). Let us give our life to fame. If we fall in combat, we gain the glory of being renowned for our courage. If we triumph in combat, we shall be honoured for the remainder of our life and beyond. Let us either gain glory through victory, or grant that glory to the man who is victorious over us in a free act of generosity'.

The verbs in the third line of the extract are presented as alternatives in a subtle extension of antithesis. To 'pay' is to 'render (something that is due)'; to 'surrender (something figured as owed, e. g., one's life)' (*OED*, pay v. 7a). To 'bestow' is to 'confer as a gift, present' (*OED*, bestow, v. 6). 'Bestow' is thus a joyful and positive stronger version of 'pay': the difference puts the bestower in a position in control of the transaction, seizing fate rather than simply paying up when required to do so. It is a movement from passivity to activity—the essence of heroism as a belief underlying what it is to live rather than merely exist.

The second line of this couplet follows by a similar semantic contrast-cum-extension of its verbs, 'give' and 'owe'. To bestow implies a willing 'gift', while to pay implies a due rendering of a debt, that which we 'owe'. However, the verbs in the second line are put in reverse order to the verbs in the first line. They thus form a chiasmus across the couplet: 'pay'/'bestow'/'give'/'owe' (abba). The second line is itself also chiastic, with the two antithetical nouns 'fame' and 'nature' located within the two verbs. We 'owe' our life to 'nature' and so we all must surrender it in re-payment. But if we take control of the process and give our life freely to 'fame', we—to a degree—defeat the power of nature by granting it to an abstract force that extends beyond the individual's life to something of broader meaning, a kind of afterlife through memorialization. The extraordinary subtlety here is that the second line is *grammatically* a chiasmus, but *semantically* an antithesis across the line: 'give to fame / 'to nature owe'. This line is, therefore, the crux, the very heart of Pope's intense stylistic compression.

The third and concluding couplet pursues this intensity into a summary expression of Sarpedon's alternatives, thus maintaining while varying a high level of rhetoric appropriate to such an exhortatory speech. Its overall structure is another chiasmus: if we 'fall' we 'give' glory to another warrior; if we 'live' we 'gain' glory for ourselves. Within the individual lines, the order is simply antithetical: 'brave, though we fall' / 'honoured if we live'; 'glory gain' / 'glory give'. Pope's repetition of the verb 'give' across the two couplets equates giving to fame with giving glory to another warrior. The implication is that giving glory to our victorious adversary constitutes another way of giving our lives to fame through an act of supreme generosity. Victory or defeat, whichever shall be the case, both yield the renown due to heroic endeavour. The epic poem that enshrines this definition of true fame is Homer's. The translation that enables the vision to be read and acknowledged by other people in other times and other places, however, is Pope's. The great translation extends the span of the great original and, by so doing, shares in an act of literary glory.

Both Homer's lines and Denham's translation emphatically locate the heroic code as a response to the ineluctable fact of human mortality. The narrative of *The Iliad*—and of *The Odyssey* and then Virgil's *Aeneid*—has at its heart a vision of the human and divine worlds functioning alongside each other and interacting with each other. Epic values are thus shared, entered into by both realms. Both have, in their own ways, to be asserting their presence, their values and, indeed, their frailties in a continuing struggle. For humans, however, such a continual combat has limits. Their epic values are founded on a willing embrace of inevitable defeat, the acceptance of the tragic. This is heroic but also futile. Humans know this: to maintain status they must engage in relentless battle, but no-one can win every battle. Also, the divine realm, with or against which humans fight, lacks any wider moral vision. The human condition is to be both isolated and heroic. Pope sets up the extraordinary finale to Sarpedon's speech with an intensification of Denham's rendering of Homer's acknowledgement of the inevitability of death. He adopts the word 'disease' from Denham, but places it at the head of a direful march: 'Disease, and death's inexorable doom'. Pope indeed sees and convincingly expresses the tragic nature of epic as an existential basis for human action.

***

Heroic style, then, is the major mode in *The Iliad*. However, the poem's texture is varied by liberal use of its celebrated similes. There are over three hundred of these, which, according to Peter Jones's calculations, occupy about 1100 lines or 7 per cent of the whole. They range in type from short similes with a single point of comparison to more extended examples in the form of 'as when Y happens, so X happened'. As Jones observes, they frequently occur at 'moments of high emotion, drama and tension'. Pope's similes 'introduce worlds of peace and plenty into a martial poem' and 'impose the unchanging world of nature on temporary, fleeting human existence, dignifying and adding significance to it' (Jones, 2003, pp. xxxvii—xxxviii).

Book 8, lines 371–74

> As full-blown poppies, overcharged with rain,
> Decline the head, and drooping kiss the plain;
> So sinks the youth: his beauteous head, depressed
> Beneath his helmet, drops upon his breast.

The Trojan hero Hector is here at the height of his power and achievements. His eventual death at the hands of the Greek hero of the poem, Achilles, in book 22 represents the key, tragic turning point of the entire epic. At present, though, Hector appears to be invincible. The Greek warrior Teucer launches two arrows at him, but both miss their target, inadvertently killing instead two other Trojans. The first of these is Gorgythion, another of the sons of Priam, the king of Troy. E. V. Rieu's classic Penguin prose translation records the simile that illuminates Gorgythion's death thus (1950, p. 136):

> As a poppy's head tilts to one side, weighed down in the garden by its seed and the showers of spring, so Gorgythion's head, weighed down by his helmet, dropped to one side.

William Cowper's blank-verse translation (1791), which was consciously intended as a rejoinder to Pope's freer version, aims to combine a more faithful account of the original with dignity of style conferred by judiciously selected and placed poetic techniques:

> As in the garden, with the weight surcharged
> Of its own fruit, and drenched by vernal rains
> The poppy falls oblique, so he his head
> Hung languid, by his helmet's weight depressed.

Notwithstanding his intention to distance himself from the precedent, Cowper is content to follow elements of Pope's translation. Like him, Cowper manages his version in four lines; he follows the Homeric formula—broadly, for he moves the position of 'so'—into-line sections ('As ... so'); and he adopts vocabulary from Pope. 'Surcharged' is the equivalent of 'overcharged', and each has 'depressed'. Cowper also borrows from Miltonic epic practices. He reverses prose syntax: 'with the weight surcharged / Of its own fruit', rather than 'surcharged with the weight of its own fruit'. He fuses adjectival and adverbial functions into a single word: 'languid' is an adjective in form, but adverbial in position. Such registers of language and variations of syntax add formality, dignity, and resonance. This is, the style tells us, a moment of poetic force appropriate to the epic context.

Before directly addressing Pope's own version, I would like to extend our present range of reference by introducing a twenty-first century perspective, with a view to considering how different ages might locate ancient epic within modern cultural conditions and concerns.

Alice Oswald's *Memorial* (2011) explicitly avoids any claims to be a 'translation' of the *Iliad*. Instead, she distils the poem to a remorseless catalogue of its multiple acts of violence and seemingly never-ending destructive cycle of retribution. Through its unflinching record of voluntary victims and studied objectivity of narrative stance, Oswald's poem lays bare the consequences of the heroic code. It is neither a glorification of battle nor an easily-donned anti-war fabric. It is much more authentic and revealing than either posture: it *is* the code in its stripped and unvarnished state. But it is also something infinitely richer. Oswald alternates the succession of killings, where she observes and follows their narrative order, with lyric sections where Homeric similes are extracted and diffused through the texture of the work. These focus on natural rhythm: falling of leaves, swell of water, growth and decay of flowers, the cycle of seasons. They serve as welcome and recurrent moments of repose where one style (direct and stark) is replaced by another: gradated versions of beautiful and elegiac refrain, usually in reiterated stanzaic forms. Further, they also make human activity a part of nature over an extensive time period, thereby—without any overt commentary, for none is necessary and any would be intrusive—exposing human littleness and even irrelevance.

The effect of Oswald's engagement with its Homeric original is not to patronize it by pretence of moral superiority, but, on the contrary, to bring out something vital at the very core of *The Iliad*. The conflicting yet co-existing poetic styles of *Memorial* express both the magnetic and mechanical drive of its male-centred warrior code and its powerful concomitant voices. Her version of the poppy simile, which follows the death of Gorgythion, runs:

> As if it was June
> A poppy being hammered by the rain
> Sinks its head down

> It's exactly like that
> When a man's neck gives in
> And the bronze calyx of his helmet
> Sinks his head down
>
> Oswald 2011, p. 32

Oswald's stanza—for as such it is presented typographically—is then echoed by an exact repetition, so that the moment is paused upon, granted a moment of stillness within the hectic action around. It occupies a very different poetic world from Cowper's. Line lengths vary between four and ten syllables. All punctuation is omitted, so that only the spaces at the ends of each line—the words, as it were, temporarily entering into emptiness—are left to invite breath pauses. We have neither blank verse nor the formality of Pope's pentameter couplets but something freer, less precise.

However, self-consciously prosaic formulations, notably, 'It's exactly like that', reduce the level of poeticism. Yet the result is certainly not simply 'prosaic'—understated, yes, but still discreetly, quietly offering controlled expression. The seven lines are as symmetrically shaped as Pope's, and more so than Cowper's, since the latter, as we have noted, shifts his 'so' to mid-line, whereas Oswald places her extended simile marker ('It's exactly like that') in the middle line of the seven. Her whole stanza is unified by poetic techniques, always deployed so as to produce the lightest of touches. Subdued echoes are brought by para-rhymes (or half-rhymes), that is, agreements of consonants with variation of vowels: 'June'/'down'; 'gives in'/'down'. Triple rhythms of the form unstress/unstress/stress predominate, sometimes given impetus by an initial shorter, two-syllable starter: 'As if it was June'; 'by the rain'; 'Sinks its head down'; 'It's exactly like that'; 'When a man's neck'; 'of his helmet'. These are not aggressively marching anapaests but more gentle rhythms. The near-repetition of the third and seventh lines provides closure to each half of the stanza and, more emphatically, to the stanza as a whole.

These techniques result in a distinctly elegiac note, a plangency appropriate for a moment of death. Most strikingly, however, Oswald adds a further level of imagery to her broad simile. She does so symmetrically, with a metaphor in each half. These metaphors within a simile are significantly related. The first is 'hammered', an intensification of the strength of the rain and an anticipation of—also in the second line of the triplet—the 'bronze calyx of his helmet'. Rain is transformed into a smith's hammer, while the product of this mechanical activity, the warrior's helmet, is rendered as the shape of a calyx, the outer casing of a closed poppy-head. The botanical term is characteristic of Oswald's precision of vocabulary. The season, as in Homer, is spring. June contains the longest day, but high summer is usually thought of as July and August. June is certainly before the late summer and autumn flowering of poppies. The 'hammered' helmet actually becomes, fuses with, the incipient flower. That figure identifies—to use the common critical terminology—vehicle and tenor: that is, the literary image we encounter in the poem (the poppy's calyx) and what the poet is describing by means of that image (the helmet). The image 'carries' the meaning over to illuminate the plain object. The martial world is thereby softened into the natural world. The warrior's head is subsumed within nature; his life is ended before its flowering, its potential denied.

Pope's two couplets give equal substance to both sides of the simile:

> As full-blown poppies, overcharged with rain,
> Decline the head, and drooping kiss the plain;
> So sinks the youth: his beauteous head, depressed
> Beneath his helmet, drops upon his breast.

The young man's helmet reflects in inverse shape the poppy-flower, rather than the calyx of spring. As Rieu does in his modern prose translation, Pope repeats the word 'head'. But, by doing so within a strong march of /d/ sounds across the couplets ('Decline', 'drooping', 'depressed', 'drops'), Pope emphasizes the connection between poppy and warrior. The death of the youth and the weighing down of the poppy—itself caused by a natural force, and one vital to its initial existence—are merged into a single process. The human (and Pope's adjective 'beauteous' adds pathos to emphasise the human) is not just imaged in the natural; in striking anticipation of Oswald's modern viewpoint, it becomes part of the natural. War and water, death and life-giving, are strikingly fused. Human violence (of which Pope's preceding succession of nouns and verbs—'weapon', 'pierced', 'drenched in royal blood'—gives full rendition) becomes part of a pattern by which earthly processes enfold each other, however unlike their aims and functions. The blow is not exactly softened—although the verb 'kiss' does this to some extent—but is brought into, contained within, a larger whole. Even Pope's use of the plural (poppies) in place of the Homeric singular quietly adds to that sense.

Pope, like Oswald after him, adds to and re-envisages the original. A new age requires a new heroism. Pope's decision to apply the essence of Sarpedon's speech on the nature of truly heroic honour to Clarissa in the final canto of *The Rape of the Lock*—a decision he took while engaged on his *Iliad* translation—assumes, we can now see, major significance. Pope's translation re-locates epic to the sphere of human potential and human vulnerability within nature, and, in the case of *The Rape of the Lock*, specifically female experience within society. Alice Oswald's 'oral cemetery', its 'antiphonal account of man in his world'—to cite her own prefatory words—does something similar yet wholly original. Both, in their own ways, remain faithful to the inner voice of the original while adapting to 'a new audience, as if its language ... was still alive and kicking' (Oswald 2011, p. 2).

10. *Epistle to Robert Earl of Oxford and Earl Mortimer; To Mr Addison; Epitaph on James Craggs, Esq*

Examples: *Epistle to Oxford*, lines 13–20; *To Mr Addison*, lines 45–52, 67–72

The Scriblerus Club was formed in the autumn of 1713 and was meeting pretty regularly by January 1714. As mentioned in the Introduction, the group's main members were Jonathan Swift, John Arbuthnot, John Gay, Thomas Parnell, and Alexander Pope. They were occasionally joined by Robert Harley, Earl of Oxford, leader of the Tory ministry from 1710 to 1714. Previously, Pope had been an occasional visitor to a larger and Whiggish group centred on Joseph Addison, who met at Button's coffee house in Covent Garden. Pope's association with this group dated from the period during which he contributed to *The Guardian* and *The Spectator* (in which, with the assistance of Richard Steele, his *Messiah*, a fusion of passages from Isaiah and Virgil's fourth eclogue, appeared). Addison was 'warmly supportive' of Pope's project to translate Homer's *Iliad* when it was announced in October 1713 (Mack 1985, p. 275). But, 'as autumn wore into winter, Pope found himself drawn away from the Whig group at Button's to the magnetic Toryism of Swift' (Mack 1985, p. 235). A process of divergence was under way.

The aims of the Scriblerus Club were to mock the follies of pseudo-learning and, especially, to expose abuses of language in all forms of poor writing. The vehicle of this satire was to be a character called Martinus Scriblerus, a learned fool who had ranged widely, but shallowly and ineffectually, in the arts and sciences (see *Memoirs of the Extraordinary*

Life, Works, and Discoveries of Martinus Scriblerus, ed. by Charles Kerby-Miller 1966). The most significant effect of the project was to infuse later works with a Scriblerian spirit. Pope's *Peri Bathous* (1728) and *The Dunciad*, and Swift's *Gulliver's Travels* (1726), are notable outcomes. For a more sceptical view of the extent and significance of the Scriblerus Club, see Marshall (2008), and Damrosch (2013, pp. 245–46).

Pope sent his *Epistle to Robert Earl of Oxford and Earl Mortimer* to Harley in October 1721. Harley replied in November, giving Pope permission to print it as a dedicatory introduction to an edition of the works of Thomas Parnell, who had died in 1718. The volume appeared in December 1721. Harley himself, following the fall of his ministry in 1714, had been impeached and imprisoned in the Tower of London, accused of treasonable activities during the negotiations leading to the Treaty of Utrecht in 1713. While he was awaiting trial, charges were dropped and he was released. He retired to his Herefordshire estate until his death in 1724.

Epistle to Oxford, lines 13–20

> Absent or dead, still let a friend be dear,
> (A sigh the absent claims, the dead a tear)
> Recall those nights that closed thy toilsome days,
> Still hear thy Parnell in his living lays,
> Who, careless now of interest, fame, or fate,
> Perhaps forgets that OXFORD e'er was great;
> Or deeming meanest what we greatest call,
> Beholds thee glorious only in thy fall.

This eight-line verse-paragraph faces in two directions. The first two couplets look back to what Harley, and Pope, have lost in order to celebrate what remains in the present. The principal markers of loss forcefully open the paragraph. 'Absent', with its reversed opening stress—in classical metrics a trochee not an iamb—refers to Swift, who had long been settled in Dublin as Dean of St Patrick's; and 'dead' refers to Parnell. The chiastic second line repeats the words, enclosed in their sad effects: a 'sigh', a 'tear'. The second couplet returns Harley to those days when his 'toilsome' immersion in politics and government could be relieved by the club's enlivening activities. That memory is then placed against the second line of the couplet, which exults in the power of poetry to revive the voice of the dead man. The double-stressed 'Still hear' (a spondee) places emphasis on the repetition of 'still' and extends the 'dear'/'tear' rhyme: publication of Parnell's poems, his 'living lays', gives voice to remembrance and transforms grief into pleasure. That final phrase, 'living lays', concludes a steady build-up of /l/ sounds through the two couplets, notably in the repeated 'still' and the name, Parnell, which appropriately lies at the heart of its line. 'Thy Parnell' answers 'thy toilsome days', the familiar form of address asserting the closeness of the friendship signalled in the paragraph's opening line.

The second half of the quartet of couplets moves the perspective onwards. Pope has invited Harley to recall Parnell through the latter's poems. Now, Pope gives Parnell a voice to recall Harley. Parnell has moved beyond the human concerns of 'interest, fame, or fate'. For Harley, notably in his former prominence in the body politic, the adjective Pope chooses is 'great', the rhyme-word in the third couplet. Raised to a superlative in the fourth couplet, it is antithetically set against 'meanest'. Parnell is perhaps no longer conscious of mere worldly status (the name 'Oxford'—Harley's title—counters 'Parnell' earlier); or, perhaps, his superior vision can now review the whole of Harley's career, which came to an abrupt end, as does the verse-paragraph, with his final 'fall' from power. This is not, however, to spin a common morality tale about the fragility of ambition. The great paradox of the final line is that Harley's most 'glorious' moment was his fall.

What does this mean? Geoffrey Tillotson's essay 'Pope's "Epistle to Harley": an Introduction and Analysis' (*Augustan Studies*,1961, pp. 162–83) draws attention to Pope's blunt and fearless review of Harley's chequered history. The concise 'fall' with which our paragraph ends is followed up in the remainder of the poem by 'disgrace' and 'cloud', and a reminder of Harley's perilous time in the Tower ('the scaffold, or the cell', lines30–39). The vicissitudes of an ambitious life are indeed extreme. But the other side of the coin, and the poem's core message, is that a human being can show his true merit under such stress, as Harley has done. The quality of an individual is found 'in each hard instance tried' (line 23). The force of poetry, now elevated to 'The Muse' (line 28) as it was earlier raised in poetic register to 'living lays' with reference to Parnell's poems, lies in how it can trace 'the brave man's latest steps .../ Rejudge his acts, and dignify disgrace' (lines 29–30). The epistle's finale resoundingly affirms that the Muse both 'shades thy evening-walk with bays' and declares Mortimer to be 'truly great' (lines 35–40). Pope's use of the word 'bays', the classical symbol of poetic prowess, aligns Harley with Parnell. The Muse's voice speaks clearly through Parnell's works and Pope's dedicatory poem. Harley, Parnell, and (discreetly, for the poem has no 'I', no first person) Pope are all reunited through the power of creative language, the medium of friendship.

Reunion of the parted in poetry features in Pope's contribution to another collected works of 1721, Thomas Tickell's edition of the writings of Joseph Addison, who had died in 1719—reunion to the extent, even, of reconciliation. According to his own note on the poem, Pope originally wrote *To Mr Addison* in 1715. By then, relations between Pope and Addison had begun to cool. The cause was literary rather than political, though a personality clash may have played a part: the older Addison gained something of a reputation for reticence or, to be harsher, stand-offishness. Devotees of the Muse are not, alas, always free from petty jealousies. Pope signed his contract for a translation of *The Iliad* with the printer Bernard Lintot in March 1714. Two months later, Tickell, who was a member of the Buttons group led by Addison, signed a contract with another publisher, Jacob Tonson, for his own translation. Although Addison did not publicly withdraw his initial encouragement of Pope's project, he transferred his support to Tickell and lent him assistance (Mack 1985, p. 276). He did not, it seems, inform Pope of this rival venture and his role in it.

Notwithstanding the state of relations between them—and the true details are inevitably unclear—Pope's epistle contains at its climax a generous tribute to Addison. The poem traces a brief history of 'medals', by which is meant coins from the classical period usually bearing an inscription or a head of the figure being celebrated (see *OED*, 'medal' *sb.* 2).

Pope's commentary on the medals themselves is not lacking in satirical touches. These focus on the ironies of greatness and the absurdities of collectors. A personified figure of Ambition is represented as sighing over the inadequacy of larger-scale monuments to preserve the glories of those whose vanity raised them: 'she found it vain to trust / The faithless column and the crumbling bust'. Instead, she 'contracts her vast design' into the form of a medal that can be held in the palm of a hand, small being not just more beautiful but more resistant to time: 'And all her triumphs shrink into a coin' (lines 19–24). 'Shrink' here wittily and tellingly both celebrates the power of the artificer to devise something that might last and wryly observes the reductive scale of the product. Then Pope turns his attention to the 'pale antiquaries' who pore over their collections and the 'sacred rust of twice ten hundred years' (line 38). Here, the oxymoron 'sacred rust' brings the collectors' obsession into comic alignment with the fame sought by emperors and heroes inscribed on the coins. The past and the present share human foibles, which the satirist is compelled to expose by ridicule.

At this point, Pope changes the tone of the epistle as he turns to address Addison and his book in another four-couplet paragraph:

> Theirs is the vanity, the learning thine:
> Touched by thy hand, again Rome's glories shine;
> Her gods, and godlike heroes rise to view,
> And all her faded garlands bloom anew.
> Nor blush, these studies thy regard engage;
> These pleased the fathers of poetic rage;
> The verse and sculpture bore an equal part,
> And art reflected images to art.
>
> *To Mr Addison, lines 45–52*

These lines have rhythmic balance and grace, and they contain a eulogistic register of language. For example, the first couplet is metrically balanced to form a reflective pattern of a six/four division of syllables in the first line and a four/six division in the second. That rhythmic chiasmus itself reflects the semantic chiasmus in line 1, where 'Theirs' is answered by 'thine' at either end and the key antithetical terms are held in between, swinging on either side of the comma. By this means, Pope emphasizes his distinction between the irrational mania of collectors ('Theirs') and the sober knowledge and scholarship contained in Addison's book on the subject ('thine'). Pope's heavy satire of collectors, such as poor Vadius (meaning Dr John Woodward, an antiquarian and regular victim of Scriblerian ridicule) who is 'long with learned spleen devoured' (line 41), is answered by praise for Addison as a true scholar whose lightness of 'touch' (line 46) adds lustre to the medals as products of Roman splendour. To 'shine' is, thus, both literal and metaphorical: the coins are restored to their original brightness and reflect the good qualities of the classical civilization which produced them.

Smooth lines of verse render their assertions attractive and engaging. Thus 'And all her faded garlands bloom anew' uses the positive language of pastoral, graced with a lyric impetus of /l/ sounds: 'all', 'garlands', 'bloom'. The final couplet neatly encapsulates these qualities of the poetry. 'Verse and sculpture' (that is, the inscriptions and representations on the coins) are brought into a state of equality, an assertion exemplified in the balanced phrasing of 'And art reflected images to art'. Pope here virtually quotes his own earlier *Epistle to Mr Jervas* (1716; see Chapter 6): 'While images reflect from art to art' (line 20). That poem was written to accompany Dryden's translation of Dufresnoy's verse treatise on painting. By means of this self-allusion, Pope imports the most laudable of literary precedents into his praise for Addison's book. Like its subject, the medals of the classical period, Addison matches in his words the attractiveness of the coins as visual objects.

This paragraph paves the way for the poem's noblest and most generous compliment to Addison. Pope concludes with a call for contemporary Britain to emulate the creative splendours of the classical periods by producing representations of its intellectual heroes, so that its 'laurelled bards' may take their place alongside those of Greece and Rome: 'A Virgil there, and here an Addison' (line 62). Joseph Addison and the great Roman epic writer share space in the line, 'here an Addison' reflecting 'A Virgil there'. This is praise indeed, but parallels between the past and the present do not end there. Poets need patrons. Virgil had his in G. Asinius Pollio, whose memory also deserved preservation on a coin. As for the present age, Pope proffers the name of James Craggs (lines 63–64) and ends the poem by actually writing a six-line inscription to accompany the head of Craggs on this proposed, virtual, medal:

> Statesman, yet friend to truth! of soul sincere,
> In action faithful, and in honour clear;
> Who broke no promise, served no private end,
> Who gained no title, and who lost no friend;
> Ennobled by himself, by all approved,
> And praised, unenvied, by the Muse he loved.
>
> *To Mr Addison, lines 67–72*

James Craggs was a politician who became Secretary of State in 1718. He and Pope were near neighbours at Chiswick, then at Twickenham, and 'held each other in high esteem' (*TE*, IV, 1939, ed. by Butt, p. 356). Craggs gave Pope some shares in the South Sea Company at a time when they were highly sought after. That action soon became compromised by what gained notoriety as the South Sea Bubble, the prototype of all future capitalist scandals, and, for many people thereafter in the eighteenth century, a defining moment in the growth and morally ambiguous status of a financial economy. Both Craggs and his father (also James) were inevitably implicated in the affair. The scandal was still at its height when Craggs junior died suddenly of smallpox in 1721 at the age of thirty-five. A month later Craggs senior committed suicide.

These distressing events should cast a dreadful retrospective shadow over Pope's adulatory lines. But Pope remained as faithful to Craggs and his memory as his poem describes Craggs's actions to be. 'There never', he wrote in a letter to John Caryll, 'lived a more worthy nature, a more disinterested mind, a more open and friendly temper than Mr. Craggs' (Elwin and Courthope, VI, 1871–79, p. 276). Pope was prepared, also, to make such fidelity public. The six lines proposed as the inscription to a medal were turned (with only the touching emendation of 'And praised, unenvied' to 'Praised, wept, and honoured') into an epitaph for Craggs in Westminster Abbey and published in the Pope-Swift *Miscellanies* in 1727. That same volume also contained an initial version of the celebrated portrait of 'Atticus' in Pope's *Epistle to Dr Arbuthnot*. Significantly, Pope omitted from that epistle a couplet which, all too strongly, alluded to the questionable behaviour of Addison in the matter of the contending versions of Homer's *Iliad*: 'Who, if two Wits on rival Themes contest, / Approves of each, but likes the worst the best' (*Fragment of a Satire*, lines 59–60; Butt 1963, p. 492)

The key word in the eulogistic lines on Craggs that close the *Epistle to Addison* and formed his epitaph is 'friend'. In the first line, it is used to define the moral imperative of truthfulness which should underlie the public role of the politician and statesman; 'should' because Pope's wry conjunction 'yet' nods at the (all too common?) alternative. In the fourth line, 'lost no friend' is a tribute to Craggs's own admirable constancy toward those dear to him. Thus, public life and private life are effortlessly conjoined in the great man's nature and actions. This unbroken continuity is itself a definition of integrity, a virtue opposite to the hypocrisy which so frequently occupies satirists. Pope in satiric mode often fittingly employs forms of antithesis to expose and represent such double-dealing. The *Epistle to Addison* does not do this. Instead, Pope's highly personal feelings of resentment towards Addison hang ironically over his formal encomium of Craggs: 'in action faithful', 'broke no promise', 'lost no friend'. 'In honour clear 'also casts reflection on an earlier line in praise of Addison: 'Touched by thy hand, again Rome's glories shine' (line 46). 'Clear' derives from the Latin 'clarus', meaning in the first instance 'bright, shining', but very commonly used of the character of a person or an act in the sense of 'distinguished, renowned, famous'—deservedly, clearly, famous, that is. Does Pope recall an earlier, highly striking use of 'clear' in a first line of another classically aware poet, Ben Jonson? 'Brave infant of Saguntum, clear', the poet apostrophizes in allusion to a story told by Pliny. A child who, in the year in which Hannibal captured the city of Saguntum and so began the second Punic War, having been born and 'looking then about', as Jonson puts it, immediately returned to the womb. The Ben Jonson poem so beginning is one of the great poems of loss and friendship, 'To the Immortal Memory and Friendship of that Noble Pair, Sir Lucius Cary and Sir H. Morison' (1640), inspired by the early death of the latter and devoted to consoling the former by arguing for the greater value of ethical integrity over mere length of life. Pope's epitaph to Craggs is his public demonstration of fidelity to the memory of a man who died too young and whose memory shines with full ethical clarity. Placed at the end of an epistle to Addison, the same lines exert retrospective irony on Pope's relationship with Addison. Fidelity and infidelity: two sides of the same coin?

11. *An Essay on Man*

Examples: 'Epistle 1', lines 1–6, 17–34, 77–90; 'Epistle 2', lines 1–18, 59–60, 133–34, 275–82; 'Epistle 3', lines 303–06; 'Epistle 4', lines 387–98

The poems considered in Chapters 1 to 10 are products of the first two decades of Pope's career, the 1700s and 1710s. The focus from now on will be on poems of the early 1730s and mid-1740s, a period in which Pope wrote an astonishing series of masterpieces. It is worth noting, however, that he was by no means inactive during the 1720s. Indeed, he engages on a number of large-scale and significant projects. He edited the poems of Thomas Parnell (1721). He followed up his translation of Homer's *Iliad* with a translation of the *Odyssey*, sharing the task with his friends William Broome and Elijah Fenton. He produced an edition of Shakespeare (1725), with controversial outcomes. Lewis Theobald, a prolific and versatile writer and translator, responded with *Shakespeare Restored: or, a specimen of the Many Errors . . . Committed . . . by Mr Pope* (1725). In punishment for such impudence, Pope put Theobald in a pair of poetic stocks by making him chief of the dunces in *The Dunciad* (1728), where he mockingly called him 'Tibbald'. Pope revised and expanded *The Dunciad* in the 1740s, replacing Theobald with Colley Cibber. We shall look extensively at both versions in Chapter 26.

The four epistles that make up *An Essay on Man* were published successively in February, March, and May 1733, and January 1734. A letter from Bolingbroke to Swift tells us that Pope had actually completed the first three epistles by August 1731 and was working on the fourth (cited in Mack, III, Part 1, 1950, pp. xiii–xiv). Pope added to the first collected edition of these epistles (1734) a short introduction entitled 'The Design'. He there explains that *An Essay on Man* is intended to be only 'a general map', tracing the extent, limits and connection of 'the greater parts'. The 'particular' will be 'more fully delineated in the charts which are to follow', that is, a further series of epistles on which he was currently engaged. Extending the geographical metaphor, Pope adds that, in the *Essay*, he is 'opening the fountains, and clearing the passage'. The later poems—he had, in fact, already published the epistles to Burlington and Bathurst, with Cobham to follow—will trace the course of individual 'rivers' and 'observe their effects'.

Pope supplies a prefatory summary of all four epistles comprising *An Essay on Man*. He calls them 'Arguments' or 'Contents': a concise table of the philosophical propositions of each section. The first epistle examines 'the nature and state of man, with respect to the universal system'. The other three epistles consider the human being as an 'individual, and as a member of society'. A *précis* here of the content of each of the epistles will provide a framework within which a reading of selected passages may be fruitfully carried out.

'Epistle 1'

Humanity's place is considered within the order of creation. The whole depends on the co-existence of all its parts, so there must be a settled place for humankind within the larger system. Disruption arises whenever there is desire for movement. Such a will derives from pride or presumption. We need to accept our role and adopt an appropriate humility.

'Epistle 2'

Acceptance of the limits of human perception and understanding necessarily includes admitting our lack of knowledge of higher forms of creation and, *a fortiori*, of the creator or creative force itself. At the heart of our divided nature ('Created half to rise, and half to fall', line 15) is the co-existence within our nature of reason and passions. These passions are forms of 'self-love' (line 93). Reason, by contrast, is a 'God within the mind' (line 204). By self-love, Pope does not mean what we today might understand by the term, that is, a selfish concern with our own being. Rather, he intends something closer to 'self-fulfilment', or a principle which provides us with the energy to activate ourselves (see John Laird, *Philosophical Incursions into English Literature* (1946), cited in Mack, ed., *TE*, III, part 2, 1950 p. 62). This antithesis between aspirational and regulatory elements within human nature is traditional and long lasting: see, for example, Cicero's *De Officiis*, I, xxviii.

Reason is powerless to prevent or oppose whatever forms of passion rule in each of us as individuals, but it can, and does, 'rectify' (line 163) them through whatever virtue is possible within our nature, the 'virtue nearest to our vice allied' (line 196). Each person's individual fusion of vice and virtue, good and ill, is part of the divine pattern which co-ordinates the whole. 'Each individual seeks a several [particular, separate] goal, / But HEAVEN's great view is one, and that the whole' (lines 237–38).

It is worth observing at this stage that Pope pursues and illustrates these philosophical positions with touches of humour that lighten the mood, and with lines blending elements of the serious and the comic. Consider, for example, the poetic shrug of the shoulders in lines 221–24 (the Orcades are the Orkneys; Zembla is Novaya Zemlya, an archipelago off Russia's arctic coast):

> But where the extreme of vice, was ne'er agreed:
> Ask where's the north? At York, 'tis on the Tweed;
> In Scotland, at the Orcades; and there,
> At Greenland, Zembla, or the Lord knows where.

'Epistle 3'

At its halfway mark, the poem pauses on its central truth: 'The universal cause / Acts to one end, but acts by various laws' (lines 1–2). It then launches into its next argument, that the same principle—the mixed nature of individual people is formed into a whole by 'heaven'—also operates at the level of society, including political and religious organisations. 'Self-love' and 'social' are co-existent in the 'state of nature' (line 148), and co-operative in human society. What is 'instinct' (line 170) in birds and animals is copied by human 'art' (line 169). Thus, the entire 'general frame' of creation confirms that 'self-love and social' are 'the same' (317–18).

'Epistle 4'

The subject of the final epistle of the poem is the nature and state of man, with respect to happiness. The principle argued in the earlier epistles is also productive of happiness: it resides not in any individual but is more general. So, happiness cannot derive from material goods or the gifts of nature, as these are not equally distributed. Nor does happiness follow from human actions, because 'ills or accidents … chance to all' (line 98). Rather, Pope endorses a traditional ethical principle: 'Act well your part, there all the honour lies' (line 194). Achievements such as public renown are ephemeral, as are all *outcomes* of human activity. Indeed, happiness lies only in the exercise of virtue *for its own sake*: 'Know then this truth (enough for Man to know) / 'Virtue alone is happiness below' (lines 309–10).

In short, the ideas presented in *An Essay on Man* are neither new nor arresting. They are gleaned from a variety of sources, classical, scientific, theological, and philosophical. Many of them have commonly appeared in literary forms, whether poetry, books of ethics, or popular essays, such as *The Spectator* and other journals have provided. Or, at least, more or less close versions of the ideas have so appeared. *An Essay on Man* is an amalgam, a large-scale gathering of Enlightenment ideas—in the widest sense, as some are inferential and experiential while others (notably that of the universe being a hierarchical chain of being) are *a priori* and derivative. Mack's *TE* volume provides full reference to sources and parallels (1950). It is the force of Pope's poetry that energizes these and fuses them into a formal entity of remarkable intensity and expressiveness, rising at many points to magnificence.

Further, there is an inherent tension in the philosophical mode of proceeding in the poem between, on the one hand, the *a priori* assumptions of the theory that Pope proposes with respect to the nature and structure of the universe, and, on the other hand, the empirical method to which the illustration and application of the theory are committed. See 'Epistle 1', lines 17ff: we can only reason 'from what we know' and we can only see, and therefore judge and argue from, what our position within the system permits; from this we 'reason' or 'refer'—i. e. operate via logical inference or analogy (lines 17–20). The *a priori* assumption is, of course, not Pope's invention; it is an inherited and traditional conception. See the introduction to Mack, ed., *TE*, III, part 1, 1950, pp. xli–xlvi; Willey 1940, chapter 3.

This tension is, however, consistent with the direction of Pope's writing as a whole. At the heart of his method lies a flexible capacity to maintain two attitudes or points of view and to express them in the complexity of his use of language, structure, and verse form. The truth is rarely pure and never simple because our lives exist within a multiplicity of contingencies. A single vision is therefore rarely, if ever, a possible or defensible response to experience; and poetry must accurately reflect this. This is why, for all its philosophical naiveté, if that is not too strong a way of putting it, the theory adopted by Pope in *An Essay on Man* is highly creative and appropriate for his mature vision. Its shortcomings and limitations constitute an essential element of his material, since naïve philosophical theories (like naïve political theories) are a part of the epistemology that surrounds us. This paradox arises at the very outset of the poem:

'Epistle I', lines 1–6

> Awake, my ST JOHN! leave all meaner things
> To low ambition, and the pride of kings.
> Let us (since life can little more supply
> Than just to look about us and to die)
> Expatiate free o'er all this scene of Man;
> A mighty maze! but not without a plan.

Pope begins the poem with a grand gesture, countered by a confessional intimation of humility. The opening couplet's exclamatory clarion call to Bolingbroke is resonant and gloriously dismissive of the ephemera of political and public engagement. As such, it is highly fitting for its addressee. Bolingbroke's career, like that of Robert Harley, his colleague in the Tory administration of 1710–14, embodied the vicissitudes of the pursuit of power. Secretary of State in that government, he enjoyed authority and influence. But then, with the Hanoverian accession, Bolingbroke lost all power, became the object of legal action, and fled to continental Europe to join the Pretender's court. His exile ended with the granting of a partial pardon in 1723 and a re-entry into political struggle along with the opposition to Walpole. After the failure of that movement, Bolingbroke was to retire again in 1735. Pope's appeal to him to place philosophical observation and reflection above the business of the state may be seen as a prophecy and, ultimately, a vindication of scholarship and ethical investigation over the diurnal realm of day-to-day governance.

Line 2's oxymoron, 'low ambition', gives rhetorical expression to this challenging attitude: the paradox is that aiming for the heights of power is actually tantamount to descending into the pit of mean activities. This is what people such as kings, and, by extension, their acolytes–the politicians–do. 'Pride' in this social context is ethically dubious. The gauntlet is thrown down: pride and ambition are really meaner than the noble task of philosophical investigation. To 'expatiate'—to engage and speak at length, and to range at will—is a nobler activity, and an expression of freedom in its enjoyment of liberty of thought rather than the narrow focus enjoined by political humdrum. The Latin root of 'expatiate' is 'spatium', that is, 'space'. 'Expatiari' thus means 'to walk about'. Pope opens up the poem's landscape for free exploration.

However, a parenthesis is placed between exclamation ('Awake, my ST JOHN!) and appeal to join with the author in this nobler task ('Let us ... expatiate'). 'Since life can little more supply / Than just to look about us and to die' casts a tone of disillusion over lofty assertion. Pope's vocabulary here is notably monosyllabic in advance of the trisyllabic 'expatiate'. In this, and in its chastening message, lies another and equally important rejoinder to assertive 'pride'. Genuine humility involves acknowledging the severe limits to knowledge inherent in the human situation. These contrary couplets lay down parameters within which Pope's philosophical venture will divagate. *An Essay on Man* is at once his most declarative affirmation of truth and a continual avowal of inadequacy. We know, and we do not know, in equal measure. The poem will wander freely and, by so doing, expose contradictions which a more controlled or orthodox method might be tempted to ignore or wish away.

In the first edition of 'Epistle I' (1733), the sixth line—at first sight rather oddly—ran 'A mighty maze of walks without a plan'. Apparently, some, or even many, readers interpreted this wording as indicating that there was no order, no system, to the 'maze'; whereas Pope's real meaning was more carefully nuanced than this. A maze does, indeed, have a 'plan' in the sense of a scheme of arrangement (*OED*, 'plan' sb., sense 2): this, after all, is what a maze in the Hampton Court, human-made, sense does have. What the maze of the universe does not have is a ready-made chart or drawing for human beings to consult at ease (*OED*, 'maze', sb., sense 1). It must, I think, be admitted that Pope's original phrasing was, at least, not entirely clear. At any rate, he altered it to 'but not without a plan' in the first collected edition of 1734.

William Empson cites the couplet in *Seven Types of Ambiguity* (1953) as an example of his seventh type, that of full contradiction, but one in which, actually, both the original and revised readings 'are very nearly the same: a *maze* is conceived as something that at once has and has not got a *plan*' (p. 204). As Mack explains clearly in the *TE*, it all depends on which meaning of plan you see (Mack, ed., III, part 1, 1950, p. 12). It does have a plan in *OED*'s sense 2 'a scheme of arrangement'; but it might not have a plan in *OED*'s sense 1, 'drawing, sketch, or diagram'—or the plan might have been lost, or at least not be in your possession.

Mazes are tricky things; and trickier still are human powers of perception and interpretation. Actually, as this small textual problem turned out, there could scarcely have been a more relevant and salutary beginning to what is, arguably, Pope's most ambitious and yet most problematic poem. As Pope himself wryly observes in many of his poems, human ambition is bound to end in failure or, at least, to encounter difficulties not readily overcome. The real achievement of *An Essay on Man* is to enact in its style, form, and language the simultaneous existence of that which is grand in humankind and that which shows up all too clearly our limitations. That is the meaning of both its model—the universe itself—and our intellect, our attempts to understand it.

'Epistle I', lines 17–34

> Say first, of God above, or Man below,
> What can we reason, but from what we know?
> Of Man what see we, but his station here,
> From which to reason, or to which refer?
> Through worlds unnumbered though the God be known,
> 'Tis ours to trace him only in our own.
> He, who through vast immensity can pierce,
> See worlds on worlds compose one universe,
> Observe how system into system runs,

> What other planets circle other suns,
> What varied being peoples every star,
> May tell why Heaven has made us as we are.
> But of this frame the bearings, and the ties,
> The strong connections, nice dependencies,
> Gradations just, has thy pervading soul
> Looked through? Or can a part contain the whole?
> Is the great chain, that draws all to agree,
> And drawn supports, upheld by God, or thee?

The argument is 'that we can judge only with regard to our own system, being ignorant of the relations of systems and things' (Mack, ed. *TE*, III, part 2, 1950, p. 9). The eighteen lines are divided by punctuation into three six-line sentences, each subdivided into couplets with either a comma or a question mark at the end of each. This structure produces a frame that is both clear in its whole and intricate in its parts.

Clarity is most obvious where Pope's manner is at its most expository, particularly in the first sextet. Here, he keeps his vocabulary at its simplest and his syntax at its most direct. There is little or nothing to get in the way of, or to adorn, the plain argument. A prose paraphrase could scarcely be more explicit: 'we can only argue from what we know, and what we know is restricted to what we can see from where we stand'. The syntax admits only slight variations from the very plainest, such as the inversions of the third line ('of Man what see we' rather than 'what see we of man' and the fifth ('worlds unnumbered' reversing adjective/noun order). These are felt as scarcely more than the slightest of tremors, very low on the syntactic Richter scale. As for vocabulary, the one word which may give us slight pause is 'station'. It holds a number of technical applications that may echo relevantly: to surveying or astronomy, say. But these are simply two among several significations deriving straight from the word's direct etymological meaning: the place where we 'stand'. The commonest thread through the six lines is the very simplest, the pronoun 'we' and its grammatical variant 'our'. Pope's habitual poetic manner is, accordingly, at its most restrained, the metrical balance of the fourth line ('From which to reason, or to which refer') just gently reminding us that he is still there. In the main, we are simply all in it together.

However, in the second sextet, the perspective shifts. 'We' are relegated to the very end, the concluding item of a sentence wholly dominated by an opposite subject, 'He'. It is possible, as Mack's volume of the *TE* notes, to take 'He, who' to mean 'only that man'—implying that there is no such man—but I think most readers naturally take it to refer to 'the God' in the earlier lines (vol. 3, part 1, 1950, p. 15). 'He' is certainly granted a grander sentence structure, an epic-like deferral of the main verb for six lines while the syntax spans several subclauses. These are granted, too, an altogether grander vocabulary, the cumulative force of which is to stress plurality as a reverse of the human single point of view. So, 'vast immensity' boldly goes into tautology, for display purposes; repetition ('worlds on worlds', 'system into system', 'other planets ... other suns') showily outshines our monochrome state; and verbal variety ('pierce', 'see', 'observe', 'tell') conveys excitement and discovery.

The third sextet now crowds its 'frame', its structural equivalent of the massive structure of the universe, with metaphors. Architecture is, indeed, the principal field of reference ('bearings', 'ties', 'gradations'), as the lines explore the multiple interconnections which hold together in various ways the many parts that, together, constitute the whole. Three rhetorical questions, *via* a sardonic address to a solitary reader ('thy pervading soul'), reinforce the lesson in humility. Pope seems to say, 'You, you see, are but one small part, and no part can possibly aspire to the vision required to see the whole. Are you absurdly presumptuous enough to imagine that you are the viewer, let alone the architect, of this great and complex construction?'

To ram home this stark message, Pope's language at the very end reverts to the expository method of the beginning of the paragraph. His questions 'Can a part contain the whole?' and 'Is the great chain ... upheld by God, or thee?' resume a largely monosyllabic and direct level of vocabulary that circles back to 'What can we reason, but from what we know?' The lesson is emphatic and determinate, and it firmly puts us in our place. And yet the paragraph's broad range of perspective has been conveyed through the medium of language, and language, too, that has been put together by a single being, the poet himself. The texture of the poem, its own frame, has indeed been created by a metaphorical architect; and one whose area of reference and variations of style—even within this relatively short passage—are enterprising and impressive. This, after all, is a didactic poem, one which aims to stamp its magisterial force on its subject—even when that subject is the limitations of human capacity. A presumptuous task in itself? The very next line of the poem (line 35) begins with an exclamatory 'Presumptuous Man!' 'Presumptuous? *Moi?*'

'Epistle I', lines 77–90

> Heaven from all creatures hides the book of fate,
> All but the page prescribed, their present state;
> From brutes what men, from men what spirits know:
> Or who could suffer being here below?
> The lamb thy riot dooms to bleed today,
> Had he thy reason, would he skip and play?
> Pleased to the last, he crops the flowery food,
> And licks the hand just raised to shed his blood.
> Oh blindness to the future! kindly given,
> That each may fill the circle marked by Heaven;
> Who sees with equal eye, as God of all,
> A hero perish, or a sparrow fall,
> Atoms or systems into ruin hurled,
> And now a bubble burst, and now a world.

This paragraph is the opening of the third section of the epistle, the argument of which, as Pope's résumé runs, is that 'it is partly upon [man's] ignorance of future events, and partly upon the hope of a future state, that all his happiness in the present depends (Mack, ed., TE, III, part 1, 1950, p. 9). The great chain of being—the theory that creation is a fixed hierarchical structure—entails each stage being inferior to those above and superior to those below. The devastating implications of this for humankind will be explored strongly in epistle two. For the moment, Pope begins by setting out the limitations the model necessitates for all sentient life. The fourteen-line paragraph is structured in three parts. The first four lines set out the proposition that all parts of creation are formed to know only their 'present state', which differs according to their place on the scale. The next four lines provide an exemplum, the lamb's ignorance of what human beings know. The final six lines present the wider context, that is, the 'kindness' of a structure in which 'God' alone—as the top of the scale—has knowledge of everything. This four/

four/six structure resembles a couplet-based version of sonnet form (quatrain, quatrain, sestet).

At first, Pope's manner is, again, expository. It is when he reaches his exemplum that his language changes. 'Dooms' brings with it dark associations, and, what is worse, those connections uneasily involve human beings' actions. 'Riot' in the sense of revelry usually comes with baleful attributes and uncomfortably implies that, if this is indeed all written in the 'book of fate', it is we who are inscribing at least some of the disturbing consequences. The 'bleed/blood' repetition marks the event as inescapably painful. The addition of 'licks the hand' provides a dramatic touch difficult to dismiss as merely sentimental. There is, too, a further level of (in this case, unstated) implication. If the lamb is ignorant of what we are about to do to it, what are we ignorant of that may be done to us?

The paragraph's final lines declare a perspective that ought to be reassuring. Heaven/God's eye is 'equal' as a temperament in musical terminology is equal: the semitones of creation, so to speak, are evenly located. But also, the eye of the beholder of all things is even in its regard for what it oversees. Thus, the relatively greater or lesser within the scale are flattened to a single level when viewed *sub specie aeternitatis*. Items that appear larger or smaller from one perspective appear uniform in significance, value, and meaning from another. Add the fragility of, in the final example, 'a bubble', and desperate vulnerability is transmitted to 'a world'. Mack defends Pope from such disturbing implications by glossing the line 'A hero perish, or a sparrow fall' as an allusion to verses in St Matthew's gospel: 'Are not two sparrows sold for a farthing? and one of them shall not fall on the ground without your Father. But the very hairs of your head are all numbered. Fear ye not therefore, ye are of more value than many sparrows' (Matthew 10. 29–31; Mack, ed. TE, III, part 1, 1950, p. 24. Shakespeare refers to the same biblical text in Hamlet's observation that there is 'special providence in the fall of a sparrow (*Hamlet*, act 5, scene 2). It is possible that Pope intends a reader to pick up this echo. Jesus's words are comforting, and specifically include the notion of value to that end: God is present even when a single sparrow falls, and a human being is of much more value than many sparrows. So, Mack argues, Pope's point is that 'God's providence embraces both sparrow and man, and not ... that man and sparrow are of equal value' (*TE*, III, part 1, 1950, ed. by Mack, p. 24n). Pope's line is carefully divided into two equal metrical halves, separated by a comma: five syllables in each, and matching stresses ('A hero pérish, or a sparrow fáll'). God's 'equal eye' is transferred to the page as a demonstration of His universal vision, not as a challenge to hierarchy. However, by juxtaposing heroes and sparrows in the metrical texture of his verse, Pope at the same time admits a sense of equivalence. Are heroes clearly of more importance than sparrows, or is such evaluation a philosophical (or even cultural) assumption dictated by the chain of being model, but uncomfortably felt, rhythmically, to be in conflict with the line of poetry as we see it, read it, hear it? I suspect most readers will detect ambiguity here. Pope's syntax and versification allow both interpretations as valid, if incompatible. Rather than seeing this as an inadvertent error of expression, should we not respond positively to it as a creative demonstration of a mind expatiating freely, and so able to contemplate co-existence of contraries?

'Epistle II', lines 1-18

> Know then thyself, presume not God to scan;
> The proper study of mankind is Man.
> Placed on this isthmus of a middle state,
> A being darkly wise, and rudely great:
> With too much knowledge for the sceptic side,
> With too much weakness for the stoic's pride,
> He hangs between; in doubt to act, or rest,
> In doubt to deem himself a god, or beast;
> In doubt his mind or body to prefer,
> Born but to die, and reasoning but to err;
> Alike in ignorance, his reason such,
> Whether he thinks too little, or too much:
> Chaos of thought and passion, all confused;
> Still by himself abused, or disabused;
> Created half to rise, and half to fall;
> Great lord of all things, yet a prey to all;
> Sole judge of truth, in endless error hurled:
> The glory, jest, and riddle of the world!

'The proper study of mankind is man' is a famous and memorable example of Pope's aphoristic style. An aphorism is language at a point where it cannot be revised. To paraphrase David Morris (1984, pp. 161–65), it is succinct, sharpened, honed to such a state that it achieves a crystalline quality of finish where any further attempt to improve it would appear impossible, or self-defeating. The result is a statement offering a convincing intellectual and linguistic finality, representing or proposing the last word, all that need be said. That this is one complete line of verse, a pentameter with no real caesura, assists such an expression: it is whole, a complete sentence and line with no intruding fussiness, and its verb is that of the most direct and simple definition ('is'). Its most important word, 'man', is where it comes to rest. This is, after all, the poem's declared topic, and so the line also justifies the entire work. The subject of the sentence, 'proper study', is boldly assertive and semantically assured: an 'essay' is a form of 'study' with aspiration to some kind of scientific certainty, and a 'proper' study sets out to reveal the constituents that are inherent within, proper to, its topic. This exact etymological sense of 'proper' (from the Latin *preposition*) was the original English meaning, and still resounds in our word 'property': that which belongs to a person or, as here, the whole of mankind. We are searching for that which is essential within ourselves and our human nature.

And yet a 'study' is also a rough sketch, a preliminary outline, an initial drawing. Pope, the enthusiastic amateur artist, knew this, as he also knew that such a sketch might, if luck is with the artist, capture a rapid essence of its subject with a vitality and brevity perhaps lost in a more 'worked' version. Pope's line, then, has an admirably finished surface, but also a marvellously concise and direct vigour that may, or may not, get to the heart of the matter. The aphoristic style manifests both possibilities. Its rhetorical completeness masks, or can mask, what Morris calls a 'potent contradiction': it 'convinces us of a completeness it cannot ultimately deliver' (1984, p. 163). Perhaps 'might not' rather than 'cannot'? Only the whole poem can fully answer that question, but even in the microcosm of this one line both completeness and something like its inverse are hauntingly present. 'The proper study of mankind is man'. Well, yes, it would be, wouldn't it? 'Man', after all, is integral to 'mankind'. Is this really a statement of the obvious, a tautology? To define the sentence's complement as an answer to a prepositional phrase in its subject looks a little like going round in a circle. Is this to achieve 360-degree perfection, or simply to end up where we began, with no progress made?

A further feature of the aphoristic style is, for Samuel Johnson, 'inexactness and inexplicitness'. He wrote in the essay on the *Bravery of the English Common Soldier* (1760) that 'in all pointed sentences some degree of accuracy must be sacrificed to conciseness'. Johnson, the great essayist, after all should know: he is famously no slouch himself at the pointed sentence, as this pointed sentence demonstrates. Paradoxically, inexactness is one of the great strengths of successful aphorisms because they contain 'an undisclosed reservoir of sense that a single reading cannot exhaust' (Morris 1984, p. 165). An aphorism without such implicit, if initially concealed, truth is its most extreme opposite, an opposite that pretends to be the real thing: a truism or a cliché where all is explicit and, as Morris puts it, 'gives up all of its sense at a single glance'.

An earlier lover of aphorisms, Francis Bacon, wrote that they represent 'a knowledge broken', and so 'invite men to inquire further' (Bacon, *The Advancement of Learning* (1605), cited in Johnston 1974, pp. 135–36). True aphorisms represent the 'pith and heart of sciences', he explained, because they are expressions emptied of exemplification and illustration. By cutting away these adjuncts, only the core observation is left. This exposure enables a reader to see the idea plain and unencumbered, and so question it. The discontinuity lurking in the true aphorism, the 'degree of accuracy' sacrificed to conciseness, is precisely that which demands continuing, and continual, enquiry. It is, as Dustin H. Griffin writes of the whole vision of *An Essay on Man*, 'both pattern and puzzle' (Griffin 1979, p. 162).

Further, there is the so-far-unexamined business of context. In an essay—as opposed to a sound-bite—there is always context. In Pope's *Essay*, context is inescapable: no line is an island entire unto itself, for it always has a simultaneous life as half of a couplet. 'The proper study of mankind is man' is the response to 'Know then thyself, presume not God to scan'. That opening line is, in several ways, an antithesis of its partner. Rather than offering a polished completeness, it foregrounds its caesura by its division into two separate clauses, with two separate verbs, at the fourth syllable. The first clause is, yes, a truism, one repeated time after time from classical times to the Renaissance (see Mack, ed., *TE*, III, part 1, 1950, pp. 53–54n), so often as to have been shorn of any real prompt to enquiry. The second clause is, by contrast, one to bring a reader up short. Though still a familiar idea, it is both a stimulus to real thinking and a joke. As Samuel Johnson has shown us, the real essayist—from Montaigne onwards—is both completely serious and self-depreciatingly aware of the absurdity of what is being proposed. Pope's clause is profoundly aware, and genuinely sceptical, of any theodicy: claiming an ability to observe and define (through our senses) a 'God' is a presumption, a typical manifestation of that primitive human fault, one which Pope's satirical muse is repeatedly and remorselessly committed to explore: pride. You cannot even calculate a notional 'God' by *a priori* methods, as is shown in Samuel Johnson's humorously savage exposé of the basis of the 'great chain of being'—the philosophical cliché lying behind much of the material of book 1 of *An Essay on Man* and Johnson's immediate target, Soame Jenyns's prose version of the theory. For no step up from a finite number can ever get us to infinity. Pope really knows this: hence 'scan' as the rhyme-word of the line, its point of rest. What else has he been doing but putting the theory into scansion? Poets are no less absurdly proud than the rest of us; but good poets know they are subject to pride; and great poets make that knowledge the subject of their poetry.

Pope's verse operates by means of an intricate maze of half-lines, lines, and couplets; but it also operates by larger structures, by verse-paragraphs built up from individual couplets. The second epistle of *An Essay on Man* begins with an enigmatic but assertive couplet. It is only when we read it along with the remaining sixteen lines of what has become one of his most celebrated and awe-inspiring paragraphs that we can begin to see a fuller picture. As T. S. Eliot wrote of Milton's verse-paragraphs, 'the full beauty of the line is found in its context' ('Milton II', *On Poetry and Poets*, 1957, pp. 157–58; cited in Ricks,1963, p. 28).

The eclectic force that galvanizes this verse-paragraph into extraordinarily powerful vitality is a deep paradox, one that burrows into the entire passage and then expands within it. A massive collection of the strongest possible assertions, expressed with all the certainty rhetoric can muster, is put at the service of demonstrating that everything, just everything, we know about ourselves is a matter of the deepest doubt. We do not just suspect we may be unsure about ourselves; we are totally certain that we are profoundly ignorant of ourselves. This is because everything we know is negated, or counterbalanced, by its opposite. The result is not an equipoise of controlled, human and philosophical—in the general sense—checks, but a highly disruptive set of contrapositions.

Pope draws on a quiverful of rhetorical figures in order to inject his paragraph with all the force of dynamic variation. The topographical metaphor of an 'isthmus' (line 3) puts humankind onto tenuous, vulnerable ground on which the succeeding dance of intellectual death will be performed. A pair of oxymorons, 'darkly wise' and 'rudely great' (line 4), occupy equal space within the second line of this couplet, with 'great' serving as a sardonic rhyme with 'middle state'. This phrase, or a version of it, is usually in neo-classical poetry a positive, representing the moderate 'golden mean' which comes down to us from Aristotelian ethics. Now Pope attenuates it so that it conveys something far less comfortable: a 'state' neither one thing nor the other.

The third couplet uses strong anaphora ('With too much ...') to introduce not a mutually reflective parallel, as this syntactic pattern usually does, but antithetical abstract nouns ('knowledge', 'weakness') which are matched against a counter-set of antitheses. Sceptics claim that we know nothing; but we do know something, as the paragraph keeps hammering home. The problem is that this something is profoundly negative and disturbing. Conversely, stoics claim that, by the force of reason, we are able to take control of our being and remain invulnerable to all circumstances. But, in reality we lack the strength of intellect and character to adopt this behaviour, and so the stoics' claims are exposed as mere 'pride'—itself a moral failing, as in 'presume not God to scan'.

The imitative syntax of lines 6 and 7, where the couplet rides over the end-stopping that marks the rest of the paragraph's versification in order to dangle as dangerously as our intellectual/topographical plight, introduces a triadic syntax. 'In doubt' (lines 7–9), as well as emphatically sounding a keynote for the paragraph, aims its destructive dart at three different but related propositions: that we know when and how to take action, that we can define our nature, and that we can distinguish our essential being. The second and third of these shots are particularly telling in the light of our habitual self-definition. Are we really made in God's image, as supposedly benevolent modes of faith assure us? And the entire idea of the 'great chain of being', consisting of comfortingly equal steps in a steady-state universal model (the very model that the first epistle of *An Essay on Man* has itself been insisting on), is set in question because its location of humankind as right in the middle ('this isthmus of a middle state') is the very cause of our sense of constant displacement. That we are, in some sense, 'divine' pulls us in one direction; that we are in another sense 'animal' pulls us in the contrary direction. This is not equipoise, but a constant strife of conflicting dislocations.

The chiasmus of lines 9–10, the fifth of the nine couplets and so the mid-point of the paragraph and its own isthmus, articulates with complete clarity the hopeless self-contradiction in which we find ourselves. If we 'prefer' our mind, we rely on its power of 'reason'; but that is fatally undermined by continual error. If we 'prefer' our body, we put our faith in that which, we know for certain, is temporary, destined to corruption.

Lines 11 to 14 assert that human faculties are flawed however we use them. Our 'reason'—the noun links back to the central couplet—is employed either 'too little, or too much'. If the former, we fail to think a question through; if the latter, it teases us out of thought. In either case, our final state is ignorance. The neat balance of 'too little, or too much' is a deception, not a resolution: like the great chain of being, its structure proposes a balance, a place of stillness, denied by its implementation. Then, our thoughts and feelings—our mind and body—impinge on each other, leaving neither pure. The result is confusion, just as a state of self-deception and realization of our fallacy are constantly ('still') in a rotation whereby we end up where we started, or swinging back and forth like a pendulum. We need to note here that 'abuse' and 'disabuse' both have specific senses. To 'abuse' has a meaning that the *OED* defines as obsolete, its last citation being, by chance, 1734, the year in which the fourth and final epistle of *An Essay on Man* was published. It signifies, as a reflexive and passive verb, to 'be deceived, mistaken' (*OED*, v. 4b). The contrary verb, 'disabuse', has remained in regular English usage, with an active meaning of 'freeing from abuse, error or mistake'. The *OED*, curiously, cites Pope's line in its entry for 'disabuse', but not that for 'abuse'.

A straight antithesis opens the final four lines of the paragraph. 'Half to rise' and 'half to fall', like the earlier 'darkly wise' and 'rudely great', occupy equal physical spaces within a balance of two half-lines. Thus, they appear, formally, to promise equipoise; however, they actually signify constantly opposite forces, reflecting yet again on the unresolvable paradox of the chain of being's joke (in bad taste) on us. The second line of the couplet follows up the consequences of this fatal division. We are both 'lord of all things' (the tone of irony aimed at our 'pride' is unmistakable in the context) and 'a prey to all'. This contradiction carries over into the last couplet, 'sole judge of truth' complementing 'lord of all things' in meaning and tone, and 'endless error' spelling out the consequences of being a prey to everything, including our own capacity for self-delusion: that is, our state of abuse, our natural attraction to being deceived. The verb which closes line 17 is striking: 'hurled' vigorously and forcibly throws us into error: it is not a gentle fall, but a fall on the grand scale of Milton's rebel angels:

> Him the almighty power
> Hurled headlong flaming from the ethereal sky
> With hideous ruin and combustion down
> To bottomless perdition, there to dwell
> In adamantine chains and penal fire,
> Who durst defy the Omnipotent to arms.
>
> *Paradise Lost*, book 1, lines 44–49

We have met this strong verb, and its rhyming partner, 'world', back in 'Epistle 1', lines 89–90: 'Atoms or systems into ruin hurled, / and now a bubble burst, and now a world'. The two contexts share a similar tonal quality; both are examples of Pope's style at its grandest and most gestural. In the earlier passage, the couplet resoundingly completes a paragraph marked by rhetorical crescendo. In the opening of 'Epistle 2', however, the power implied in the verb is, though highlighted by its position as rhyme-word in the couplet, a momentary flash of anger. The tone of the very last line is, as is more habitual for the sophisticated and sceptical eighteenth-century poet, wry and self-conscious, not engaged and unrelenting as is his distinguished predecessor's. 'Glory' picks up, phonically as well as semantically, the earlier 'lord'; 'jest' is mockingly self-aware (there are no jokes in the Milton passage describing the fall of Satan); and 'riddle' ends the paragraph with a big question-mark or a sign of unknowability (there is no such uncertainty in Milton's narrative). Perhaps this comparison sums up as well as any other the difference between the great English epic of the seventeenth century and the new, enlightened ethical examination which is Pope's attempt to construct an epic whole from many parts.

'Epistle 2', lines 59–60

> Self-love, the spring of motion, acts the soul;
> Reason's comparing balance rules the whole.

This couplet sets out concisely the different basic, essential functions of the two principal factors the *Essay* defines in man, 'Self-love' and 'Reason'. They are stated at the beginning of each line, and are so placed in antithesis and also joined together in the spatial configuration of the couplet.

The self-love line is energised by rhythmic invention, irregularity, and vitality. Two caesuras, marked by two commas, produce an unusual 2/5/3 rhythm and point up emphatically the opening hyphenated noun. Strongly vital language adds vigour. 'Spring' is a term from watch-making, and is widely applied to human psychology (*TE*, III, part 1, 1950, ed. by Mack, p. 62n). But it also suggests 'spring' as a source of water and so life. 'Acts', that is, to move to action, to impel, is a strong verb that sustains motion. This is coming to life, beginning, the life-force itself. The reason line is, conversely, rhythmically smooth, with no caesura. Its language is logical and abstract ('comparing'), while continuing the watch-making imagery ('balance'). The line's calm itself complements and balances the energy of its partner.

'Epistle 2', lines 133–34

> As Man, perhaps, the moment of his breath,
> Receives the lurking principle of death;

This is an example of how Pope can infuse an idea with devastatingly forceful expression. The first line hesitantly ('perhaps') sets up the proposition; then the second powerfully delivers it. The verb 'receives' makes us the passive objects of action: our very first breath takes in, accepts the inevitability of our last breath. We die from the moment of our inception. A single adjective ('lurking') sums up the dark, insidious truth that the 'principle of death' is lying malevolently in wait for us. The couplet enacts their inevitable co-ordination in the rhyme ('breath/ death'), which traps the lines into an inescapable bond.

'Epistle 2', lines 275–82

> Behold the child, by Nature's kindly law,
> Pleased with a rattle, tickled with a straw:
> Some livelier plaything gives his youth delight,
> A little louder, but as empty quite:
> Scarves, garters, gold, amuse his riper stage;
> And beads and prayer-books are the toys of age:
> Pleased with this bauble still, as that before;
> Till tired he sleeps, and life's poor play is o'er!

Sitting alongside passages of rhetorical splendour and portentous import, the poem frequently presents lines of a very different character. These reflect a pull towards the comic or satiric that Pope's muse so often exerts. A laugh, or at least a smile, is usually not far away. In the context of *An Essay on Man* such passages are not simply incidental. On the contrary, they are essential exemplifications of man's state as the 'glory, jest and riddle of the world' (line 18). It is jest time.

Like a miniature version of the seven ages of man, this four-couplet paragraph skips through four stages, the child, the youth, the (delicately if ironically put) 'riper' man, and old age. The effect is to render each of his activities, at every point, equivalent in their triviality and emptiness. Do we learn, do we mature ('riper'), do we grow? No, we remain distinctly immature, wedded to the farcical and meaningless. This parody of the notion of progress allows Pope to indulge in a few short, sharp, satirical cuts. Sashes worn by doctors of divinity are belittled as 'scarves'; garters are reduced from noble symbols of the Order of the Garter to just plain garters without the 'Order'; the rosary of Catholic observance is shown up as, empty of meaning, merely a few beads. Each is as much a bauble, a mere plaything for immature minds, as the rattle and straw with which we begin our journey through life.

There is a theatrical element here as well. Our most famous 'Seven Ages of Man' speech is found in *As You Like It*. 'Riper' summons up Edgar's consolatory, or resigned, aphorism in *King Lear*: 'ripeness is all'. 'Life's poor play' explicitly echoes Macbeth's final soliloquy in act 5: 'Life's but ... a poor player / That struts and frets his hour upon the stage'. All these Shakespearean instances of belittlement point to echoes in other poems. So, the child's toy will be found again in his dismissal of verse as 'rhymes and rattles of the man or boy' in another poem addressed to St John, Pope's *First Epistle of the First Book of Horace Imitated* (line 18); and the reduction of 'all the world's a stage' to the level of farce is also enacted in the finale to *The Dunciad*, in both versions. The running idea, then, is that life has no real essence or existence; rather, a sham display of vacuous insignificance. Jokes can be serious.

'Epistle 3', lines 303–06

> For forms of government let fools contest;
> Whate'er is best administered is best:
> For modes of faith, let graceless zealots fight;
> His can't be wrong whose life is in the right:

The couplets are parallel in syntax. The first lines set up the subject ('government', 'faith') through parallel syntax ('For ...') and semantic equivalence ('let fools contest', 'let graceless zealots fight') whereby the verbs are synonyms; the second lines are, by contrast, varied in syntax, but both represent the poet's answer to the implied questions, what constitutes the 'best' form of government and the 'best' mode of faith. 'Best' and 'right' are the two clinching rhymes, in response to the synonyms of 'contest'/'fight'. In both cases, the answer is that the 'best' is that which produces the best practical outcome. The poetry avoids engaging in theoretical or ideological disputation in favour of a pragmatic conclusion. Note that Pope does not say that there is no difference between the various 'forms of government' and 'modes of faith'; but that such differences are meaningless or insignificant when considered apart from their effects upon the actual lives of people. Pope himself explicitly made this distinction in a manuscript note (*TE*, III, part 1, 1950, ed. by Mack, appendix B, p. 170). There is, he contends, no point in wrangling or speculating about forms of government unless the 'preferred' form is 'well and uprightly administered'; and, equivalently, modes of faith are only of significance if they have a beneficial effect on how a believer acts. It is the moral outcome that matters, not the belief itself. In secular and religious, and theoretical and ideological areas, Pope's argument has earlier philosophical points of reference: Aristotle's *Politics*, the Cambridge Platonists and Sir William Temple (*TE*, III, part 1, 1950, ed. by Mack, pp. 123–24 n and appendix B). As is commonly the case, Pope is not thinking originally, but is producing concise, economical, and memorable expressions of existing thought: 'What oft was thought, but ne'er so well expressed'. His arguments are nonetheless strongly significant in terms of their meaning: Pope is always on the side of the pragmatic and sceptical of the abstract. In this he is in tune with the main tenor of Enlightenment thought. His couplets are fine, and representative, examples of his unparalleled capacity for intense and economical expression. Consider the epigrammatic power of simple linguistic repetition ('is best ... is best') and contrast ('wrong ... right'). Further, the couplets enact the meaning of Pope's statement. Whereas the language attributed to those who do spend their time mired in political and religious dispute is divisive, about conflict ('contest'; 'fight'), Pope's couplets resolve the lines into rhyme, the language of harmony and reconciliation. So 'contest' leads to 'best'; and 'fight' to 'right'. The rhythm, the movement of the couplets are expressive of their meaning.

'Epistle 4', lines 387–98

> When statesmen, heroes, kings, in dust repose,
> Whose sons shall blush their fathers were thy foes,
> Shall then this verse to future age pretend
> Thou wert my guide, philosopher, and friend?
> That urged by thee, I turned the tuneful art
> From sounds to things, from fancy to the heart;
> For wit's false mirror held up Nature's light;
> Showed erring pride, 'WHATEVER IS, IS RIGHT';
> That REASON, PASSION, answer one great aim;
> That true SELF-LOVE and SOCIAL are the same;
> That VIRTUE only makes our bliss below;
> And all our knowledge is, OURSELVES TO KNOW.

For his finale, Pope concisely brings together the central messages of each epistle. Lines 394 to 397 accord each book in turn a single line. The first epistle sets out the fixed, immutable structure of creation according to the traditional idea of the chain of being, or the scale of nature. Human beings occupy their allotted place, which they must accept. 'Whatever is, is RIGHT' (epistle 1, line 294), and to challenge this is to give way to pride. The second epistle defines two ruling agencies within individual men and women: 'Self-love, to urge, and reason, to restrain' (epistle 2, line 54). Modes of self-love we call our passions, which move us to action; reason is the force that controls. In the third epistle, Pope expands these definitions to encompass our roles within society, and finds that 'self-love and social' are the same essential forces ('Epistle 3', line 318). In the fourth epistle, happiness is shown to lie within virtue alone; virtue for its own sake and not its consequences, as these are acted upon by ills or accidents over which we have no control ('Epistle 4', line 310).

This quartet of summaries at the poem's close is preceded by invocation of the term which marks the condition of our being: 'Nature' is the 'natural' state of humanity, of both our own selves and our earthly context. And the quartet is rounded off by a re-statement of the guiding aphorism for any proper study of our existence: 'Know then thyself' ('Epistle 2', line 1). This, then, is Pope in magisterially didactic mode: the essayist signing off his work.

But there is much more than such succinct messaging in *An Essay on Man*. In spite of Pope's stern denial in line 393, there is much 'wit' to the poem. It just all depends what we understand by 'wit'. Etymologically, the word signifies knowledge, but it has come to cover many wider connotations, some positive, some negative, and some questionable. Wit can be, line 393 asserts, a false mirror, a distorting image or reflection: itself a reflection, it may be, of our desire to assert our own brief authority over our perceptions, to mould them into forms that may please but really flatter to deceive. On the other hand, as Pope himself will imply in Dr Busby's speech in the fourth book of *The Dunciad*, 'rebel wit' can be the very principle of our intellectual being: not so much an aspect of our pride in the sense of presumption but of our pride in the possibilities of genuinely enlightened agency: our nature's 'light', as line 393 itself allows. There are gradations and subtleties within our intellectual being, and the poem needs to show this if it is to reveal in its fullness our nature.

And there is something else, too, which shines through and mitigates the rigours of what might, if dogmatically asserted, become a cage for our fixed position within the scale of being. By making happiness available to humans, the concluding sections of 'Epistle 4' warmly assure us, the universal cause offers a benign and welcome message. The purpose of the human soul in its individual and social being begins and ends in 'LOVE OF GOD, and LOVE OF MAN' ('Epistle 4', line 340). A word that resounds through the ending of the poem is 'friend' ('Epistle 4', lines 367, 373, 390). Fittingly, its final statement is in the moving and celebrated appeal to the poem's addressee and patron. Pope proclaims (the core meaning of 'pretend', from Latin 'praetendere'—literally to 'hold out before') Bolingbroke as 'my guide, philosopher, and friend'. From Pope's earliest poems onwards (see *An Essay on Criticism* in Chapter 3) through all his later epistles, friendship has been his continuing solace, inspiration, and—in the true sense—pride.

12. *An Epistle to Richard Boyle, Earl of Burlington*

Examples: Lines 23–38, 57–64, 113–20, 191–94

The *Epistle to Burlington*, published in December 1731, was the first poem written in Pope's plan for a philosophical magnum opus, a grand survey of the ethical, political, and social concerns defining a mature and enlightened account of human beings and their place within creation. This epic for the modern age was to be constructed out of a series of individual works. Parts answering parts would slide into a whole. It was an ambitious undertaking, and its scope and its constituents changed and developed as the 1730s proceeded. It may never have achieved a final shape, but the sets of major poems produced—the *Epistles to Several Persons*, *An Essay on Man*, the *Imitations of Horace*—represent a substantial accomplishment in themselves. And, indeed, it may be argued that, like the Enlightenment itself, its status as an ongoing project is fitting for its underlying principles. Miriam Leranbaum's *Alexander Pope's 'Opus Magnum 1729–1744* (1977) remains the standard and definitive account of the design and implementation of the scheme.

Although the *Epistle to Burlington* eventually became the fourth of the four *Epistles to Several Persons* in the 1735 *Works*, its position in order of composition is instructive. It is Pope's major contribution to a debate on creativity and represents a keystone definition of the magnum opus's aesthetic structure. The poem's subtitle is 'Of the Use of Riches'; its principal role is to define, in Pope's inimitable comic manner, an artistic formula for judgement. In Pope's poetry, art itself is always paramount.

Lines 23–38

> You show us, Rome was glorious, not profuse,
> And pompous buildings once were things of use.
> Yet shall (my Lord) your just, your noble rules
> Fill half the land with imitating fools;
> Who random drawings from your sheets shall take,
> And of one beauty many blunders make;
> Load some vain church with old theatric state,
> Turn arcs of triumph to a garden-gate;
> Reverse your ornaments, and hang them all
> On some patched dog-hole eked with ends of wall,
> Then clap four slices of pilaster on't,
> That, laced with bits of rustic, makes a front:
> Or call the winds through long arcades to roar,
> Proud to catch cold at a Venetian door;
> Conscious they act a true Palladian part,
> And if they starve, they starve by rules of art.

The opening couplet of this verse-paragraph is an epigrammatic statement of principles at the heart of the neo-Palladianism espoused by Burlington and championed here by Pope. 'You'—Burlington—'show us' because he, together with William Kent, had published the designs of Inigo Jones and Andrea Palladio in, respectively, 1727 and 1730. Jones was the earliest English advocate of Palladianism, as exemplified by his designs for the Queen's House at Greenwich. Palladio's own *Quattro Libri dell'Architettura* (1570) were the standard reference work for the English Palladian Revival movement of the early eighteenth century (see Harris 1994, chapter 1).

The couplet's economy exemplifies the first element of its proposition: Rome, the architectural centre of classicism, showed that buildings could be 'glorious'—magnificent in their visual splendour—without spilling over into the grandiose. Poetry, by analogy, achieves beauty of form by eschewing verbosity. To avoid meanness, it is not necessary to embrace extravagance, as happens in the cautionary fictional example of Old and Young Cotta in Pope's next epistle, *To Bathurst*. There exists a golden mean, a state of equipoise between extremes.

The second line defines another element of the foundation principle. 'Pompous' buildings—splendid, magnificent buildings—can, at the same time, be 'things of use'. Classicism is defined by a capacity to balance beauty with utility, to combine a regard for visual pleasure with practical value. That we have to pause to remind ourselves of the core meaning of the word 'pompous' is itself an implicit acknowledgement of how easily human endeavours to attain splendour can slide into ostentation. Indeed, the history of the word 'pompous' demonstrates the precariousness of such balance: the negative meaning of 'exaggerated display, vaingloriousness' has accompanied the 'good' meaning from the beginning of its usage in the late medieval period (see *OED*, 'pompous', adj., senses 1 and 2). 'Facilis descensus averno', as the Virgilian tag has it. Today, of course, the derogatory meaning has triumphed, and its alternate virtually disappeared.

The couplet in its entirety enacts a proper predominance of good taste over bad. Its statement of a negative—'not profuse'—is squeezed into three syllables, bracketed away by its succession of positive clauses ('You show us', 'Rome was glorious', 'pompous buildings once were things of use'). That brief negative is trenchantly answered by the blunt rhyme-word that concludes the end-stopped couplet: 'use'. The conjunction of beauty and utility was a maxim familiar from its Horatian source in the *Ars Poetica*, the third of the three epistles in book 2: 'omne tulit punctum qui miscuit utile dulci, / lectorem delectando pariterque monendo (lines 343–44) [he who mixes the useful with the pleasant wins the vote, charming and advising the reader in equal measure]. Horace is advocating an economical fusion of instruction and delight when writing in the didactic mode. Pope's application of the idea to the practical business of building is duly effected in a couplet that displays the very axiom in action within his own poetic formulation: Burlington and Pope, each in his own sphere, show how to do it.

This principle is implicit throughout Pope's epistle, as in his immediate response to the excessive scale on which Timon's villa is constructed ('What sums are thrown away!', line 100) and his wry observation of Timon's library ('In books, not authors, curious is my lord; / To all their dated backs he turns you round', lines 134–35). As the poem approaches its finale, Pope re-states his main theme in another end-stopped couplet: 'Tis use alone that sanctifies expense, / And splendour borrows all her rays from sense' (lines 179–80). Such pragmatism is, as we saw in Chapter 11, echoed at the social level in *An Essay on Man*: 'For forms of government let fools contest; / Whate'er is best administered is best'

('Epistle 3', lines 303–04). Cut the superfluous theorizing: what makes people's lives better is a properly functioning system. The true value of books lies in their content—the author's words—not in the date and quality of their binding. Timon strips books of their human reference, so reducing them to inactive material objects. Buildings are places for people to live in, and people respond best to whatever best serves their needs and adds pleasure to their lives.

Would that life were that simple and straightforward. We get only as far as the second couplet in our paragraph before gentle notes of satirical comedy slide in: 'Yet shall (my lord) your just, your noble rules / Fill half the land with imitating fools'. The parenthesis has a touch of mock-solemn deference, and 'noble' quietly puns on Burlington's rank. Pope remains delicately hesitant, but fools rush in without observing any caesura or any decorum. The rhyme of 'noble rules' and 'imitating fools' is a telling wound. And not only are the fools many and we, my lord, few; but 'one beauty' engenders 'many blunders'. You may condemn the fools' lack of taste, but you cannot deny their industry.

The imitating fools are energetic in their misapplied activity, and they are versatile in the scope of those misapplications. These range from inappropriate choice of decoration for the function of the building ('Load some vain church with old theatric state') to abuse of enhancing materials ('Reverse your ornaments'); from inappropriate use of whole structures ('Turn arcs of triumph to a garden gate') to misplaced architectural structures ('call the winds through long arcades to roar'). Pope's range of language matches the wild reach of the fools' imaginative disarrangement: from demeaning nouns ('dog-hole', defined in *OED* as a 'hole fit for a dog; a vile or mean dwelling or place, unfit for human habitation') to disrespectful verbs ('clap'); from startling oxymorons ('vain church') to slangy colloquialisms ('on't'). At the heart of the fools' perverse activity lies a repeated lack of attention, an inability—or refusal—to apply the care required for art to emerge. So, the drawings they take from Burlington's architectural sheets are 'random', ornaments are put on back to front or in reverse, and 'rustic' (rough-hewn) stonework is cut up into small interlaced 'bits' rather than used as contrasting blocks within an overall surface.

The paragraph's final couplet rounds off the entire farrago. The fools' ignorance of what they are doing is exposed by the undermining implications of 'act' and 'part'. There is a world of difference between conscious enactment of noble principles and unauthentic game-playing. Rules of art—the last line picks up on those 'noble rules' placed in ironic rhyme to 'fools' at the beginning—are rendered absurd by being invoked as justification for self-destructive squandering of riches. Like the crazed creatures who are gathered into Dulness's vortex in book 4 of *The Dunciad*, the fools suffer from an incapacity to see how parts should answer parts to 'slide into a whole' (line 66). Everything is left in pieces. But, unlike the sleep-walkers to oblivion in that later, devastating, satire, these representatives of chaos are alert, busy, and unflagging. It is all so exhausting.

How, then, is order to be restored and the integrity of Burlington's example re-established? At the centre of the next paragraph (lines 39–46) lies the word 'sense'. It concludes the fourth line and begins the fifth, so acting as amid-point fulcrum: 'Something there is, more needful than expense, / And something previous even to taste—'tis sense: / Good sense, which only is the gift of heaven'. To exemplify the power of good sense to reinstate order, Pope turns to another art-form, one that frequently accompanies architecture: landscape gardening, or the arrangement of the grounds of a building to match and support architectural forms:

Lines 57–64

> Consult the genius of the place in all;
> That tells the waters or to rise, or fall,
> Or helps the ambitious hill the heavens to scale,
> Or scoops in circling theatres the vale;
> Calls in the country, catches opening glades,
> Joins willing woods, and varies shades from shades;
> Now breaks, or now directs, the intending lines,
> Paints as you plant, and as you work, designs.

The syntax of this eight-line paragraph repairs the centrifugal flight to chaos in the 'imitating fools' passage. It restores order by defining a proper and respectful relationship between human activity and natural principles. The result is integrity of vision, a harmonious hierarchy which embraces creation and creativity.

The principal means by which Pope renders this is his choice and placement of verbs. The would-be landscape gardener is addressed directly by the imperative 'Consult'. The verb derives from Latin 'consulere', with its central meaning of taking counsel. Legal connotations are to the fore in its English application, but the Latin verb was equally open to religious usage. Pope's 'genius of the place' is his classically conscious version of *genius loci*, the attribution to place of a spirit, an inherent principle of animation. This idea of taking advice from the quasi-divine ordering within a landscape reverses the imitating fools' wanton and self-defeating imposition of their solipsistic and hubristic irrationality on whatever they touch. 'Consult' enhances a contrary humility: our first duty is to observe the proper order of creation, in which whatever force does animate nature is respected and acknowledged. The whole line serves to reset human deference and return calm to the fools' aimless bustling. The analogy also serves, discreetly, to re-establish Burlington's authority in the sphere of architecture. He is, as it were, the 'genius' of modern neo-Palladianism; his editions of Jones and Palladio were the aesthetic movement's authoritative texts to be consulted and not ripped asunder.

From this point on, all the principal verbs in the paragraph are those for which 'the genius of the place' is subject. These represent the advice we should seek to follow. The sequence of verbs is semantically varied to reflect the particular aspects of nature addressed. For example, the verbs in the second couplet are set in parallel across the lines ('Or helps', 'Or scoops'), but are antithetical in meaning as the features of landscape are opposites. Hills reach towards the skies, and can be metaphorically rendered as aiming high, as if animated by hope. 'Scoops', by contrast, elegantly breaks into the ground with an orderly motion implicit in 'circling'. The couplet in its entirety balances rising and descending ground as nature always does: a rise looks forward to a matching declivity in a visually harmonious created landscape. The role of human activity is to respect and co-operate with the resultant symmetry, and Pope's lines follow in their simultaneous balance and antithesis.

Pope deploys these verbs in varying and gently accelerating rhythm: one per line in 59–60 ('helps', 'scoops'), doubling up in 61–62 ('Calls/catches', 'Joins/varies'). This restrained increase in pace as the paragraph proceeds reaches its climax in the final couplet, where human agency is explicitly brought into proper relationship with the forces of animating nature. Pope appropriately reserves his most stylistically intense and virtuosic rhetoric for this couplet: his art rises to the challenge of an aphoristic conclusion. The first line follows the dual verb format of the preceding couplet and connects both to an object ('intending lines'), which strikes an inspired and appropriate classical note. 'Intending' has its roots, via French 'entendre', in Latin 'intendere', meaning to stretch out, to endeavour to attain, to purpose (*OED*, 'intend', v. 2, sense 5). Latin applied it to various semantic fields, starting from the literal reaching out of arms towards or in the direction of an object of wish or attention. Most significantly for Pope's purposes, 'intending' referred to the cognate ideas of turning one's thoughts or attention to a fitting end. Horace, for example, writes of directing the mind to one's studies: 'animum studiis'. In Pope's context of visual experience, the implied direct object is 'eyes', from the Latin 'intendere oculos'. So, the lines of nature lead our eyes in an expressive and intentional direction.

This classicism prepares for the final line of the paragraph, where Pope sets out one of his favourite structures, a chiasmus. Here the two verbs deriving from the genius of the place are located at the beginning and end: 'Paints', 'designs'. Human corresponding activity is enclosed within these twin verbs: 'as you plant, and as you work'. The key semantic and philosophical point is that humans take on the humble and laborious roles, while truly artistic activity is the sphere of the animating spirit infusing the whole. 'Paints' and 'designs' ordinarily operate within the realm of human creativity. Within the wider vision of this paragraph, that principle is transferred to its proper agent. Human activity is put in its place: valuable and satisfying, but secondary. Humility (in contrast to the fools who are 'Proud to catch cold', line 36) is restored. It all makes sense, really. So, the first line of the next paragraph picks up that word, which by now has gathered together its physical and mental meanings (what we perceive visually and what we grasp intellectually) and chimes the line with a central definition of harmony: 'Still follow sense, of every art the soul, / Parts answering parts shall slide into a whole' (lines 65–66).

However, Pope's satirical mind cannot leave matters there. It is not that easy to shake off a desire to give rein to, and simultaneously deride, the objects of satire that paradoxically are its bread and butter as well as its poison. The *Epistle to Burlington* has seen off one set of fools and restored 'nature' (line 50) and Burlington to their rightful places. But there is still room for the biggest fool of the lot. A tour of Timon's villa makes up the largest part of the poem (lines 99–168). It was also, in its time and for long afterwards, the poem's most controversial section, as gleeful gossips and curious commentators ventured at guessing the model for Timon. Time alone has allowed the likely truth to emerge: that the vulgarians' vulgarian was a fictitious composite rather than a specific target.

The principal ironic message of Pope's account of Timon's estate and house is that the hubristic scale of his villa and gardens has, as its direct consequence, a diminution of the human, and, so, of Timon himself. Pope's reference to Brobdignag (line 104), the land of the giants in his friend Swift's recently published *Gulliver's Travels*, makes the point while also connecting this section of the poem to the satirical ends of the Scriblerus Club. The giant fool is really a 'puny insect' (line 108), like the devotees of Dulness who swarm around their Great Mother in book 4 of *The Dunciad* (see Chapter 26).

A specific satirical point is made in the course of the description of his gardens. However hard you try to get fools to think straight about an aesthetic principle, their infinite variety will twist it out of shape again:

Lines 113–20

> His gardens next your admiration call,
> On every side you look, behold the wall!
> No pleasing intricacies intervene,
> No artful wildness to perplex the scene;
> Grove nods at grove, each alley has a brother,
> And half the platform just reflects the other.
> The suffering eye inverted nature sees,
> Trees cut to statues, statues thick as trees.

Harmony and its Palladian architectural equivalent, symmetry, are the ideals underlying a balanced view of the place of humans within nature, but trust a fool to grab the wrong end even of this stick. Harmony, in short, may have distortion as its obvious opposite, but it also has monotony as its lop-sided extreme. The true ideal is an Aristotelian golden mean, as Pope frequently reminds us. For example: 'Like good Erasmus in an honest mean, / In moderation placing all my glory, / While Tories call me Whig, and Whigs a Tory', *The First Satire of the Second Book of Horace, Imitated* (lines 66–68.)

Timon knows that proportion lies at the heart of taste. He may even have read Pope on this very topic in, say, the St. Peter's section of *An Essay on Criticism* (lines 247–52). But he has missed a crucial element of true classicism, as surely as the imitating fools who snatch randomly from Burlington's designs. The aim and definition of true beauty are the 'joint force and full result' of all constituent parts (*An Essay on Criticism*, line 246). Yes, a wall is an essential element in, well, a walled garden. Simply building four walls and leaving it at that, however, is to confuse parts with whole. At first glance, Pope's use of the verb 'perplex' as the counterbalancing effect of 'pleasing intricacies' may itself appear perplexing if read in its more common negative sense of 'confuse'. However, Pope is here digging into his language to expose its own intricacy. Latin 'perplexus' can indeed mean 'confused', but it also means 'intricate', as 'plexus' was used of a plaited, interwoven texture, such as a garland of flowers. The straight lines of a wall require to be set off by the variation of pattern plantings bring.

The final couplet of these lines invokes chiasmus to perform its other, satirical, function, matching its primary creative use, as in 'Paints as you plant, and as you work, designs' (see above, line 64). In 'Trees cut to statues, statues thick as trees', artistic taste is, as its preceding line has it, 'inverted' rather than positively illustrated. Back in 1713, Pope had written an essay in the *Guardian* (no. 173, 7 September 1713) mocking the fashion for topiary work, shaping of plants into sculptural forms. Here, Pope adds an inverse distortion by telling us that Timon crowds his actual, stone statues together as if they were a grove of trees. Statues, being three-dimensional works of art, require space for the viewer to observe them from all perspectives. If you cannot do this, then, again, the artistic event is stripped of all its elements. The aesthetic values of trees and statues have been inverted in a mutually negating act of ignorance. Pope's highly compressed chiasmus is as sharp in its expression as Timon's garden is obtuse in its.

Lines 191–94

> You too proceed! make falling arts your care,
> Erect new wonders, and the old repair;
> Jones and Palladio to themselves restore,
> And be whate'er Vitruvius was before:

This final paragraph returns, after the satirical centre of the poem, to where we began: with a direct address to the Earl of Burlington. 'You show us', 'You too proceed'. Focus now, though, is on Burlington's active involvement in the public sphere. The poem has dealt with the theory, the 'noble rules' which he has set out in his editions of the designs of Inigo Jones and Andrea Palladio. But Burlington is not just a mere theorist. He is himself a practising architect, one who builds, who engages in the real world, and so puts his ideas to the test. 'Proceed!'—progress, march on—is the imperative now.

The future works, which the poet both hopes and expects will enrich the architecture of contemporary Britain, are to be solidly based on a full and proper understanding of the achievements of the past. These lines provide the pedigree. Vitruvius was the Roman architect who built the Augustan city. Palladio's work in Renaissance Italy was itself based on Vitruvian precedent; and Jones has initiated the revival of classicism in seventeenth-century England. Now the responsibility moves on to our present eighteenth century. This endeavour will include and improve the past—'the old repair'—and, at the same time, 'erect new wonders'. Neo-classicism is a present acknowledgement of its responsibility to tradition and to the future. Pope's poem sets this out, and, in this radiant finale, brushes aside the fools whose stupidity has been so witheringly and wittily exposed. He, too, begins the 1730s with *The Dunciad* of 1729 behind him and engages on his task of building an epic for the new age. He, too, proceeds. Confidence and optimism are to the fore here. But will those fools confess their defeat and stay away? Does their presence as objects of satire at the heart of this poem's manifesto remain a worrying, niggling reminder?

13. *An Epistle to Allen, Lord Bathurst*

Examples: Lines 161–62, 187–92, 203–04, 209–12, 223–28, 249–50, 263–68, 299–310

Pope's planning for a large-scale study of ethical, philosophical, economic, and sociological principles began at least as early as 1730. The *Epistles* to Burlington and Bathurst were the first two individual contributions, alongside the lengthier composition of the four epistles of *An Essay on Man*. Given Pope's perennial tendency to revise drafts and to attend to appropriate times for publication, it is difficult to ascertain exact completion dates. The Bathurst *Epistle* is theoretically closely linked to the Burlington *Epistle*, as studies of the use and abuse of wealth in, respectively, the newly rich merchant classes and the aristocracy. By delaying publication until 1733, Pope signalled an equally important relationship between the specific and personal Bathurst poem and the philosophically ambitious *Essay on Man*. The *Epistle to Bathurst* was published on 15 January 1733; the first epistle of *An Essay on Man* on 20 February that year, closely followed by its second and third epistles.

That link is textually emphasized by clear cross-references, as in the first of the following extracts. These have been selected to describe, broadly, the shape of the poem's argument.

The Maxim: Lines 161–62

> Extremes in nature equal good produce,
> Extremes in man concur to general use.

Pope here adopts the aphoristic manner frequently seen in *An Essay on Man*. He thereby effects a stylistic interplay between the two poems, which would have been a crucial integrating factor for the magnum opus, had it been completed. The role of an aphorism is to express an idea in its most concentrated form (Chapter 11's examination of *An Essay on Man* contains a full discussion of aphorisms.) A single line of verse is perfect for this; its separate and integrated state is rendered both visually by naturally embracing a single syntactic unit and by the empty spaces preceding and succeeding it on the page. When made one half of two such lines in an end-stopped couplet, as here, the force of each line is enhanced by the other's contiguity. The semantic relationship between these two lines wavers between similarity and antithesis.

'Nature' is different both from 'man' and from a larger whole of which 'man' is a part. 'Man' thus 'fills out' (the etymological meaning of 'complement') a space within 'nature'. The subjects of the two lines then lead to antithetical predicates. Extremes in nature—the 'reconciled extremes of drought and rain, seedtime and harvest, life and death, change and permanence ... on which, in the traditional view, the well-being of the world is founded' (*TE*, III, part 1, 1950, ed. by Mack, p. 79)—balance out to create the 'equality' that is creation's equilibrium. Extremes in man, as the poem will go on to illustrate, form a series of opposites, such as the miser and the prodigal. As far as these individuals are concerned, there can be no reconciliation: they are either one or the other, as in the characters of Old Cotta and Young Cotta (see below). Only at the social level may they be seen as 'concurring' to 'general use'; and, even there, it is arguable that the outcome is mutual destruction rather than any form of social balance.

Pope's careful choice of verb, here, is telling. To 'concur' originally meant to 'run together violently; to come into collision' (*OED*, 'concur', *v*. 1; from the Latin 'currere', meaning 'to run'). The latest usage in this sense cited by the *OED* is 1692, a date close enough to Pope's poem to suggest that its shock waves might still be felt rippling through, even as the more modern sense of 'combine in action', 'co-operate' (*OED*, sense 3) was becoming firmly established. Telling also is Pope's metrical variation between the two lines. The pause between subject and predicate in the first line is at the halfway mark, dividing the line into two equal parts. An equivalent pause in the second line divides it into four and six syllables. Both are, of course, common rhythmic divisions and are therefore felt as variations rather than violent disruptions; and both lines divide the stresses into two in the first part, three in the second. The couplet as a whole, then, ends in harmony.

But the differences remain as at least a tremor. Especially is this so when compared with the couplet's fellow in *An Essay on Man*: 'Extremes in nature equal ends produce, / In man they join to some mysterious use' ('Epistle 2', lines 205–06). The first lines in both poems mean the same: the 'ends' produced by nature are 'good'. However, the second line in *An Essay on Man* means something different. Pope's theory there is that a single human being can, or does, contain at least the potential for both extremes to mingle to some degree. As Mack asks, 'in an ambitious statesman, how much is desire for self-aggrandizement and how much is public spirit'? (*TE*, III, part 1, 1950, p. 80.) This is a mystery indeed. The more philosophically inclined *Essay* digs somewhat deeper as a result of its argument that human beings are a compound of self-love and reason: two forces that pull in opposite directions. The *Epistle to Bathurst* is less searching, more concerned to entertain and amuse with a series of portraits of comic or satirical types. However, both couplets end up in the same place: 'use', a link between the *Epistles to Burlington* and *Bathurst*, both of which have as their sub-title, 'Of the Use of Riches'. These variations between the *Epistles* and the *Essay* perhaps provide a clue to how Pope might have wanted his complete magnum opus to have looked. By building it up through bringing together differing genres, and so differing voices, Pope would have presented an intellectual epic appropriate for a modern, diverse world.

The Examples: Old Cotta and Young Cotta: Lines 187–92, 203–04, 209–12

> Like some lone Chartreux stands the good old hall,
> Silence without, and fasts within the wall;
> No raftered roofs with dance and tabor sound,
> No noontide-bell invites the country round:
> Tenants with sighs the smokeless towers survey,
> And turn the unwilling steeds another way:

lines 187–92

When Pope turns from general maxim to specific examples, his poetry shifts from abstract to concrete. His example of the tendency of generations to swing from one extreme to the opposite is a fictional one of Old and Young Cotta. We can feel Pope relaxing into a mode he finds congenial: the comic portrait. The verse expands from aphoristic economy into satirical extravagance. His language sparkles with the glee of inventing and representing, cartoon-like, the sights and sounds of human absurdity.

To depict Old Cotta's miserly frugality, Pope reaches for the old country-house ideal of charity and hospitality as exemplified in poems such as Ben Jonson's *To Penshurst* (1616), a paean to the social conscience and generosity of the Sidney family. This social vision rested on the duty and responsibility of the great and the good to serve as the hub of a well-ordered community in the 'country' (in the sense of the surrounding area, the estate). In terms of *An Essay on Man*, such behaviour exhibits a chain of social order, which 'Connects each being, greatest with the least' (*An Essay on Man*, 'Epistle 3', line 23).

Old Cotta, alas, has mislaid his principles, abandoning 'his fortune and his birth' (line 177) as surely as his manor. His 'good old hall'—Pope's adjectives summon up the glib nostalgia of a creed conveniently agreeable to those favoured by fortune—instead adopts the isolationism ('lone') of a Carthusian monastery, whose contemplative austerity acts as an anti-type, rather daringly for a Catholic writer, however notionally so. 'Silence', appropriate for a place of prayer and meditation, is set against the 'dance and tabor' of social pleasures or the inviting 'noontide-bell'. Everything at Cotta Hall is framed in negatives, in absences: no sounds, no merriment, no invitations, no warmth (the 'smokeless towers' that would indicate a once-vigorous and welcoming hearth). Repulsion replaces attraction, turning away displaces warm greeting. And it is not only his tenants who face rejection: Cotta is turning his back on the traditional role that alone can sustain and justify such a social model.

Cotta's son, however, inverts his father's frugality into flagrant displays of indulgence. But it is narrowly focussed indulgence:

> Whole slaughtered hecatombs, and floods of wine,
> Fill the capacious squire, and deep divine!

lines 203–04

Old Cotta's monkish habits sink beneath 'hecatombs' (literally, the sacrifice of a hundred cattle or oxen in Greek or Roman feasts) and 'floods of wine'. Young Cotta's pagan rituals and extravagance replace his father's austerity and isolationism. He shares his plenty with a narrow (in range, if not in girth) and dubious set, secular and ecclesiastical, far removed from the idealized society summoned up by long-lost country-house principles.

Nor is Young Cotta's sense of national duty accurately aimed:

> The woods recede around the naked seat,
> The sylvans groan—no matter—for the fleet:
> Next goes his wool—to clothe our valiant bands,
> Last, for his country's love, he sells his lands.
>
> lines 209–12

Such is his 'zeal for that great house'—the House of Hanover, now reigning in the person of George II—that he despoils his own house of its estate's natural resources. Pope's irony is precise and remorseless: the 'country'—now in the sense of the nation—receives from Young Cotta the gifts of the entire estate which traditionally (and rightly if one subscribes to the code) ought to furnish and maintain the wealth and health of 'the country' in that earlier sense of the surrounding neighbourhood (line 190).

Pope's language is also tellingly precise. The 'sylvans groan' in the multiple senses of the men and women who live in the woods as foresters, the creatures whose habitat is thereby destroyed, and the symbolic deities or spirits of the woods. The resonance of classical mythology joins with modern economic and environmental well-being to lament their destruction in the service of national naval and military glory. But what price a 'country' devastated at the altar of the 'country'? Cotta's own resultant bankruptcy follows logically: he has sold out, sacrificed himself for that chimera; his actions are both generally and personally destructive. The structure of the lines of verse, too, is put under stress. The dashes that appear in lines 210 and 211 break up the rhythm in stylistic sympathy with the plight of the groaning sylvan and the empty pastures.

The Mean: Bathurst: Lines 223-28

> To balance fortune by a just expense,
> Join with economy, magnificence;
> With splendour, charity; with plenty, health;
> Oh teach us, BATHURST! yet unspoiled by wealth!
> That secret rare, between the extremes to move
> Of mad good nature, and of mean self-love.

Addressees of Pope's epistles generally represent a standard by which the comic or tragic failures can be measured. Allen, Lord Bathurst was one of the twelve peers created by Queen Anne in 1712 to ensure a majority for her Tory government. Pope addresses him as both a close personal friend of long standing and a public, political figure (Mack 1985, pp. 371-73). He stands as a generous, living counter to the wildly fictional parodies of Old and Young Cotta.

Pope's poetry accordingly reverts from the spirited burlesque manner of the two paragraphs on the Cottas to poetry which measures out the calming influence of his friend. The opposite of the Cottas' destructive extremes is simply and directly stated: 'balance', 'between the extremes'. Words and phrases are organized in the lines so that they effortlessly occupy places that represent spatial and rhythmic equilibrium: 'economy'/'magnificence' are ample words of the same metrical form; 'With splendour, charity'/'with plenty, health' expand into phrases that fill out a complete line through exactly balanced syntax; 'Of mad good nature, and of mean self-love' are prepositional phrases shaped, with the conjunction, into equal halves—whether the reading voice stresses two syllables in each (mád, náture; méan, lóve) or three ('mád good náture'; 'méan sélf-lóve'). Harmony is welcomingly soothing after the disruptive hustle and bustle of the lengthy Cotta passages. The poem could, one feels, end here. Indeed, some of Pope's epistles, such as *An Epistle to a Lady*, do use their direct appeal to addressees as a satisfying resolution. The overtly ethical language Pope uses ('virtue' in line 220; 'self-love' at the close of the paragraph) ensures an elevated tone and set of references. But, in fact, the poem is little more than halfway done: 228 out of 402 lines. Further exemplification and exploration seem to be demanded. Why is this?

The Exemplar: The Man of Ross: Lines 249–50, 263–68

Lord Bathurst stands at the top end of the social and economic spectrum. Pope neither hides nor apologizes for this, so forestalling one obvious objection to the implication that Bathurst and his privileged like are specially fit and able to exhibit gracious and rational behaviour. Bathurst has the 'sense to value riches' (line 219), and our extract is full of words emphasizing his blessed position within modern society: 'fortune', 'magnificence', 'splendour', 'plenty', 'wealth' (note the quiet, so quiet as to pass almost unheard, 'yet' before 'unspoiled by wealth' in line 226). 'It's all very well for you, Bathurst, enjoying the prestige of your status and the lustre of your Cirencester estate', we may well murmur. Pope—no heir to privilege himself, and never a landowner—is ready with a due response:

> But all our praises why should lords engross?
> Rise, honest Muse! and sing the MAN of ROSS.
>
> lines 249–50

The verb 'engross', highlighted as the rhyme word, is subtly cogent here. Its primary meaning in the context is 'occupy, take up'; it suggests the thought 'why should we spend all our time, and all our poem, praising aristocrats, of however recent formation?'. 'Engross', though, also has a specific financial meaning and one not without an ambiguously moral side. It means 'to buy up wholesale', from the French phrase *en gros*, signifying 'in one whole'. As the *OED* notes, the English verb particularly implies the business practice of buying up 'the whole stock, or as much as possible, of (a commodity) for the purpose of "regrating" or retailing it at a monopoly price' ('engross', *v.* 2, sense 3). This sense was very much in contemporary usage and could be extended to include land: the *OED* cites Swift and Arthur Young, the eighteenth-century English writer on agriculture, as examples. It is a rather uneasy word to apply to substantial landholders, however virtuous.

Step up, then, the 'Man of Ross'. Pope wrote his own note to identify the real-world figure who inspired the character. 'The person here celebrated, who with a small estate actually performed all these good works ... was called Mr John Kyrle. He died in the year 1724, aged 90, and lies interred in the chancel of the church of Ross in Herefordshire'.

Howard Erskine-Hill's *The Social Milieu of Alexander Pope* (1975; pp. 15–41) provides further information on Kyrle.

> Behold the market-place with poor o'erspread!
> The MAN of ROSS divides the weekly bread:
> He feeds yon alms-house, neat, but void of state,
> Where age and want sit smiling at the gate:
> Him portioned maids, apprenticed orphans blessed,
> The young who labour, and the old who rest.
>
> lines 263–68

Direct and simple acts of charity invite a direct and simple style of narration. Pope's depiction of Kyrle is itself 'neat, but void of state'. Verbs are undramatic but precise ('divides', feeds'), nouns humble but with their own dignity ('man', 'bread'). Actions are fair and even-handed, young and old equally benefiting as the bread is equally distributed. Everything is in proportion in a supportive society, where maids with their dowries and orphans with their apprenticeships are granted what they need for taking their place within a stratified but clear social organization. The result is equilibrium, measured out like the weekly bread and the balance of 'The young who labour, and the old who rest'. This is a functioning society underpinned by deeds, not a philosophical system of abstractions.

But is this all, well, idealized if not outright naïve? Yes, it is, in the way that pastoral presents an unpretentious and artless image of nature by means of a graceful and felicitous style. That is what makes an ideal standard by which any blemish or insufficiency can be measured. An exemplar is a model, a pattern for imitation, which is what the Man of Ross offers within the structure of the poem. Antithesis and severe logic demand an equivalent representation of a ruinous extreme, and the poem soon provides one.

The Warning: 'great Villers': Lines 299–310

> In the worst inn's worst room, with mat half-hung,
> The floors of plaster, and the walls of dung,
> On once a flock-bed, but repaired with straw,
> With tape-tied curtains, never meant to draw,
> The George and garter dangling from that bed
> Where tawdry yellow strove with dirty red,

> Great Villers lies—alas! how changed from him,
> That life of pleasure, and that soul of whim!
> Gallant and gay, in Cliveden's proud alcove,
> The bower of wanton Shrewsbury and love;
> Or just as gay, at council, in a ring
> Of mimicked statesmen, and their merry king.

This is George Villiers, Duke of Buckingham (1628–1687), Pope's actual anti-type to the real figure of John Kyrle. Here, again, Pope supplies his own note: 'This lord, yet more famous for his vices than his misfortunes, after having been possessed of about £50,000 a year, and passed through many of the highest posts in the Kingdom, died in the year 1687, in a remote inn in Yorkshire, reduced to the utmost misery.'

Pope's picture of the declined and debauched aristocrat is painted with precision and abundance perfectly matched to its structural role as encapsulating all that is the opposite of the Man of Ross. The latter, Pope tells us, performed his charitable actions on an income of 'five hundred pounds a year' (line 280). Buckingham's fortune was a mathematically convenient hundred times greater (the adverb 'about' is Pope's apologetic nod to the lure of approximation). So, the scene depicted is a distillation of anti-pastoral, ironically located against wry invocation of the language of its idealized opposite ('gay', 'bower').

Pope does not hold back, giving rein to his developed sense of the grotesque. It is not enough that the scene of the Duke's degradation is the worst inn: it is the worst room you can find there. Think of the worst, then think of something worse. Everything is askew, a riot of imbalance and squalor. The mat, itself a coarse fabric, is precariously only 'half-hung'. The flock-bed is bad enough, as a crude decline from fashionable feathers to bits of cloth of any sort; 'repaired with straw' takes it down a further step. Curtains need tape to keep them together, but then they can't even be drawn, anyway. As for the walls, other products of the stable make do.

Pope's couplet about Villiers's 'George and garter' sums it all up. The article of clothing no longer graces an elegant leg to represent the highest order of English knighthood; it 'dangles' uncertainly from the wretched bed, displaced and demeaned. Its gold buckle and emblem of 'Honi soit qui mal y pense' embroidered in gold (*OED* 'garter', sb., sense 2) are now mockingly matched to the bed's 'tawdry yellow' fighting for pride of place with 'dirty red' (best not to enquire further). It is all a far cry from the insouciant, cavalier balance of 'That life of pleasure, and that soul of whim' and the 'merry King'—Charles II—whose notorious behaviour served as model and excuse for his society. 'The mob of gentlemen who wrote with ease' is how Pope will sum up the 'wits of either Charles's days' (*The First Epistle of the Second Book of Horace Imitated*, lines 107–08). Now, he proceeds, there is 'No wit to flatter' (line 311) the lonely, exposed, and rejected Duke of Carolean misrule.

The vigour with which Pope depicts his debauched nobleman is compellingly attractive, even as its materials are nauseatingly repellent. This combination is at the heart of those forms of satire that plunge all too deeply into human ugliness. It is paradoxical, but true. And truthfulness is Pope's aim. But where does this leave a poem whose maxim is 'Extremes in man concur to general use'? What on earth could be the 'general use' served by Buckingham? An answer to this question requires us to step back from the immediate and particular to the context and the whole. This is true of the *Epistle* taken by itself, where ideal and antitype belong equally to the form of the complete poem. And it is true of the larger project of Pope's 1730s corpus. The challenge to us is as ambitious as it was to him.

14. *An Epistle to Sir Richard Temple, Lord Cobham*

Examples: Lines 23–30, 184–85, 256–61

The *Epistle to Cobham* was the third of the four *Epistles to Several Persons* to be written, but it was placed first in the group in the 1735 *Works* and subsequent editions. The Twickenham editor, F. W. Bateson, argued that Pope wrote specifically to take that leading position, as part of his emerging magnum opus (*TE*, III, part 2, p. xxxiv). Its first publication date, 16 January 1734, ties it very closely to *An Essay on Man*, the fourth and final epistle of which came out just eight days later.

That the *Epistle* makes minimal reference to its addressee, as compared with the other three (Burlington, Bathurst, and Martha Blount), also suggests that its aim was more to set out general principles than to make full use within its argument of that addressee's private character or public status. Lord Cobham acts as a suitable figure for Pope to reach for, given the eulogy for Cobham's landscape garden at Stowe he had written in the *Epistle to Burlington*. However, compared with the significant role played by Burlington in his poem, and, in particular, the resonant finale where Pope hails and encourages him as a force for good, Pope's nod towards Cobham in the *Epistle*'s last two couplets has, unusually, a somewhat perfunctory air.

In the revised 1744 quarto edition, the so-called 'deathbed' edition, some changes were made in the order and structure of a number of verse-paragraphs (Rogers 2006, p. 655). Critics have disagreed about the extent to which William Warburton was responsible for these alterations, and the declining Pope merely acquiescent. Editions thereafter differ. The Twickenham follows the original, 1734, version;

whereas the Oxford editors, Herbert Davis and, later, Pat Rogers, took the 1744 route. Given the likelihood that the 1744 text was prepared with at least some consideration of the lapsed magnum opus project (*An Essay on Man* was also prepared for a 1744 edition), the following extracts employ that revised order.

Lines 23–30

> Our depths who fathoms, or our shallows finds,
> Quick whirls, and shifting eddies, of our minds?
> On human actions reason though you can,
> It may be reason, but it is not man:
> His principle of action once explore,
> That instant 'tis his principle no more.
> Like following life through creatures you dissect,
> You lose it in the moment you detect.

The eight-lined paragraph is not structured as two complementary quartets, as Pope often chooses to do in such paragraphs. Rather, it has the more ambiguous form of a large chiasmus. The middle four lines spin abstract terms around in self-negating order. You can exercise your reason on 'human actions', but, if you do, you end up cherishing your 'reason' but letting 'man' slip away. You end up with a negative: 'it is not man'. Within this self-defeating process, the word 'reason' suffers a belittling diminution conveyed by the change in auxiliary verbs: yes, you 'can' reason if you want to, but, though it 'may' be what you intended, its inability to do the business leaves it a weakened possibility. The two uses of the word 'reason' uneasily fill the centre of a chiastic couplet: 'human', 'reason'/'reason, 'man'. In the second of the middle couplets, too, the word 'principle', proudly up front in the first line, is relegated to a negative as it crosses to the conclusion of the second line: 'his principle no more'. Once again, you have lost it (see line 30, above).

Chiasmus is the most semantically flexible of rhetorical figures, its cross-over pattern allowing either a satisfying sensation of parts agreeably falling into place or a jarring feeling of disjunction of meaning. The two outer couplets enclosing the shifting abstracts of lines 25–28 provide, respectively, one metaphor rapidly exemplified in four variations ('depths', 'shallows', 'whirls', 'eddies') and one simile threading its way through. The first couplet leaves our minds out of their depth, lost in contrary movements. The final couplet phonically connects a self-defeating process ('Like', 'life', dissect') with a self-defeating outcome ('lose', 'detect').

How, then, can we learn anything about what makes human beings think and act? The poem's proposed solution is that, although our principles for action may be hard to grasp and their unceasing variability difficult to keep up with, everyone has, however lost in the *mêlée* of apparent contradictions, a single 'ruling passion' (line 174). Track that down, and you have the 'clue' that 'once found, unravels all the rest' (line 178). The word 'clue', originally 'clew', meant a ball of yarn or thread, which could be used to 'thread' one's way into or out of a maze or labyrinth.

After the statement of this principle, Pope applies it to a series of actual and fictional figures, varying his tone from comic to tragic. The first, and longest, such example is Philip, Duke of Wharton, whose highly public career as poet, Catholic convert, and gentleman of pleasure had come to an untimely end with his death in 1731 at the age of thirty-three. His ruling passion Pope defines as 'lust of praise' (line 181), which motivated his behaviour without any discrimination of the value of that praise when heterogeneously sought and gained.

Lines 184–85

> Though wondering senates hung on all he spoke,
> The club must hail him master of the joke.

Wharton's gift for effective oratory is applied to contrary ends in contrasting contexts. Pope's satirical scalpel dissects by means of a tellingly sharp antithetical couplet. Senates, gatherings of the most distinguished voices in the *polis* (at least theoretically), are set against 'the club'. Pope may be thinking here of the notorious Hell Fire Club, of which Wharton was reportedly a member, rather than the (at least theoretically) more sedate environments of London clubs. The verbs 'hung' and 'hail' phonically link the exercise of power to both stages. The concluding rhyme-words of each line, 'spoke' and 'joke', play the (again, at least theoretical) dignity of a parliamentary speech against the triviality of making a crowd laugh. Thus, apparently contradictory behaviour is linked by the pursuit of rhetorical renown, no matter where or why or to what end. A strength declines into a weakness because of an absence of judgement, an unhealthily random employment of a real gift.

Lines 256-61

At the other end of the tragic/comic spectrum is this concise and witty imaginary death-bed scene between a rich man and his legal representative:

> 'I give and I devise' (old Euclio said,
> And sighed) 'my lands and tenements to Ned.'
> Your money, Sir; 'My money, Sir, what all?
> Why,—if I must'—(then wept) 'I give it Paul.'
> The manor, Sir?– 'The manor! hold,' he cried,
> 'Not that—I cannot part with that'—and died.

Legal terms ('devise'—to assign by a will—and 'tenements'—lands, properties) provide the formal and serious context. Old Euclio, however, is unable to respond with due dignity. Pope disrupts the rhythm of his lines and couplets to dramatize the breaking up of Euclio's rational grasp on realities. The passage concludes with death converted into bathos, a radical diminution of solemnity into farce. We are left with a sense of the sheer absurdity of human attitudes of mind and behaviour, conveyed by a poet with a gift for comic scenarios.

There is something unsatisfactory about the *Epistle to Cobham*. The 'ruling passion' (line 174) is briefly asserted, and appears conceptually at odds with the main tenor of the various character sketches and scenarios. As Brower puts it, the ruling passion explanation 'is attempted only in a small number of examples, and then applied quite mechanically and perfunctorily', and most of the poem 'demonstrates the deceptions of appearance, the difficulty of getting at reality' (Brower 1959, pp. 260–61). If 'life's stream' will not 'for observation stay' (line 37), and 'Not always actions show the man' (line 109), how can we get to the stability required for defining a fundamental 'reality'? The poem is really far more concerned to illustrate the sheer unpredictability and absurdity of humankind; and it is to these depictions that its vitality and energy are principally directed. The poem's paradox is that it lives most fully when it is itself engaged in dissection. This is what gives it comic and satiric force. No wonder that both the real Wharton and the fictional Euclio were both, as the poem was published, dead.

15. *Epistle to Miss Blount with the Works of Voiture; Epistle to Miss Blount, on her Leaving the Town after the Coronation; An Epistle to a Lady*

Examples: *Epistle to Miss Blount with the Works of Voiture*, lines 49–56, 37–48; *Epistle to Miss Blount, on her Leaving the Town after the Coronation*, lines 13–18, 41–50; *An Epistle to a Lady*, lines 249–56, 235–42, 115–26

An Epistle to a Lady was the last of the four *Epistles to Several Persons* to be published. It appeared on 8 February 1735, three weeks before the death of John Arbuthnot. It is not clear exactly when Pope wrote the poem or over what length of time he kept and revised it. Estimated dates run from February/March 1733 when he may have begun it, or a preliminary version of it, to August/September 1734, when he may have completed it, or nearly so, while staying at Bevis Mount at the home of Charles Mordaunt, Earl of Peterborough (Mack 1985, pp. 590, 626). These dates suggest that Pope's *Epistles* to Dr Arbuthnot and to Martha Blount (the 'Lady') shared a period of composition, revision, addition, and publication during which the strength and fragility of friendship, and the vulnerability of friendship to events, were at the forefront of his mind.

Pope became acquainted with the sisters Teresa and Martha Blount as a young man, possibly as early as 1707 (Ibid., p. 242). He and Teresa were born in the same year, 1688; Martha was two years younger. They were part of the Catholic set living in various locations to the west and south-west of London. Martha was god-daughter to John Caryll, the instigator of the first, two-canto version of *The Rape of the Lock*, published in 1712, the same year as the *Epistle to Miss Blount with the Works of Voiture* appeared, also in Lintot's *Miscellany*. Charles Jervas painted a double portrait of the Blount sisters around 1716, the year in which Pope's *Epistle to Jervas* was published (Ibid., p. 246). Pope's *Epistle to Miss Blount, on her Leaving the Town after the Coronation* was first published in the 1717 *Works*, which included the final version of *The Rape of the Lock*, with the crucial addition of Clarissa's fifth-canto speech. By the time of *An Epistle to a Lady*, Martha Blount had been Pope's closest female friend for many years, and she would be his principal legatee.

The title of the *Works of Voiture* epistle in Lintot's *Miscellany* was *To a Young Lady*. The name 'Miss Blount' did not appear until its publication in the 1735 volume of Pope's *Works*. Uncertainty over which sister was intended as the addressee has concerned some editors and biographers (Rumbold 1989, pp. 52–53). Like many writers, Pope pondered and debated the question of whether satire's effectiveness is enhanced or diminished by the use of actual names rather than generic types. The problem is less pressing in the case of affectionate poetry, such as this, where friendship, whether intimate or more distant, provides the theme and the tone. Where tactfully presented, naming will probably be greeted sympathetically and even warmly by most general readers, contemporary and future. This epistle responds so to the 'charm' Pope attributes to the French seventeenth-century poet Vincent de Voiture and the object of his devotion, the Duchesse de Montausier. 'Charm' is a key linguistic thread holding the poem together, running through it from line 5 ('Sure to charm all was his peculiar fate') to the final couplet ('And dead, as living, 'tis our author's pride / Still to charm those who charm the world beside'). For a contrasting example of an unhappy woman, Pope adopts a representative figure.

Epistle to Miss Blount with the Works of Voiture, lines 49–56

> The gods, to curse Pamela with her prayers,
> Gave the gilt coach and dappled Flanders mares,
> The shining robes, rich jewels, beds of state,
> And, to complete her bliss, a fool for mate.
> She glares in balls, front boxes, and the Ring,

> A vain, unquiet, glittering, wretched thing!
> Pride, pomp, and state but reach her outward part;
> She sighs, and is no Duchess at her heart.

In both sets of four lines, appurtenances of wished-for wealth and social status are set up in order to fail at the end. The clue is right there at the beginning, in the apparent paradox of 'curse'/'prayers'. The gods have indeed accommodated Pamela's desires (the name was then stressed on the second syllable): be careful what you wish for. The material accompaniments and signs of a wealthy match pile up in list form, each item spectacular in its ostentatious display. They build towards an anticipated climax: 'And, to complete her bliss'. The double pause created by this interpolated infinitive phrase, which defers the caesura until after the sixth syllable of the line, maintains anticipation just long enough for the brutally monosyllabic final phrase, 'fool for mate', to work its disabling bathos. Top of the pile, Pamela, goes the fool you married, and all comes tumbling down. The fool and the preceding splendours are intimately linked: you can't have the others without the one; and who, in the end, is the real fool? Checkmate; or, rather, 'fool's mate'.

Pope's adjectives 'gilt' and 'shining', each implying or at least threatening, an ominous superficiality, provide the link to the second quartet. Here, the first three lines present, in turn, three places for fashionable display, four adjectives ranging over Pamela's physical and emotional state, and three abstract nouns summing up her achievement. Each line has its signifier of emptiness: the glaring of a ball's unforgiving luminescence, the glittering of momentary radiance, the pomp of showy display. At their heart lies the adjective 'vain', with its etymological force of 'empty'. Again, these lists build up; only this time the game is up as early as the end of the third line, leaving the last line to bring a note of sadness in. The early caesura (this time) puts emphasis on Pamela's sigh of acknowledged inner grief, leaving the rest of the line to decline into a simple negative and emotional poverty. All that superficiality is bought at a vital and supreme cost: 'at her heart'.

Society and its vacuous core, thus described, are unmistakably reflected in the artificial attractiveness of the world in which the unfortunate events of *The Rape of the Lock* take place. Details reflect from art to art. For example, the 'Ring' here (line 53) is a circular route in Hyde Park for parading 'gilt' coaches and their 'glittering' owners. A simple metathesis (transposition of sounds or letters, here 'il' to 'li') in the adjectives connects Pamela's superficiality with her means of display. It reappears in the 1712 *Rape of the Lock* as 'Hide-Park Circus' (canto 2, line 35), and, in the 1714 expanded version, figures in the sylph Ariel's account of Belinda's guardian spirits: 'These, though unseen, are ever on the wing, / Hang o'er the box, and hover round the ring' (canto 1, lines 43–44). Juxtaposition of clauses picks up the epistle's listing of 'front boxes' alongside 'the Ring'. Both poems imply, through the circular form of the course, the emptiness of a round of movement with no progress, only eternal repetition.

And what is the cause of Pamela's ironic loss of her heart to heartless display? The paragraph tells us, of course: 'Pride, pomp and state', a vanity in the truly moral sense. But, in the immediately preceding lines, Pope projects a searchingly social cause to add to, or perhaps impel, its falsely glittering result. 'Marriage', he writes, may indeed be entered into in an endeavour to secure the pleasures which 'your sex' envisages as worthwhile goals. But such pleasures can prove 'tyrants', controlling lives.

Epistle to Miss Blount with the Works of Voiture, lines 37–48

> Marriage may all those petty tyrants chase,
> But sets up one, a greater in their place;
> Well might you wish for change by those accursed,
> But the last tyrant ever proves the worst.
> Still in constraint your suffering sex remains,
> Or bound in formal, or in real chains:
> Whole years neglected, for some months adored,
> The fawning servant turns a haughty lord.
> Ah quit not the free innocence of life,
> For the dull glory of a virtuous wife;
> Nor let false shows, or empty titles please:
> Aim not at joy, but rest content with ease.

This presents another, and darker, version of a list building up to its inevitable, but unlooked-for, trap of a conclusion. If you chase pleasures, you end up with the last pleasure that each wish for something costlier eventually necessitates: a rich catch, which in fact catches you; a loveless union in which all your power is ceded by the rules of marriage as defined by social edicts. The writer's moral is that it is better to avoid such 'dull glory' and 'false shows'. But does this sound a little glib, all too 'easy'? If so, then perhaps Pope will recall this epistle when writing the crowning passage to the evolving *Rape of the Lock*, Clarissa's speech. There, motifs from the present poem are brought into supremely powerful expression: for example, Clarissa's recommendation of 'good humour' (canto 5, line 30) echoes line 61 of this epistle: 'Good humour only teaches charms to last'. Pope's study of women's moral, emotional, and social chains (formal or real) is only just beginning.

***

Epistle to Miss Blount, On her Leaving the Town after the Coronation, lines 13–18

The coronation of George I took place on 20 October 1714. Martha Blount had caught the dreaded smallpox and missed the ceremony itself, and the whole family had to leave London straight afterwards. This epistle, first published in Pope's 1717 *Works*, is addressed to Teresa Blount, under the romanticized name of Zephalinda. The poem imagines the plight of a young lady dragged off to the country:

> She went from opera, park, assembly, play,
> To morning-walks, and prayers three hours a day;
> To part her time 'twixt reading and bohea,
> To muse, and spill her solitary tea,
> Or o'er cold coffee trifle with the spoon,
> Count the slow clock, and dine exact at noon;

The principal joke here is Pope's reversal of the convention of rural idyll, as enshrined in myriad poems from classical times to the present day. His own early *Pastorals* have at least one foot on this ground; though they also serve, as we have seen, as poetic exercises in an easily accessed existing genre. These spirited lines scintillate with comic tricks: bathos in the first couplet; hyperbole (though the time spent praying may feel like three hours a day); in the second couplet, tautology of 'bohea'/'tea' ('bohea' being a variety of tea—or 'tay' as the word was then pronounced) to express tedious routine; comic transferred epithets of the P. G. Wodehouse kind ('solitary tea', 'slow clock'); in the third couplet, unmelodious ('Or o'er') and jarring ('cold coffee') phrasing; hopelessly unfashionable habits. Noon is the time when fashionable ladies, such as Belinda in *The Rape of the Lock*, would normally be just waking: 'sleepless lovers, just at twelve, awake' (canto 1, line 16). Later lines add to the pleasures of retirement to the country. A neighbouring squire, for example, who 'visits with a gun, presents you birds', makes love with 'knees beneath a table', and 'loves you best of all things— but his horse' (lines 23–30). Poor Teresa is beached up in the midst of vulgarity and intellectual inadequates. Isolation is the keynote.

Epistle to Miss Blount, On her Leaving the Town after the Coronation, lines 41–50

So where is the poet who is sending this comic letter?

> So when your slave, at some dear idle time,
> (Not plagued with head-aches, or the want of rhyme)
> Stands in the streets, abstracted from the crew,
> And while he seems to study, thinks of you;
> Just when his fancy points your sprightly eyes,
> Or sees the blush of soft Parthenia rise,
> Gay pats my shoulder, and you vanish quite,
> Streets, chairs, and coxcombs rush upon my sight;
> Vexed to be still in town, I knit my brow,
> Look sour, and hum a tune, as you may now.

He is back in town, but, no less isolated, 'Stands in the streets, abstracted from the crew'. The derogatory noun here—'crew', denoting a rabble, a mob—shows that you do not have to be in the country to feel apart. London can be a lonely place, too. Why? The answer completes the couplet: 'And while he seems to study, thinks of you' (lines 43–44). The rhyme-words 'crew' and 'you' are opposites—a miscellaneous and anonymous plurality and a specified, named and loved individual. The poet's abstraction and detachment from company are both the cause and the result of his own musing. Like Zephalinda/Teresa's, his mind is elsewhere. But whereas the poet imagines Miss Blount's 'pensive thought' (line 33) to be with the elevated social world she has been obliged to leave, that of 'coronations ... lords, and earls, and dukes, and gartered knights' (lines 34, 36), his own has a single focus.

In its graceful propriety, the poet's self-depiction represents another ethos, behaviour far distant from the boorish squire's clumsy demeanour. He suggests, through a process of decorous placing of himself in a situation reflective of hers, and yet humbly different, that their characters may share, if not duplicate, aspects of temperament. She will also, Pope implies, be entertained by the same love of humour that has gone into the poem's composition. The tenderness may be (and often has been) taken by readers as implying a form of affection. It certainly conveys something at its heart which is there to counter isolation: friendship. Johnson's *Dictionary* (1755) defines 'friend' as 'one joined to another in mutual benevolence and intimacy'. Sending an epistle, a letter, is an act of mutual affinity.

An Epistle to a Lady, lines 249–56

> Ah! friend! to dazzle let the vain design;
> To raise the thought, and touch the heart be thine!
> That charm shall grow, while what fatigues the ring
> Flaunts and goes down, an unregarded thing:
> So when the sun's broad beam has tired the sight,
> All mild ascends the moon's more sober light,
> Serene in virgin modesty she shines,
> And unobserved the glaring orb declines.

The final movements of Pope's *Epistles* to Martha Blount and John Arbuthnot begin in the same way: with an exclamatory address to a friend he has known for well over twenty years. In the case of Arbuthnot, the poem's last paragraph is both a farewell and a vision of Pope's own love and duty of care for his aging mother ('Me, let the tender office long engage / To rock the cradle of reposing age', lines 408–09). By turning the closing notes of the epistle to private matters, Pope drains the poison engendered by the public world. In the case of Martha Blount, who has many years of prosperous life ahead of her—she lived until 1763, nearly twenty years longer than Pope himself—the finale to her *Epistle*'s can be more extensive (forty-four lines) and joyfully adopt a tone of respectfully tranquil celebration.

Our extract, the first paragraph of the finale, again displays the satisfying balance so agreeably produced by two linked quartets. The first contrasts Martha's intellectual nobility and emotional grace to 'the vain', echoing his description of Pamela in the *Epistle to Miss Blount with the Works of Voiture* he had written years earlier. Vanity, a moral blemish so endemic in the social world, reflects the word's own inherent statement of vacuity thanks to its Latin root of 'vanus' ('empty'). Also, as in the earlier epistle, Pope connects morally hollow behaviour with the 'ring', the Hyde Park setting that appropriately defines its own tedious and pointless circularity.

The second quartet adds an analogy whose elemental force directly and simply endorses the moral value Pope is attributing to his friend. The glare of untempered exposure to unrelieved sun (cf. *Epistle to Miss Blount with the Works of Voiture*, line 53, in Chapter 15) echoes the excessive, self-defeating endeavours of the vain to shine ('dazzle', 'fatigues'). By contrast, Martha Blount's more discreetly attractive 'charm'—the theme word of the *Epistle to Miss Blount with the Works of Voiture*—of person and behaviour still 'shines' but does so in the form of the moon, whose purer light is given the force of the adjectival phrase, 'Serene in virgin modesty'. The cultural familiarity of the analogy does, indeed, imbue it with the strength of uncomplicated value. And, if it has been often thought, then it surely has been 'ne'er so well expressed' (*An Essay on Criticism*, line 298):

> So when the sun's broad beam has tired the sight,
> All mild ascends the moon's more sober light.

The absence of caesura, the chiming liquidity of 'All mild … light' encompassing the harmonious alliteration in 'the moon's more sober', the stately succession of long vowels in 'All mild … moon's more … light'— these all combine to radiate euphony. There is an effortless equanimity here, defined in the adjective 'serene' and also concisely summed up in the phrase that opens Pope's following paragraph: 'blessed with temper'—with, that is, 'due or proportionate mixture or combination of elements or qualities', 'mental balance or composure' (*OED*, 'temper', n. 1, 3). Balance is there in the antithesis of the sun/moon couplet, as it is in the first quartet's 'To raise the thought, and touch the heart be thine!', where intellectual elevation and pleasing sympathy effortlessly occupy the same syllabic and rhythmic space.

An Epistle to a Lady, lines 235–42

The context provided by Pope's full-scale epistle serves to enhance, by contrast, the values enshrined in Martha Blount. When describing the future which awaits all those women who devote their youth to thoughtless pursuit of unobtainable pleasures, Pope writes with both a sharp pen and a comic imagination:

> At last, to follies youth could scarce defend,
> It grows their age's prudence to pretend;
> Ashamed to own they gave delight before,
> Reduced to feign it, when they give no more:
> As hags hold sabbaths, less for joy than spite,
> So these their merry, miserable night;
> Still round and round the ghosts of beauty glide,
> And haunt the places where their honour died.

In age, women prudently pretend to follies that are scarcely defensible in youth. Being ashamed to admit that they once gave pleasure at all, they are reduced to feigning pleasure when they now give none. As witches hold sabbaths out of spite rather than pleasure, so women when older keep up a pretence of enjoying the pleasures of the night when they really supply only misery. They drift round and round, like ghosts haunting the places where they lost their virtue. Pope's lines are acutely observed. For example, the manner in which prudence declines into shame exemplifies perfectly the thin divisions which their bounds divide, so demonstrating his deft connection of youthful and elderly behaviour with a touch whose precision is matched by delicacy. The ingredients of the verse combine to render moral specificity and hard, cool observation with a sheer beauty of expression, while maintaining the grossness of the picture he paints. The final couplet is the climax of this procedure. The choreography is exquisite, the moral point mortally wounding. Obsessed in youth with the 'Ring' and all its ethical lumber, they are condemned in age to an eternity that parodies and mocks their former world. And yet how beautifully their movements are described and how memorably the sheer grace of 'glide' shares its space between ease and aimlessness before sinking into the finality and judgement of 'died'.

An Epistle to a Lady, lines 115–26

The principal parts of the *Epistle*, leading up to the unremitting image of the hags' midnight dance of death and the contrasting elegance of Martha Blount's quiet ascent to moral elevation, are formed by a succession of female types, all exemplifying the self-destructive divisions with which Pope characterizes them and by which he satirizes them. He produces a linguistic gallery of portraits, after the manner of some seventeenth-century poems, notably Andrew Marvell's *The Gallery*. In the memorable phrasing of Pope's own earlier *Epistle to Mr Jervas*, 'images reflect from art to art' (line 20). Three of these portraits were omitted from the 1735 text: the characters of Philomela (lines 69–86), Atossa (lines 115–50) and Cloe (lines 157–98). These were first included in the so-called 'deathbed' edition, which Pope distributed to friends but which was suppressed until 1748, after his death. The reasons behind these omissions have long been mulled over by critics, the usual cause being located as sensitivity to, or fear of, the harms and dangers of readers' possible identification of the portraits with actual contemporaries rather than acceptance of them as types only. (See Bateson, ed. *TE*, III, part 2, pp. 155–64 (1951); Rogers (2006), pp. 667–68). The sheer power of the poem is clearly enhanced by their inclusion, especially that of Atossa from which our extract is taken:

> But what are these to great Atossa's mind?
> Scarce once herself, by turns all womankind!
> Who, with herself, or others, from her birth
> Finds all her life one warfare upon earth:
> Shines, in exposing knaves, and painting fools,
> Yet is, whate'er she hates and ridicules.
> No thought advances, but her eddy brain
> Whisks it about, and down it goes again.
> Full sixty years the world has been her trade,
> The wisest fool much time has ever made.
> From loveless youth to unrespected age,
> No passion gratified except her rage.

Two stylistic and structural features dominate these lines and others in the extensive, indeed exhaustive, description (thirty-six lines in total): continuing images and motifs proposing coherence, and chopped-up couplets shattering the portrait into bitingly hurtful pieces. These qualities are themselves at odds, so manifesting the divisiveness Pope is ruthlessly exposing within his own text. The result is a passage that is thoroughly exhausting to read: we share in, experience something like, the self-destructive life Atossa lives.

The centre of the imagery is the metaphor 'one warfare upon earth'. From this emerge words such as 'hates', 'rage' and, as the full passage proceeds, 'fury', 'hit', 'revenge', 'hell', 'violence', 'storm'. Related to this ever-shifting but paradoxically unchanging succession is that of harsh movement, without progression: 'her eddy brain / Whisks it about, and down it goes again'; and, later, 'outran', 'turn' and—again—'storm'. Pope's syntax frequently supports and represents rhythmically this cycle seemingly without end. Thus, line 117, 'Who, with herself, or others, from her birth', keeps starting and stopping. The segments, like broken shards, penetrate the line's search for continuity and coherence, enforcing self-contradiction. The repeated prepositional phrasing ('with herself', 'or [with] others', 'from her birth') exacerbates the grating, like exposed bones rubbing against each other. Paradoxes, oxymorons, or plain self-contradictions add to the mix: 'wisest fool', 'loveless youth', 'unrespected age'. These are later expanded from phrases into lines, such as 'Nor more a storm her hate than gratitude' (line 132). Line 135 brings the jagged syntax, shattered rhythm, and contradictions together in an exclamatory burst of gunfire: 'Superiors? death! and equals? what a curse!' We end up with reactions which themselves invite a condign expression such as, perhaps, 'consistent inconsistency', or 'ever-moving immobility'.

The sources of such a portrait have been present from the outset in our linking of extracts from the Blount sisters' poems. For example, Pamela in *Epistle to Miss Blount with the Works of Voiture* is cursed by the gods insofar as they give her what she prays for. Atossa is 'cursed with every granted prayer' (line 147). The huge difference lies in the Atossa portrait's dreadful intensity, massive reduplications, and persistent, obsessive pitch.

The three epistles this chapter has been looking at form a growing concern, over a number of years, with the nature and the social positioning of women. Taking them as a continuing, evolving narrative, and thinking about how they are related to other highly significant sections of Pope's impressively increasing *oeuvre*, notably *The Rape of the Lock* and Clarissa's speech within that poem's final version, can sharpen our vision of Pope's broad and deep analysis of his society. The progress of *An Epistle to a Lady*–by far the longest of the three poems—is, after a brief, conversational acknowledgement of its addressee ('Nothing so true as what you once let fall'), a journey through a gallery of satirical portraits to the final paragraphs in which Martha Blount takes centre stage ('Ah! Friend!'). Our examination of this epistle actually began at the end, with Martha Blount herself, in order to set forward her central significance as an ideal, as a true representative of female autonomy, and as a friend. She and what she represents are the true fount, the cause, the destination, and the resolution of the poem.

16. *The First Satire of the Second Book of Horace Imitated*

Examples: Lines 111–22, 1–14, 23–28, 45–52, 91–100, 123–28

Pope wrote his imitation of the first satire in Horace's second book in January 1733, while recovering from an illness at the London home of Edward Harley, Second Earl of Oxford (1689–1741). He was prompted to do so by Henry St John, Viscount Bolingbroke, who observed that an English imitation would, as Pope reported to Spence, 'hit my case' (Spence, ed. by Osborne, I, 1966, p. 143). Pope clearly responded to the idea with alacrity, for it was published in February; and it initiated his series of such imitations running through to 1738. Here, then, is another group of poems contributing generously to the creative cornucopia of this decade in his career.

Horace wrote his poem as an introduction to the book, and it has been generally accepted as marking a completion of his work in this genre as he moved on to writing epistles. Pope followed this sequence, choosing first three of Horace's satires, then four of his epistles (1733–34 and 1737–38, respectively).

This first poem is set in the form of a conversation between the author and a legal adviser. In Horace's case, this role is played by C. Trebatius Testa, a distinguished jurist who enjoyed the esteem of the emperor Augustus but was also—or so he comes across in the letters of Cicero—a likeable man who enjoyed activities as varied as swimming and social drinking. He would, therefore, have been likely to appreciate the joking tone of much of Horace's poem, while also being well equipped to offer a sobering legal perspective from which to advise his informal client on the risks incurred in writing rather too freely about public figures (Rudd, 1966).

Pope chooses as his interlocutor William Fortescue (1687–1749), a friend of long standing, whose legal career took him to senior positions within the Walpole administration. Like Trebatius, then, Fortescue is able to join in a friendly conversation while speaking with authority when Pope ventures into dangerous territory. However, there are significant differences between Trebatius and Fortescue. Trebatius was by twenty years or so Horace's senior, whereas Fortescue and Pope were near contemporaries. Fortescue is closer to Pope: he contributed to a spoof law case written by Pope in the 1710s (*Stradling versus Stiles*) and became a neighbour at Richmond. He was still in the early stages of his legal career at that point, having been called to the bar in 1715 and appointed King's Counsel and attorney-general to the Prince of Wales in 1730. He would later achieve the heights of becoming Master of the Rolls in 1741. At the same time, he had also become directly associated with Robert Walpole, serving as his private secretary in 1715. Fortescue's ambiguous—or double—situation, then, makes him an intriguing figure in the poem. In the text, Pope and Fortescue appear as P. and F.

Pope published his *Imitations* with the Latin original on the verso (left-hand) pages and his English version on the recto (right-hand) pages facing them. Readers were thus presented with three poems at once. They were invited to read (or re-read) Horace's original, to read Pope's imitation and, by reading across double pages, to read an amalgam of both. This complex process pointed readers in the direction of observing and reflecting on how similar to or dissimilar from the Horatian model were Pope's lines. The very fact of turning Latin into English did, of course, necessitate basic variation. For a start, Latin is a much more concise language than English, with an elaborate system of case-endings and verb conjugations delineating relationships between words that English has to spell out by longer means, such as prepositional phrases and auxiliary verbs. It therefore takes Pope 156 lines to render Horace's 86.

However, these and other dissimilarities, familiar problems to all translators, were used artistically by Pope as means of articulating a complex dialogue between the poems' arguments, at the levels of detail and superstructure. Frank Stack's definitive study, *Pope and Horace:*

Studies in Imitation (1985), states clearly and precisely: 'The parallel texts repeatedly underline the essential point: that as an imitator Pope's relationship with Horace is profoundly paradoxical, involving both the minutest connections of word, tone, and nuance and the greatest freedom and individuality of expression.' By these means, 'Pope's identification with Horace and his texts in the *Imitations* involves at once an appreciation of Horace's forms, language and vision, a criticism of their limitations, and an imaginative and creative extension of their possibilities' (Stack, pp. 23–24, 25).

Lines 111–22

> Could pensioned Boileau lash in honest strain
> Flatterers and bigots even in Louis' reign?
> Could Laureate Dryden pimp and friar engage,
> Yet neither Charles nor James be in a rage?
> And I not strip the gilding off a knave,
> Unplaced, unpensioned, no man's heir, or slave?
> I will, or perish in the generous cause:
> Hear this, and tremble! You, who 'scape the Laws.
> Yes, while I live, no rich or noble knave
> Shall walk the world, in credit, to his grave.
> TO VIRTUE ONLY and HER FRIENDS, A FRIEND,
> The world beside may murmur, or commend.

Pope's lines are strongly assertive, from an opening rhetorical question, through the simple and clear 'I will', and the imperative 'Hear this, and tremble', to the reiterated determination of 'Yes, while I live, no ... knave / Shall walk ...'. The 'virtue' line (121), then, has behind it the force of personal moral outrage and it is in this context that we read Pope's linguistic and syntactic changes to it. Horace's equivalent line runs: 'scilicet uni aequus atque eius amicis' [evidently well-disposed to virtue alone and her friends]. In the original printing of Pope's imitation, the six words after 'scilicet' are also given capital letters. So, Pope draws specific attention in both Horace and his own version to virtue and friendship. He thereby aligns himself with the ethical touchstones of Horace's satire.

Horace provides a compact, epigrammatic single hexameter in which the adjective 'aequus' bears the weight of meaning and defines an attitude and, beyond that, a whole philosophical world-view. It denotes balance, impartiality, self-control, fairness, a good disposition. This range of meanings derives from its literal significance: a level, flat place (it is the root of English 'equal'). Horace uses it elsewhere: in the opening lines of *Odes*, book 2, ode 3, where it describes keeping a level (or balanced, controlled) mind ('mentem'); and in the last line of *Epistles*, book 1, epistle 18, where it qualifies 'animus', that is, the rational part of a person, their intellect, reason, understanding. In line 9 of the same epistle, Horace defines virtue as a mean between vices: 'virtus est medium vitiorum'. These extremes are servility, an unthinking acceptance of doing what you are told, and a nit-picking, argumentative engagement with the most trivial of issues. 'Aequus', then, sums up a broadly philosophical attitude to life.

Pope's line 121 converts Horace's balanced statement into a more dynamically charged version of the same fundamental outlook, an ability to look even-handedly only on virtue and her friends. He renders Horace's adjective 'aequus', which admits 'friendly' as one of its range of possible meanings, by repeating the noun 'friend' and deferring it to the end of his line by means of one of his favourite figures, hyperbaton: transposition of the normal order of words for the sake of emphasis. The energy of the line derives from the resulting striking repetition: it is both semantically balanced ('a friend to virtue and her friends') and rhythmically wildly unbalanced, its caesura being withheld until after the eighth syllable, leaving 'a friend' strongly foregrounded. That element of aggression follows on from the preceding assertive lines, while the meaning remains fundamentally well-proportioned: 'any true friend of virtue is a friend of mine'. A change in syntax and word-order signifies Pope's desire to highlight comradeship as a positive quality in the context of satire, a genre which cannot but make enemies. So, Pope sounds both friendly and hostile. Horace's more laid-back attitude is commendable and philosophically attractive, but do the present times demand more vigorously committed writing?

Pope also changes the context of the line. In Horace, it forms the climax of a passage (lines 62–70) in praise of the satiric method of an earlier writer, Gaius Lucilius, who had been writing during the last third of the second century BCE (about 133–102). Niall Rudd's translation reads:

16. The First Satire of the Second Book of Horace Imitated

> When Lucilius first had the courage
> to write this kind of poetry and remove the glossy skin
> in which people were parading before the world and concealing
> their ugliness, was Laelius offended by his wit or the man who rightly
> took on the name of the African city which he overthrew?
> Or did they feel any pain when Metellus was wounded and Lupus
> was smothered in a shower of abusive verse? And yet Lucilius
> indicted the foremost citizens and the whole populace, tribe
> by tribe, showing indulgence only to Worth and her friends.
>
> Lines 62–70. (Rudd 1979, p. 87)

Horace's point may be summarized: 'my predecessor Lucilius fearlessly attacked all people in society, including by name the great and the powerful, sparing only the virtuous; so why do people complain when I do the same?' He thereby neatly combines justification of his own satires through reference to precedent with an implied satirical dig: 'people were tougher in those days'.

Pope retains Horace's historical perspective, naming two seventeenth-century satirical poets, Boileau in France and Dryden in England, as writers who freely and directly attacked 'flatterers and bigots' and Catholic clergy, respectively, without enraging the monarchs of the time. However, these examples are rapidly given, each in a couplet, while the weight of the passage shifts to Pope himself, incorporating the climactic line we have been scrutinizing in a powerful statement of his own rights and independence.

Pope is thus engaging implicitly in a conversation with his original source. By noting this, as one can only do by reading horizontally across the two pages, a reader is drawn into the problem. How does, or should, satire adjust to the conditions within which it appears? What does the modern age demand of a writer? Does, indeed, our definition of 'virtue'—the moral excellence that becomes a person, the duty of goodness—have to adjust, or does and should it remain rooted in a timeless mean, a medium? Add to these questions Pope's firm adherence to the value of friendship, its force for good, and we are nearing the heart of the quest for what constitutes ethically responsible personal and social action; the quest that energizes the whole of Pope's poetry of the 1730s.

Lines 1–14

> P. There are (I scarce can think it, but am told)
> There are, to whom my satire seems too bold:
> Scarce to wise Peter complaisant enough,
> And something said of Chartres much too rough.
> The lines are weak, another's pleased to say,
> Lord Fanny spins a thousand such a day.
> Timorous by nature, of the rich in awe,
> I come to counsel learned in the law:
> You'll give me, like a friend both sage and free,
> Advice; and (as you use) without a fee.
> F. I'd write no more.
>   P. Not write? But then I think,
> And for my soul I cannot sleep a wink.
> I nod in company, I wake at night,
> Fools rush into my head, and so I write.

To summarize: 'We satirists just can't get it right, can we? Some people say I'm not polite ('complaisant') enough to those whom I write about, while others say my verses are too feeble.' Peter Walter ('Peter') and Francis Charteris ('Chartres') had both been referred to in Pope's *Epistle to Bathurst*, and both in unflattering terms. The colonel and adventurer Charteris was a frequent object of attack on account of his rakish lifestyle and his complicity with the Walpole administration. In *Bathurst*, Pope rhetorically asked whether riches could restore his (sexual?) 'vigour' (line 86). Since he had died in 1732, the year before *Bathurst* was published, this could be seen as a little tactless, to say the least: kicking a man when he is well and truly not only down but out. Perhaps Pope had not heard of the death, or, as he wrote the poem over a couple of years or so, had not checked up. Peter Walter was also a regular object of critical observations by writers. For, he was known as a man who made a fortune as a money-lender or 'money scrivener', defined as one who receives money 'to place out at interest' and supplies 'those who wanted to raise money on security' (*OED* 'scrivener', sb., sense 3). Henry Fielding portrayed Walter as Peter Pounce in his novel *Joseph Andrews* (1742). In *Bathurst*, Pope had, pretty sharply and sarcastically, described him as one who wisely 'sees the world's respect for gold, / And therefore hopes this nation may be sold' (lines 123–24). Fielding has his Peter Pounce state that, in his view, 'the greatest fault in our constitution is the provision made for the poor' (chapter 48). But does Pope go rather too far by virtually attributing to him treasonable sentiments?

Then, even when he turns to those who find his satire too 'weak', Pope cannot resist a jibe at another prominent Walpole supporter, Lord Hervey, vice-chamberlain and confidential adviser to Queen Caroline. Indeed, Pope goes out of his way to make a personal insult. In Horace, the poet simply complains that people have censured him for producing the kind of feeble, wishy-washy verses that anyone could spin out in the thousands. Pope introduces the name of 'Lord Fanny' as one who does just that. Hervey certainly saw this as a reference to himself and quickly responded by assisting Lady Mary Wortley Montagu to write *Verses addressed to the Imitator of Horace* (1733), a vicious no-holds-barred attack on Pope's physical and moral 'deformities'. Pope could hardly complain. Later in his dialogue with Fortescue, he throws down a scarcely concealed and unpleasant jibe at Montagu: 'From furious Sappho scarce a milder fate, / Poxed by her love, or libelled by her hate' (lines 83–84). If you dish it out, you have to be ready to take it. 'Fanny' probably did not yet have its modern vulgar sense, but Pope's use of a female name (prompted, perhaps, by the references to 'Fannius' in Horace's *Satires* 4 (line 21) and 10 (line 80) as a poet and critic of him) could only be interpreted as a snide comment on Hervey's sexual proclivities. Rather undignified all round? Where lies Pope's vaunted virtue in all this?

Or would this be to react too preciously and primly? Satire in the eighteenth century was a rough trade in all its forms–theatrical, literary, and artistic. It was so because corruption at both personal and public levels was as endemic then as it usually is in human society, finance, and governance. As Juvenal, a Roman satirist from a later generation than Horace's, put it, 'difficile est saturam non scribere' [it is difficult not to write satire] (*Satire* I). Francis Charteris, it seems, was indeed a notably unpleasant character, a gambler, usurer, pimp, and convicted rapist. Peter Walter did very well out of his financial activities, acquiring a large amount of property in Dorset and leaving £300,000 at his death (Butt, ed. *TE,* IV, 2nd ed. (1953), pp. 353 and 392). Better a society in which it is possible to attack vices with vehemence than one that represses opposition? Should not virtue, as it were, join battle even if it risks becoming to some degree compromised?

These are the very questions raised and explored with vigour in this poem, as in other of Pope's satires. As Stack observes: for Pope, 'the central question of *Horace's* poem, to be explored in his Imitation, was, how far the energy of satiric writing is fundamentally moral' (1985, p. 31). These opening lines, with their deliberate invocation of specific cases, challenge the reader and challenge the Horatian original, too. 'Horace thinks of himself in relation to a general public; Pope's lines bristle with living personalities. From the beginning we realize that the power of Pope's satire lies in its power to offend, and if it is to be defended, it has to be defended in those terms' (Stack, p. 34).

Pope's opening is also brilliantly versatile, lexically and metrically virtuosic, and just plain funny. The very first couplet, 'There are (I scarce can think it, but am told), / There are to whom my satire seems too bold', adds to Horace an outrageously mock air of disbelief. 'How could anyone find my satire too bold?' He has to repeat 'There are', whereas Horace writes a single 'Sunt quibus' [there are to whom]. Pope's tongue is firmly in his cheek when he describes himself as 'Timorous by nature, of the rich in awe'. After all, the risks he repeatedly takes in his satire are hardly the mark of a diffident faint heart; and, far from being awestruck by power and riches, he is going out of his way to call out those who prosper by morally dubious actions. There is a vital, energetic, and ironic voice at play here.

The scene is, as it is in Horace, amusingly comic and dramatic. Trebatius's legal authority is expressed in what Rudd calls the 'sententious brevity of a jurist' (1966, p. 130), blunt one-word responses. 'Quid faciam?' asks Horace; 'Quiescas' [Keep quiet] replies Trebatius. 'Are you telling me not to write poetry?' asks an incredulous Horace. 'Aio' [Yes], replies Trebatius. English, alas, does not permit quite such economy of expression, but Pope uses Fortescue's slightly longer reply to slide wittily into a marvellously comic extension of Horace's protest that he just cannot sleep (lines 11–14):

> F. I'd write no more.
>   P. Not write? but then I think,
> And for my soul I cannot sleep a wink.
> I nod in company, I wake at night,
> Fools rush into my head, and so I write.

Pope simply is a man of words; if he cannot write them, he has to think them. Refreshing one of his memorable lines, 'For fools rush in where angels fear to tread' (*An Essay on Criticism*, line 625), Pope creates a picture that is as lively as it is engaging.

His comedy is increased by extension of his witty, tongue-in-cheek satirical edge to the very legal profession whose advice he is seeking. 'I come to counsel learned in the law' treads a fine line between deference and jokiness. However, Pope steps over that line with an additional nudge in lines 9–10:

> You'll give me, like a friend both sage and free,
> Advice; and (as you use) without a fee.

Fortescue does not rise to a response: non-committal, these legal types. Or is Fortescue actually playing up to his role as straight man to Pope's humour? When we compare the scenes in the two poems, Horace's and Pope's, we can see that they share qualities and yet differ. Pope does not simply follow his original; but nor does he leave him behind. Both writers are clearly enjoying the drama, the comedy, the opportunity for a creative display of their talent to amuse. Frank Stack again: 'Every point in Pope has been inspired by Horace, and yet every point is different. And it is this lively, endlessly open, play between the texts which makes reading the poem as an Imitation so invigorating. Each poetry seems to open up the other and give it new vitality. What we are aware of is the endless play of similarity and disparity, re-creation and transgression' (1985, p. 33).

If you have to write, advises Fortescue, why not write verses in praise of 'Caesar' (i.e., George II)? You will be well rewarded with a knighthood or the poet laureateship. This is teasing advice, as George's aversion to poetry was well known. Pope rises to the occasion:

> What? like Sir Richard, rumbling, rough, and fierce,
> With ARMS, and GEORGE, and BRUNSWICK crowd the verse,
> Rend with tremendous sound your ears asunder,
> With gun, drum, trumpet, blunderbuss, and thunder?
> Or nobly wild, with Budgell's fire and force,
> Paint angels trembling round his falling horse?
>
> lines 23–28

Horace responds to Trebatius's equivalent advice with a few parodies of epic images, such as 'battle columns bristling with javelins'. Pope turns up the temperature, offering two actual models of poetic heroism. Eustace Budgell, a cousin of Joseph Addison and a contributor to the *Spectator*, had written a *Poem upon His Majesty's Late Journey to Cambridge and Newmarket* (1728), which celebrated George, as Prince of Hanover, for leading a cavalry charge at the Battle of Oudenarde (1708) even as his horse was shot from under him. This represents a twist on another of Horace's examples, a wounded Parthian falling from his horse. Pope adds the trembling angels as a further parodic touch.

'Sir Richard' Blackmore had long been a butt of Pope's derision. Most notably, he furnishes *Peri Bathous*, Pope's comic essay on how to write anti-climactic 'heroic' poetry, more instances than anyone else. For example, Blackmore thus describes a warrior's noble action:

> The mighty Stuffa threw a massy spear,
> Which, with its errand pleased, sung through the air.

The second line's assertion that the huge spear was actually mightily pleased with itself, and shows it by singing like an errand-boy whistling as he goes, presents, not epic grandeur, but inept anti-climax. This couplet is just one of many others in Blackmore's attempts to achieve the high style of epic, but which actually sink into absurdity. (The lines, incidentally, are from Blackmore's *King Arthur* (1697), not, as Pope's note states, *Prince Arthur*. See Cowler 1986, p. 264.) Pope now stuffs his lines full of onomatopoeia in a bravura display of fatuous hyperbole. Line 26 is the highpoint: 'With gun, drum, trumpet, blunderbuss, and thunder'. Six reverberant short /u/ vowels, mouthfuls of clashing consonants and a lineful of commas result in a proper plethora of painful panegyric. Arise, Sir Alexander?

After the comic bravura of Pope's demonstration of how to praise the royal family as they deserve, Fortescue (enjoying the joke or despairing of getting his client to take anything seriously?) explains that the more satire he (Pope) writes the more enemies he is making. 'Look, you may mock,', a paraphrase of Fortescue's advice might run, 'but it's really better to toe the line like Colley Cibber'—the actual poet laureate, frequent butt of Pope's mockery, and future anti-hero of the revised, four-book *Dunciad*—'than to "Abuse the city's best good men in metre,

/ And laugh at peers that put their trust in Peter"' (lines 39–40). This is a reference, again, to Peter Walter. 'And it's no good making up names because, if you do, you manage to rile even more people by encouraging them to imagine they must be the intended victim of the fictitious name.' But Pope goes blithely on, mixing real and invented names with the ease and delight of a poet really enjoying himself.

Lines 45–52

> P. Each mortal has his pleasure: none deny
> Scarsdale his bottle, Darty his ham-pie;
> Ridotta sips and dances, till she see
> The doubling lustres dance as fast as she;
> Fox loves the senate, Hockley Hole his brother,
> Like in all else, as one egg to another.
> I love to pour out all myself, as plain
> As downright SHIPPEN, or as old Montaigne:

The Fox brothers, Stephen and the later more-famous Henry, are nonchalantly caught in a chiasmus that places Parliament ('the senate') alongside Hockley Hole, a celebrated bear-baiting garden in Clerkenwell, near the Fleet, a river long converted into a stinking sewer (see Rogers 1980, pp. 146–47). 'Ridotta', meanwhile, is a generalised name for a society woman frequenting a *ridotto*, a social assembly for dancing and music, introduced into England in 1722. She trips along in a couplet that exuberantly dances with her. With it, Pope conveys the message, 'You see, everyone takes innocent pleasure in some activity. Mine just happens to be writing a stream of verses in which I make no attempt to hide or pretend to be what I'm not.' Rather, he names his models as 'downright SHIPPEN' and 'old Montaigne'. William Shippen was a longstanding MP, an uncompromising and unrelenting critic of the Walpole administration who had strongly attacked the financial corruption of the South-Sea Company and who was admired by all political sides for his principled stand. Montaigne is the sixteenth-century French writer whose free-thinking and wide-ranging *Essais* had established him as a model for honest self-examination and independent investigation of ethical, social, and religious questions and problems. Pope's couplet here has the direct ('plain') lucidity and rhythmic limpidity of a clear stream. Better this than a foul ditch: Pope is, with graceful, lightly-worn facility, building a moral case whose natural product is satirical poetry.

Lines 91–100

> Then, learned Sir! (to cut the matter short)
> Whate'er my fate, or well or ill at court,
> Whether old age, with faint but cheerful ray,
> Attends to gild the evening of my day,
> Or death's black wing already be displayed,
> To wrap me in the universal shade;
> Whether the darkened room to muse invite,
> Or whitened wall provoke the skewer to write:
> In durance, exile, Bedlam, or the Mint,
> Like Lee or Budgell, I will rhyme and print.

Line 45 begins the longest speech in the poem, placed at its heart. This verse-paragraph is its climax, its peroration. The half-line that ends it, 'I will rhyme and print', is Pope's most resonant declaration of the satirist's intent. The paragraph's structure is based on Horace's syntax and its assertive conclusion:

> Ne longum faciam: seu me tranquilla senectus
> Exspectat, seu mors atris circumvolat alis;
> Dives inops, Romae seu fors ita iusserit, exul,
> Quisquis erit vitae, scribam, color.
>
> lines 57–60

> [In brief: whether a peaceful old age
> awaits me, or whether death with black wings hovers round;
> rich or poor; whether in Rome or, if chance so orders, in exile;
> whatever will be the 'colour' [that is, condition] of my life, I will write].

Pope extends and intensifies Horace's rhetoric. The first unknown, whether his later days will be peaceful or be haunted by the ominous bird of death hovering above, becomes two couplets in Pope, and is given additional metaphorical warmth (in the former case) and sombreness (in the latter). Is there a touch of sentimentality, of basking in the sunlight of the 'evening of my day'? If there is, then surely it would be a hard critic who would deny a man a little self-indulgence as he contemplates the future? Pope is depicting himself as a genuine, frank conversationalist, opening his heart and mind to his critical friend. And he is honest enough to balance such a rosy picture with the rather gruesome alternative, that Horace's black-winged bird might not just be hovering but be all set to 'wrap' him—a shiver of physical contact with mortality here—in the finality of the classical idea of death as an eternal darkness. No trembling angels here.

Pope then adds a further dimension. The prospect that a darkening room will at least provide an archetypal environment friendly to meditation and the contemplative poetry which might result is set against, in the second line of the couplet, a far less welcome picture of a madman scrawling on the blank walls of whatever Bedlam might await. Better a comfortable darkening room than the bright lights of lunacy is a wry inversion of the usual light/dark antithesis. Lest the reader should wonder whether the forceful satirist is growing a little too soft-centred, at least this less appealing image of the isolation of old age allows a quick re-emergence of the poet for whom fools rush into his head. He name-checks the Restoration dramatist Nathaniel Lee, who did indeed spend five years in Bethlehem Hospital ('Bedlam') and, once again, poor old Eustace Budgell.

Pope saves his final expansion of the original Latin for the very end. Horace's 'quisquis erit vitae, scribam, color' is brilliantly effective as a terse (Latin's facilitation of brevity again) assertion of his resolution, despite all of Trebatius's warnings and advice ('quiescas'), to carry on writing: 'scribam'. Latin's system of defining grammar through forms of words rather than syntactic conventions of word-order enables ready employment of hyperbaton. 'Scribam' occupies a central place in the full line in Horace's poem:

> HOR. Quisquis erit vitae, scribam, color.
>   TREB. O puer, ut sis
> Vitalis, metuo

> [HOR. Whatever will be the condition of my life, I will write.
>   TREB. O young man, that you are
> Likely to live, I fear]

Horace's assertion induces Trebatius to interrupt the full line. Pope marks the ending of his speech in another way, by doubling the verbs so that he completes his full line: 'I will write and print'. There are no limits to production and dissemination in eighteenth-century England. Printing allows for a huge extension of the reach of literature when compared with the pre-Caxton world. This can only strengthen its potential to exert influence. And printing is, of course, the medium through which we are reading Pope's satire.

The line we began with, 'TO VIRTUE ONLY and HER FRIENDS, A FRIEND', is the climax of Pope's next speech, which occupies most of the final third of the poem. Straight after it comes a calm passage, expressing a mood of comfortable and undisturbed pleasure in the company of friends gained through friendship to virtue.

Lines 123–28

> Know, all the distant din that world can keep,
> Rolls o'er my grotto, and but soothes my sleep.
> There, my retreat the best companions grace,
> Chiefs out of war, and statesmen out of place.
> There ST JOHN mingles with my friendly bowl
> The feast of reason and the flow of soul:

Enter Henry St John, Lord Bolingbroke. He is the poem's progenitor and, hence, instigator of the entire series of *Imitations* as well as the addressee of *An Essay on Man*, which sits alongside them and the other epistles as the great achievement of Pope's fifth decade of life. There is a philosophical air to these lines, rendered in smooth rhythms, euphony, seamless lines and couplets, and the balanced language that is Pope's stylistic embodiment of Horace's 'aequus'. The line 'The feast of reason and the flow of soul' encapsulates all these qualities. The stressed syllables ('feast', 'réason', 'flow', 'soul') form a justly famous resumé of a life, a mind and body, a whole being, at ease with itself. Long open vowels internally chime, spreading the line out in agreeably luxurious length.

From such heights the less than ethically perfect world beyond may be contemplated with a mixture of Horace's Epicurean contentment and a Stoicism which motivates Pope's determination to engage actively in the social and political life of the nation. Satire is his means to that end, and this—whatever its flaws, its descents into demeaning ways, its dyer's-hand involvement in the corruption of which it treats—must be its justification.

One further note needs to be sounded or, rather, re-sounded. Both Horace and Pope end their poems by returning to the comic dialogue with which they began. The lawyers give their clients one last warning: 'There are laws and courts, there are statutes against libel; so do be careful.' The poets reply: 'But if we poets compose works that Caesar himself must judge as good (Horace), that a King might read and Sir Robert [Walpole] approve (Pope), then, surely...'. The relieved lawyers respond: 'Oh, well, in that case, any legal action will collapse'. Pope renders this: 'In such a cause the plaintiff will be hissed, / My lords the judges laugh, and you're dismissed' (lines 155–56). Pope here follows Richard Bentley's allocation, in the latter's 1711 translated edition, of the last line of Horace's poem to Trebatius: 'The case will dissolve in laughter, and you'll be dismissed and walk away'. Modern texts all accept this reading. So, the two lawyers cannot resist having the last word, which draws attention to the influence of the great and powerful (Caesar Augustus, Robert Walpole) over the courts. However, by so doing, the lawyers end up actually exemplifying the poets' sceptical commentary on the 'independence' of the law. They thus inadvertently become the satirists they have been counselling their clients all along not to be. The truth will out; and the poets have the last laugh.

17. *The Second Satire of the Second Book of Horace Imitated. To Mr Bethel*

Examples: Lines 45–48, 61–66, 129–50

'Bethel's sermon': Moderation

The larger part of the satire, published in 1734, is given over to Bethel's oration in praise of traditional virtues and avoidance of extremes (lines 11–128). These qualities are woven into the structure of the verse in various ways. An excessively self-indulgent lifestyle, marked by an absurd pursuit of rich food and gourmandism, is set against an equivalently relentless and irrational frugality (lines 17–44 and 49–60; and compare Old Cotta and Young Cotta in the *Epistle to Bathurst*). The outcome of Bethel's account of such mutually defeating modes of life is his praise of temperance, which occupies lines 67–90, framed by a direct opposition of 'temperance' (line 67) and 'intemperate' (line 90). Then a vision of the good old days of sturdy countrymen's habits is contrasted to a critique of urban modernity (lines 91–122). In all this, Bethel—an old friend of Pope's and member of the Burlington circle in Yorkshire—speaks as a bluff, self-avowedly sensible landowner, a contemporary up-market version of Horace's no-nonsense, blunt Ofellus. Pope calls Bethel's speech a sermon, a transliteration of Horace's 'sermo', which actually means speech or conversation. Bethel's principal concern is to draw clear lessons from his observations and examples of flawed human behaviour.

> 'Tis yet in vain, I own, to keep a pother
> About one vice, and fall into the other:
> Between excess and famine lies a mean;
> Plain, but not sordid; though not splendid, clean.

lines 45–48

The voice is that of a plain-speaking man, as plain as the 'mean' he defines. He speaks colloquially, his first line topped and tailed by an informal abbreviation ('Tis) and a blunt register (pother, meaning fuss, disturbance), each within two-stress verbal constructions ('Tis yet in vain; to keep a pother). Between them, 'I own' curtly takes responsibility for Bethel's adherence to, and expression of, the absurdity of extremes. He will not fall into the trap of being so occupied avoiding 'one vice' that he ends up in 'the other'.

The second couplet is more elevated in language, more stately in structure, and more moralizing in attitude. The two extremes of 'excess' and 'famine' spread across the line to end in their 'mean', a resolution which forms an impressive assertion. The second line presents, as a complement, the most complex structure of the four, its elevated status lying in its echo of a time-honoured and often imitated original, the 'Thames couplets' in Sir John Denham's *Cooper's Hill* (1642):

> O could I flow like thee, and make thy stream
> My great example, as it is my theme;
> Through deep yet clear, though gentle yet not dull;
> Strong without rage, without o'erflowing full.
>
> lines 189–92

Denham's lines constitute the rhetorical high-point of his poem. They express desire for a moderate attitude to be adopted between a lazy, 'frozen', absence of principled or committed statesmanship and a zealous, 'torrid' (line 140), pursuit of political aims at any cost. Published as it was in the year Civil War finally broke out after a lengthy period of tense and strained relations between King and Parliament, Denham's poem carries a clear and relevant political message. These lines endow the principle with timeless authority. By locating his ideal within the natural world, Denham distances it from the contingencies of human-created artifice, thus according it an external validity and status. The values it celebrates flow through the observable world. Poetically, his balanced syntax embodies the principle in his expression of it. Pope's version of them follows his model, taking it a step closer to exact symmetry: five syllables either side of the medial semicolon; two or three stresses in each half-line, depending on how a voice internally speaks the line. The chiastic order by which the simple, monosyllabic positive terms ('Plain'; 'clean') encircle the opposed negative terms ('not sordid'; 'not splendid') and forms a mirror structure, a reflection of controlled yet natural balance. The four lines as a group thus rise rapidly from a colloquial manner to a relatively grand and formal style. Conciseness is a feature of their trenchancy, their aphoristic quality. Their position within the poem, separating a satirical description of one extreme, gourmandism, from that of its complementary opposite, frugality, makes them the pivotal lines within Bethel's sermon.

A paragraph later, Pope reverses his stylistic modulation in the service of another statement of the desirability of seeking a mean that balances extremes. This time, he begins with the more formal assertion and moves to a looser exemplification:

> He knows to live, who keeps the middle state,
> And neither leans on this side, nor on that:
> Nor stops, for one bad cork, his butler's pay,
> Swears, like Albutius, a good cook away;
> Nor lets, like Naevius, every error pass,
> The musty wine, foul cloth, or greasy glass.
>
> lines 61–66

The first couplet here nonchalantly displays an unostentatious rhetorical command of the idea it expresses. The opening assertion joins simple diction to ellipsis ('He knows [how] to live') so as not to waste words. A subordinate construction ('who ...') then pauses at the end of its first clause, so making the key phrase, 'the middle state', come to rest appropriately at the couplet's mid-point. The second line then rocks back and forth in illustration of how to find balance ('neither ... on this' / 'nor on that'). The remaining couplets present first one extreme of domestic regime—excessive fastidiousness and controlling behaviour—then the other—sloppy disregard of basic cleanliness. These examples quickly slip into comic mode with a trio of snappy adjective/noun phrases: 'musty wine', 'foul cloth', 'greasy glass'. This is writing that effortlessly combines precision and organized syntax with light-touch humorous observation and implicit judgement. This is the satire's dominant tone: a laid-back, uncensorious and amused reflection on the absurd human propensity to self-harming extremes.

Pope's Frugal Living

Pope changes the later section of Horace's satire. Ofellus continues his speech to the end of the poem. Horace adds just a brief insertion to tell us that, as a small boy, he knew Ofellus when his wealth had not yet been reduced, and that Ofellus's simple style of living was as much in evidence then as it is now (lines 112–115). Pope completely takes over the poem through to its conclusion, Bethel's example providing his model. Here is Pope's transitional passage:

> Thus BETHEL spoke, who always speaks his thought,
> And always thinks the very thing he ought.
> His equal mind I copy what I can,
> And as I love, would imitate the man.
> In South Sea days not happier, when surmised
> The lords of thousands, than if now *excised*;
> In forest planted by a father's hand,
> Than in five acres now of rented land.
> Content with little, I can piddle here
> On broccoli and mutton, round the year;
> But ancient friends (though poor, or out of play)
> That touch my bell, I cannot turn away.
> 'Tis true, no turbots dignify my boards,
> But gudgeons, flounders, what my Thames affords:
> To Hounslow Heath I point and Banstead Down,
> Thence comes your mutton, and these chicks my own:
> From yon old walnut-tree a shower shall fall;
> And grapes, long lingering on my only wall,
> And figs, from standard and espalier join;
> The devil is in you if you cannot dine:
> Then cheerful healths (your mistress shall have place)
> And, what's more rare, a poet shall say grace.
>
> lines 129–50

Pope's portrait of his modus vivendi follows on from the bluff nonchalance of Bethel's examples, 'imitating' his friend in easy and open admiration ('as I love'). This is the poet in self-depreciating mode, confessing his (relative) poverty: a rented five acres in contrast to the grandeur of 'lords of thousands'. His produce is all home-grown or locally sourced, acknowledged in the throw-away manner of a twenty-first century right-on colour magazine culinary writer. His manner of speaking matches his posture. Colloquial diction strikes a comic note. 'Piddle' is a verb meaning to trifle or toy with something, from a task to one's food. The *OED* describes it as 'always depreciatory' (v., sense 1) Pope refuses to take himself seriously or to claim any significant achievement or self-importance. Informal abbreviation ('Tis true') and chatty phrasing ('The devil is in you') keep the tone light. And yet there is more than a hint of harmless pride in the declarative nature of his projected self-image—a touch of 'look at me; see how humble I am'. It is a manner not always absent from modern-day life-style experts, but with Pope it is all a conscious part of the humour with which he presents his speaker, his shadow-self. For the relative lowliness of the fare on offer—mutton, not lamb; gudgeons and flounders, not turbots—comes with the gesturing of ownership, self-sufficiency, and a not unimpressive display of provision. A horn of moderate-plenty, a cornucopia of the middle state, showers down on us like walnuts from his tree. 'Yes, I might live simply', he seems to say, 'but there's lots of it and it's all my own.'

Ethical instruction in the manner of Aristotelian advocacy of a golden mean teaches us to discriminate between bad pride and good pride. The former is vainglory, boastfulness. The latter is a justified assertion of due dignity. To stoop to excessive display of humility is to enter the moral world of the Uriah Heeps and the Mr Collinses of literature, where professed humility paradoxically morphs into insidious pride. Pope's avoidance of such a lapse ensures due ethical integrity. Old friends are welcome to share his feast, and the poet will say grace. These are virtues of which it is right to be proud. Yet Pope can see the humour, the self-consciousness, which peeps out when actually saying this. But, after all, saying so is what ethical poets do; if they do not, they are not doing their job properly.

Comic tone is a principal means of ensuring that such acknowledgement and observation of a writer's ethical duty comes across engagingly. The poem's structure, whereby the principal role is accorded to Bethel/Ofellus and the writer (Pope/Horace) follows and imitates, is another deflecting mechanism. This order of proceeding also allows the moral assertion of Pope's contribution to flow naturally, unjarringly, from his model's—in two senses, for Pope the speaker is modelling himself on Bethel, while Pope the writer is imitating Horace. Bethel and Horace make a good team: modern Yorkshire and classical

Roman, like a neo-Palladian villa designed by John Carr on the basis of Burlingtonian principles, join to form a whole. The result is, in a word, integrity.

Bethel is defined as a model of individual integrity in the couplet that links the conclusion of his speech to Pope's essay in self-definition: 'Thus BETHEL spoke, who always speaks his thought, / And always thinks the very thing he ought.' Here, the location of 'thought'/'thinks' at the heart of the couplet sets reasoned behaviour at the core of ethical endeavour and justifies the use of speech (Bethel's and, now, Pope's) as a means of declaring principles. This is an unchanging ('always'/'always') truth. Bethel's achievement of a balance between thought, speech and action Pope summarizes as 'equal': 'His equal mind I copy what I can, / And as I love, would imitate the man.

As we noted when reading Pope's Fortescue satire, the adjective 'equal' is the equivalent of one of Horace's key ethical terms, the word 'aequus'. The Latin word literally means a place that is even, level, flat (*aequum* as a noun means a 'plain'). By transference, 'aequus' thus refers to anything that is on the level, so is fair, just, right. Of a mind it signifies calm composure, a due balance, in the face of the temporary state of human life—for both 'lords of thousands' and Pope himself, who owns 'five acres now of rented land'. This is not merely a rhetorical flourish. Pope did not own his celebrated Twickenham house and symbolically designed garden: they were leased from Thomas Vernon. Pope's poem embodies the only response which maintains a rational and composed response: that modelled by Bethel and Horace. As the final couplet of this *Imitation* declares: 'Let lands and houses have what lords they will, / Let us be fixed, and our own masters still.'

18. The Second Satire of the First Book of Horace. Imitated in the Manner of Mr Pope

Examples: Lines 39–44, 71–72

This poem has often been a source of embarrassment for solemn and humourless critics. It was published anonymously as *Sober Advice from Horace* in December 1734, between Pope's 'Bethel' *Imitation* and *Epistle to Dr Arbuthnot*. That original title gives the game away. Anyone familiar with the Horace *Satire* would have known that 'sober' it is not, and the 'advice' it gives is equivocal, to put it gently. In other words, the title is ironic and the poem itself is going to be a joke. Jokes are what strait-laced critics do not get. Warburton omitted it from his 1751 edition of Pope's *Works*, as did Whitwell Elwin and William John Courthope from their ten-volume edition (1871–89), which was the standard later edition until the authoritative Twickenham edition of the mid-twentieth century.

Horace's satire presents itself as being about the dangers of adultery, its recommendation being that it is altogether safer to have affairs with prostitutes and women of doubtful morality than with respectable married women of rank. This allows Horace to have great fun exposing the wild sexual goings-on in Roman society, with lots of examples and frank language. Pope's imitation also does not hold back, relishing its satirical portrait of the lustful dissipation of all and sundry. One remembers how unrestrained eighteenth-century satirical prints could be.

Lines 39–44

> My Lord of London, chancing to remark
> A noted dean much busied in the Park,
> 'Proceed', he cried, 'proceed, my reverend brother,
> 'Tis *fornicatio simplex*, and no other:
> Better than lust for boys, with Pope and Turk,
> Or others' spouses, like my Lord of York'.

'My Lord of London' (that is, the Bishop of London) is Edmund Gibson. His biographer, Norman Sykes, sums him up: Gibson's 'solid scholarship, his untiring industry, his practical sagacity, his sober piety, represent the best qualities of eighteenth-century churchmanship' (cited in Butt, ed., *TE*, 1939, VI, p. 362). So, he is just the man to provide official and reliable approval for the vigorous, if somewhat unconventional, outdoors activity of a fellow ecclesiastic, the 'noted dean'. Thomas Sawbridge, Dean of Ferns and Leighlin, who had been indicted for rape in 1730, is identified by the Twickenham edition as the target here. And why the approval? Well, at least it is legally sanctioned sex, rather than pederasty or adultery. 'My Lord of York', that is, the Archbishop of York, was at the time Lancelot Blackburne. The Twickenham Edition, sedulous as ever, quotes a letter of Horace Walpole's: 'I often dined with him—his mistress (Mrs. Cruwys) sat at the head of table, and Hayter [later Bishop of Norwich], his natural son by another woman, and very like him, at the bottom, as chaplain' (cited in Butt, ed., *TE*, 1939, IV, pp. 78, 347).

Pope's lines follow all this with a vigour of their own, taking their cue from Horace's quoting the great statesman Cato as commending a famous man ('notus homo') seen leaving a brothel, on the grounds that it is better that way than 'screwing other men's wives' ('alienas / Permolere uxores'). St James's Park had something of a reputation for providing erotic opportunities, as exemplified by the Earl of Rochester's lively poem, *A Ramble in Saint James's Park* (1680). Pope's lines surely cannot be accused of being lurid or explicit? On the contrary, consider the euphemism of 'much busied' and the prudent cloak of decent Latin for the actual activity. And he cannot be accused of naming names: he leaves it to others to supply the identifications. In its original version, indeed, London and York were just dashes ('L___n', in the former case), so adding a further level of mock concealment. The only name that appears is 'Pope'; unless he means…? Surely not?

Lines 71–72

> To Palmer's bed no actress comes amiss,
> He courts the whole *personae dramatis*.

A contemporary annotator, so the Twickenham edition tells us, identifies this chap as Sir Thomas Palmer, a politician whose second wife (of three), Susanna Cox, was an actress (*TE*, 1939, 2nd edn, 1953, IV, pp. 81, 376). But he died in 1723. So, no proof. Anyway, is there not something rather generous in Palmer's attitude? Again, we note Pope's polite and elegant euphemism: 'courts'. The rhyme is flamboyantly witty, as if anticipating Byron's mode in *Don Juan* (1819).

In short, Pope is having fun, as Horace did before him. He is teasing his readers by shamming prudence and caution, leaving it to them to expose their hypocritically puritanical prurience and relishing the opportunity to indulge in linguistic ingenuity and vivacity. He is also enjoying a game with his readers about authorship. The first printing as *Sober Advice from Horace* declared that the poem was 'imitated in the manner of Mr. Pope'. Well, Mr Pope's manner has been—and will again be—guided by a flexible, thoughtful, and serious inquiry into the nature of moral actions and the operation of an ethical vision in society. To 'imitate' Horace, and 'Pope' himself, by donning a comic mask in an ebullient demonstration of how *really* immoral are society and—especially—its most 'honourable' members, is both joyfully letting one's wig down and (seriously) posing intriguing questions. Does moral 'satire' actually have any effect? Is society too endemically immoral for reform to be a genuine possibility? And that includes us inquisitive readers, too.

19. *Epistle to Dr Arbuthnot*

Examples: Lines 27–32, 193–214, 317–22, 392–99

In July 1734, John Arbuthnot, one of Pope's closest friends, wrote to tell him that his own illness was terminal. Arbuthnot had been Queen Anne's physician, and a member of the Scriblerus group. Pope responded by addressing to him what has become probably his best-known verse epistle. In a letter to Arbuthnot in September 1734, Pope called the epistle 'the best memorial I can leave, both of my friendship to you, and of my character' (Sherburn 1956, III, p. 431). The poem was published on 2 January 1735 and was included in the second volume of Pope's *Works* published months later. Arbuthnot died on 27 February of that year.

As Pope acknowledged to Arbuthnot, the poem included some sections which had appeared in earlier versions. The most notable of these is the 'Atticus' passage, which Pope first wrote before Joseph Addison's death in 1719 (lines 192–214; see below). The substitute name used in the *Epistle to Dr Arbuthnot* is a reference to a patron and friend of Cicero's, T. Pomponius Atticus. But it is fair to say that the new material and the re-location of revised existing passages formed, together, a far more ambitious, moving, and complete poem. That it also contains some of his most harshly satirical passages may suggest how, for Pope, intense friendship was defined against its opposite. In his 1751 edition of Pope's works, William Warburton put the poem at the head of the *Imitations of Horace*, calling it a 'Prologue to the Satires'. However, there is no evidence that Pope authorized such a description or location.

Pope's 'Advertisement' to the *Epistle* calls it 'a sort of bill of complaint', that is, a written statement of a plaintiff's case in a judicial suit. This fits much of the poem, which amounts to a justification of his career as a poet in the light of the animosity and opposition he had stirred up. But the word 'complaint', in the context, has another reverberation. The *OED*'s first citation for it in the sense of 'bodily ailment, indisposition' is Arbuthnot himself (1705); the second is Swift (1733; sb., sense 6). Linking illness to a judicial process not only evokes the origins of the poem; it also serves as a suggestive introduction to the epistle's central metaphor, that of a state of corruption within the cultural and political body of the country.

Lines 27–32

> Friend to my life! (which did not you prolong,
> The world had wanted many an idle song)
> What *drop* or *nostrum* can this plague remove?
> Or which must end me, a fool's wrath or love?
> A dire dilemma! either way I'm sped,
> If foes, they write, if friends, they read me dead.

Pope has begun the epistle by complaining, in mock-exaggerated terms, about all the people who besiege his house looking for his endorsement of, or assistance with, their own poetical endeavours. It is as if Bedlam has opened its doors and released every madman in sight to 'fly to TWIT'NAM, and in humble strain / Apply to me, to keep them mad or vain' (lines 21–22). What medicine (*'drop* or *nostrum'*), dear doctor, can you prescribe to take this plague away? Alas, there is none. These are rhetorical questions. Pope is trapped, as line 32 demonstrates: its antitheses—foes/friends; write/read—all end up in the same deadly conclusion.

Well, all this is something of a joke, or at least a fancifully self-conscious essay in hyperbole. But the context for the epistle is serious: for both writer and addressee, death is no laughing matter, no jokey metaphor. Dr Arbuthnot has been a loyal and reliable friend to Pope's life, lengthening his days to allow the poet more time to compose more verses. 'Idle song' continues the self-depreciating manner, to be echoed in the 'rhymes and rattles of the man or boy' of Pope's *Epistle to Bolingbroke* (1738).

In the present poem, Pope goes on to begin his defence of his own poetic life and career with a further tribute to Arbuthnot's tender skills:

> The Muse but served to ease some friend, not wife,
> To help me through this long disease, my life,
> To second, ARBUTHNOT! thy art and care,
> And teach, the being you preserved, to bear.
>
> lines 131–34

Poetry has supported Arbuthnot's 'art and care' by teaching Pope to endure better the life he has protected. Now, the roles are reversed. Pope's genial, intimate, and kindly verse letter is his offering, his humble gift of words to help his friend to 'bear' the final days of his 'being'. 'Friend', indeed, is the word that resounds through to the epistle's final paragraph.

However, that alliterative antithesis in line 32—'foes'/ 'friends'— has gently planted a less wholesome seed in the poem's growth. We might overlook it on a first reading, but its ominous note of apparently incongruous pairing at least in retrospect warns us of something much darker to come. Not the least devastating of the ironies in the *Epistle to Arbuthnot* is that it is, arguably, the poem which displays most starkly Pope's capacity for all that comes with the simple monosyllable 'foe'. Hardly just an 'idle song', it contains his most violent and shattering expressions of disgust at human malignity. The tone of these expressions exhibits a range amounting to an exploration of satiric possibilities. The most subtle of these is, appropriately enough, a 'character': a description of a particular 'type' of person, as exemplified in a fictional or, as here, non-fictional figure. This is the poem's first major set-piece, the 'Atticus' passage, in which, at its heart, lies the same 'friend'/ 'foe' antithesis.

Lines 193–214: Atticus

> Peace to all such! but were there one whose fires
> True genius kindles, and fair fame inspires;
> Blessed with each talent and each art to please,
> And born to write, converse, and live with ease:
> Should such a man, too fond to rule alone,
> Bear, like the Turk, no brother near the throne,
> View him with scornful, yet with jealous eyes,
> And hate for arts that caused himself to rise;
> Damn with faint praise, assent with civil leer,
> And without sneering, teach the rest to sneer;
> Willing to wound, and yet afraid to strike,

> Just hint a fault, and hesitate dislike;
> Alike reserved to blame, or to commend,
> A timorous foe, and a suspicious friend;
> Dreading even fools, by flatterers besieged,
> And so obliging, that he ne'er obliged;
> Like Cato, give his little senate laws,
> And sit attentive to his own applause;
> While wits and templars every sentence raise,
> And wonder with a foolish face of praise—
> Who but must laugh, if such a man there be?
> Who would not weep, if ATTICUS were he!

The section in the Introduction about Pope's use of couplets showed how they could be formed into two types of semantic relationship. By manipulating language across a line and across the two lines, Pope is able to express a state of either balance or imbalance. In the former, words and phrases are complementary, 'two parts which mutually complete each other' (*OED*, 'complement' sb., sense 5). In the latter, they are antithetical, forming an 'opposition or contrast of ideas' (*OED*, 'antithesis', sb., sense 1). The Introduction also cited a couplet from the fourth epistle of *An Essay on Man*:

> Never elated, while one man's oppressed;
> Never dejected, while another's blessed.
>
> lines 323–24

This couplet demonstrates how both antithesis and complement can be present, so expressing a resolution of potential differences. Thus, the relationship between a couplet's constituent parts may be, in varying degrees, contradictory or equivalent. A couplet's energy and its challenge to the reader largely derive from the dynamic between these possibilities.

The Atticus passage illustrates how such a co-existence of likeness and unlikeness can be extended across a full paragraph. At one end of the character sketch lies concord:

> Blessed with each talent and each art to please,
> And born to write, converse, and live with ease.
>
> lines 195–96

The gifts of nature ('each talent') and the attainments of nurture ('each art') are set in the middle of line 195, with the simplest of all conjunctions, 'and', bringing them into a balanced phrase. Indeed, the very grammatical term itself embodies the action it expresses: 'union, connexion, combination' (*OED*, 'conjunction', sb., sense 1). At either end of the line, framing 'each talent and each art', are the complementary past participle and infinitive, 'Blessed' and 'to please'. The 'ease' (line 196) with which Atticus has acquired his blessings is reflected in the facility with which he pleases other people. The entire line 196 describes a man who uses his natural linguistic skills of communication, on paper and in speech, to shape a complete harmonious relationship with his society and his fellows within society. The rhymes of 'please' and 'ease' thus sound an aural note of unison, enacting and celebrating that harmony.

At the other end of the paragraph, we find a very different couplet. (In between, contraries hold sway, such as the oxymoronic 'Damn with faint praise', a trenchantly concise clause, which has entered the vocabulary of the English-speaking world. For a fuller examination of the middle part of the passage, see my *Living Poetry* (Hutchings 2012, pp. 33–39). In that analysis, no attempt is made to locate the extract in the context of the poem or in that of Pope's poetry as a whole.)

> Who but must laugh, if such a man there be?
> Who but must weep, if ATTICUS were he!
>
> lines 213–14

The verbs 'laugh' and 'weep' occupy the same position in each line, the fourth monosyllabic beat, emphasized by the two commas which constitute, in each case, a strong caesura. The meanings of the verbs, however, are clearly antithetical. On the other hand, the anaphora of 'Who' suggests a complement, confirmed by the second halves of the two lines. The simple repetition of the conditional 'if' introduces the subjunctive verbs, 'be' and 'were'. Indeed, the whole paragraph is framed in this mode. The first verb of the character sketch is 'were': 'were there one whose fires' (line 193). The syntax of the entire paragraph is resolved only in the final couplet; and this contradictory culmination rapidly changes our response from mockery to pity, the archetypal emotion of tragedy. Lines 213–14 thus exemplify, at its most forceful, a couplet which brings together complement and antithesis.

What is the cause that transforms a man blessed with such natural gifts for harmony into the divided creature he becomes? Pope gives us the answer in the third and fourth couplets of the paragraph. 'Should such a man, too fond to rule alone' (line 197) regard any other person of similar talents and arts not as a colleague, but as a rival, he will

> View him with scornful yet with jealous eyes,
> And hate for arts that caused himself to rise.
>
> lines 199–200

The *OED* has a full definition of 'jealous': 'Troubled by the belief, suspicion, or fear that the good which one desires to gain or keep for oneself has been or may be diverted to another; resentful towards another on account of known or suspected rivalry' (*OED* 'jealous', a., sense 4). Pope's character sketch echoes words in this definition: 'rise' (line 200), 'suspicious' (line 206). The whole paragraph embeds Atticus's moral failing within Pope's rigorous description. It therefore constitutes perhaps the most convincing treatment and presentation of a ruling passion, the theory proposed in the epistle to Lord Cobham (see Chapter 14).

The *Epistle to Dr Arbuthnot* is explicitly a poem of deep and reciprocated friendship. However, the friends/foes antithesis we saw in the first passage discussed ('If foes they write, if friends, they read me dead', line 32) is deeply inscribed into its structure. It is as if Pope cannot have one set without the other, a tension animating his satire at one end, and, at the other, his recurrent theme and cherishing of friendship. This uneasiness spreads throughout the poem, most explicitly in the dark, not to say vicious, treatment of Sporus (see the following extract, lines 317–22). The Atticus portrait occupies more ambiguous territory. Chapter 10 referred to the sense of betrayal Pope may have felt as a result of Joseph Addison's transference of his support for Pope's project to translate Homer's *Iliad* to that for a rival version by Thomas Tickell. The name of Addison lying behind Atticus shows how personally Pope took this slight (Mack 1985, pp. 279–82). The Atticus paragraph profoundly expresses the contradictions Pope felt in his relationship with Addison and in the heart of the man he sees as embodying such inconsistencies. It is in his deployment of couplets' potential for diverse structures and meanings, and in the paragraph energized by a series of such couplets, that Pope's art maintains both a clear dissection of the man, and a longing, lingering love for the friendship contaminated by Addison's ultimate moral failure. We all, perhaps, have the capacity to waste our potential: this consciousness simply reinforces the reader's feeling for Addison and the poet so affected.

Lines 317–22: Sporus

> Whether in florid impotence he speaks,
> And, as the prompter breathes, the puppet squeaks;
> Or at the ear of Eve, familiar toad,
> Half froth, half venom, spits himself abroad,
> In puns, or politics, or tales, or lies,
> Or spite, or smut, or rhymes, or blasphemies.

If Atticus is the most elevated of Pope's portraits in the *Epistle to Arbuthnot*, there is little doubt that the 'meanest' is Sporus, to use Samuel Johnson's adjective (Johnson, II, 1925, p. 228). The whole passage (lines 305–33) consists of a sustained and unrelenting attack on Lord Hervey, son of the Earl of Bristol and a prominent courtier to George II. He was particularly associated with the powerful Prime Minister, Robert Walpole ('the prompter') and Queen Caroline ('Eve'). Today, we would celebrate or demonize him as a 'Special Adviser'.

Pope's animosity was personal as well as political. Hervey joined forces with Lady Mary Wortley Montagu, another of Pope's former friends-turned-enemy. As noted in Chapter 16, Pope's *Imitation* of Horace's first satire of book 2 ('To Fortescue') of 1733 had viciously attacked her as 'Sappho': 'From furious Sappho scarce a milder fate, / Poxed by her love, or libelled by her hate' (lines 83–84). Pope employs Lady Mary's work on encouraging inoculation against the killer disease of smallpox to insinuate another variety of pox lying in wait for anyone who gets too intimate with her. The line entraps her in appropriately destructive consequences from whichever of the extreme emotions such people will encounter. Her response, *Verses Addressed to the Imitator of Horace* (1733), was co-authored with Hervey, and did not hold back in its attack on Pope's mind and body. There seems to have been something about perceptions of sexuality that brought out the worst in Pope. He borrowed the name Sporus from Suetonius's account of the emperor Nero's lover. The outcome for the character in the *Epistle to Arbuthnot* is a relentless obsession with Lord Hervey's probable bisexuality ('Now trips a lady, and now struts a lord', line 329). It is all, we may say, not entirely edifying.

And yet, at another level, the Sporus passage does fit, artistically, in an integrated study of a culture and a society perceived, rightly or wrongly, as fatally divided between extremes (friends and foes) and in desperate need of the healing that comes literally from good medicine (Arbuthnot) and metaphorically from good poetry (Pope)—the body and the mind.

The present extract is centred on poison ('venom'), as channelled through both physical and cultural forms. The latter operates by the lines' allusion to Milton's *Paradise Lost* (1667). In his destructive pursuit of the innocent Eve in the Garden of Eden, Satan is discovered by cherubs guarding her (like the sylphs guarding Belinda in Pope's *The Rape of the Lock*) 'Squat like a toad, close at the ear of Eve' (book 4, line 800). The allusion posits that Lord Hervey's malign influence on national governance is a specific political manifestation of a corruption endemic to divine creation. It is culturally significant myth brought into the here and now of historical reality.

Its physical actuality, as imaged in animal forms, connects it with an observable set of phenomena. These begin with the little scribblers whose imperviousness to mockery Pope likens to spiders who, if one web is broken, will spin 'the slight, self-pleasing thread anew' (line 90). They pass through the insignificant, small-minded critics whose pedantic misconceptions are preserved like grubs in amber in editorial versions of great works ('in Milton's or in Shakespeare's name', line 168); and most absurdly present themselves in the puffed-up pride of a literary patron, satirised in the character of Bufo, the Latin word for 'toad': 'Proud as Apollo on his forked hill, / Sat full-blown Bufo, puffed by every quill' (lines 231–32). In the 1729 *Dunciad*, Pope had made use of the same allusion in his depiction of the anti-hero at the beginning of book 2: 'Great Tibbald sat'. Tibbald, Pope's belittling name for Lewis Theobald, author of *Shakespeare Restored* (1725), in which he criticized Pope's own edition of the plays of Shakespeare, is one of those grubs in amber in *Arbuthnot*. Behind both is the opening of book 2 of *Paradise Lost*, where 'High on a throne of royal state ... Satan exalted sat'.

So, when the Sporus lines proceed to locate 'politics' in a bald list of demeaning manifestations of literary culture, ranging from the relatively harmless 'puns' to serious 'blasphemies' via the outright inversions of truth that are 'lies', the political becomes the cultural; and the cultural becomes the political. All order disappears in a web of miscellaneous, random expressions. Discrimination is lost in the world of 'Grub Street' (line 378).

Lines 392–99

> Born to no pride, inheriting no strife,
> Nor marrying discord in a noble wife,
> Stranger to civil and religious rage,
> The good man walked innoxious through his age.
> No courts he saw, no suits would ever try,
> Nor dared an oath, nor hazarded a lie:
> Unlearned, he knew no schoolman's subtle art,
> No language, but the language of the heart.

What, then, is the antidote to all this poison? 'What *drop* or *nostrum* can this plague remove?' (see above, line 29). The finale of the *Epistle to Dr Arbuthnot* proposes that, since the body politic is seemingly infected beyond cure, private life has to be the resource of health and purity. The last paragraph is devoted to Pope's mother, who died in 1733, and 'my friend', John Arbuthnot, whose character and presence have been the poem's unifying factor. These lines are from Pope's idealized account of his father, which occupies the penultimate paragraph. Its language is a direct rebuttal of much of what has gone before. For example, 'nor hazarded a lie' counters the 'lies' at the heart of Sporus's list of cultural confusion (lines 321–22). Pope's linguistic technique is an orderly succession of negatives. Each line contains one or more negatives: 'no pride ... no strife', 'Nor', 'Stranger', 'innoxious', 'No courts ... no suits', 'Nor ... nor', 'Unlearned ... no', culminating in the line 'No language, but the language of the heart'. There, the early caesura (after only three syllables) moves the weight and emphasis to its second part. Public language, in political and more widely cultural spaces, has become corrupt. But Pope's father's very lack of learning preserves him from contamination. Instead, he possesses natural, authentic knowledge: 'the language of the heart'. 'The' good man is a phrasing that allows, in its objectivity, Pope's father to become representative as well as personal. That he 'walked innoxious through his age' converts a negative to a positive action. 'Innoxious' here carries particular force. Its usual meaning is simply the opposite of 'noxious': not poisonous. Using it to attribute to a person the quality of being blameless is rare, as rare as a man like him. Its meaning is a single, powerful, semantic rebuttal of the poison that infects and kills.

20. The First Ode of the Fourth Book of Horace: To Venus

Example: Lines 37–48

Pope wrote just one version of a complete Horace ode. An imitation of four stanzas of another, the ninth ode of book 4, was published only posthumously, in Warburton's 1751 edition of Pope's works. The imitation of the first ode of book 4, thus, has a unique status. It first appeared unofficially and anonymously in a newspaper, the *Whitehall Evening Post*, a few days before its authorized publication on 9 March 1737 (*TE*, IV, ed. Butt, 2nd edn, 1953, p. 148; Mack 1985, pp. 672–74).

Horace's ode begins with an appeal to Venus to cease her demands on him now that he is approaching the age of fifty. Please, he says, visit instead the house of his much younger good friend Paulus Maximus, a well-born and handsome lawyer who will make an ideal lover. For Horace himself, such days are over. And yet, the poem concludes in a poignant twist: he finds a tear or two falling down his cheek and silence breaking into his speech. 'Why, Ligurinus, is this happening; and why do I dream of pursuing you over the grass of the Campus Martius?' As in Thomas Hardy's 'I look into my glass' (*Wessex Poems and Other Verses*, 1898), time 'shakes this fragile frame at eve / With throbbings of noontide'. This is Pope's version of Horace's finale:

> – But why? ah tell me, ah too dear!
> Steals down my cheek the involuntary tear?
> Why words so flowing, thoughts so free,
> Stop, or turn nonsense at one glance of thee?
> Thee, dressed in Fancy's airy beam,
> Absent I follow through the extended dream,
> Now, now I seize, I clasp thy charms,

> And now you burst, (ah cruel!) from my arms,
>   And swiftly shoot along the Mall,
>   Or softly glide by the canal,
>   Now shown by Cynthia's silver ray,
> And now, on rolling waters snatched away.
>
> lines 37–48

Or so it was in the officially published text. In the newspaper, line 37 read, 'But why, ah Patty still too dear' (*TE*, IV, 1953, p. 153). 'Patty' was Martha Blount's nickname: a moment of delicate intimacy had found its way into public print.

With or without the confessional name, Pope's finale subtly and movingly adjusts Horace's original. Up to this point, Pope has carefully, discreetly, and brilliantly followed the structure and import of the Latin text, employing octosyllabic / decasyllabic couplets to reflect Horace's alternating shorter and longer lines. The first eight lines echo Horace's vocative appeal to Venus to relent in her pursuit of him. Horace's repetition 'parce precor, precor' [spare me, I beg you, I beg you'] becomes 'let me, let me rest' in both second lines. The famous and delicately self-depreciative 'non sum qualis eram bonae / sub regno Cinarae' (lines 3–4) [I am not as I was under the reign of good Cynara] is wittily and gracefully deflected to 'I am not now, alas! the man / As in the gentle reign of my Queen Anne'. A 'sober fifty' awaits him, as Pope's forty-ninth birthday is fast upon him (21 May), too late an age to endure the paradox of Venus as 'Mother too fierce of dear desires' (line 7): in Horace, 'dulcium / mater saeva Cupidinum' (lines 4–5) [in literal order: 'of sweet / mother fierce of desires'].

The middle sections of both poems depict a future of pleasure, sociability, and love for (in Horace) Paulus Maximus and (in Pope) William Murray, a young lawyer, future lord chancellor, and addressee of Pope's 1738 *Imitation of Horace's Epistle* I, 6 (see Chapter 23). Pope's iterative 'shall' (seven times in the space of fifteen lines, 16–30) beats out the future as in the celebratory dance envisaged by both poets. Set against such joys, Horace forcefully hammers home his loss of desire in a succession of negatives ('nec'):

> Me nec femina nec puer
> Iam nec spes animi credula mutui
>   Nec certare iuvat mero
> Nec vincire novis tempora floribus.
>
> lines 29–32

> [In neither woman nor boy
> nor trusting hope in mutual feelings
> nor drinking parties, do I have pleasure
> nor garlanding my temples with fresh flowers]

Pope depicts a lost and irrecoverable past by means of a succession of equivalent negatives ('those joys are o'er', 'the vernal garlands bloom no more') and two exclamations of 'adieu!', indicating the finality of farewell' (lines 31–35). However, he leaves out Horace's 'nec femina nec puer', reacting sensitively to sexual mores less flexible than those of an earlier time. This omission creates space for a more wistful and protracted conclusion, in which present desire for another person—whether named or, as in the approved version, a vague 'too dear'—is dwelt upon longingly.

Horace's dream occupies four lines, whereas Pope's stretches out over eight. The latter describes a scene in which the beloved not only bursts from his embrace but leads his thoughts on a lyrical chase through both a contemporary townscape, one romanticized by classical light. The effect of Pope's momentary self-indulgence can be gauged by contrasting his finale with an earlier verse translation, that by Ben Jonson:

> Hard-hearted, I dream every night
> I hold thee fast! But fled hence, with the light,
> Whether in Mars his field thou be,
> Or Tiber's winding streams, I follow thee.
>
> *Ben Jonson: The Complete Poems*, ed. by Parfitt (1975):
> 'Underwoods', 86, lines 37–40

Jonson's is a more literal, tighter version. It is indicative that he keeps to the forty lines of Horace's original, whereas Pope extends his poem to forty-eight lines. Pope retains an element of topographical precision ('the Mall'), so that the vision keeps one foot in the here and now. But he transforms the scene by means of evocative verbs and adverbs: 'swiftly shoot', 'softly glide' (lines 45–46). Echoing consonants (notably liquid 'l's), and alternating short and long vowels stretch the lines into harmonious grace. The penultimate line, 'Now shown by Cynthia's silver ray', is Pope's own, an unexpected addition which maintains euphony through vowel and consonant repetitions in 'Cynthia' and 'silver'. Mythological lunar light irradiates the scene, and luminescence sheds a glow of poetic imagination, as the verse form changes from alternating octosyllabic and decasyllabic lines to a trio of octosyllabics (lines 45–47), so introducing a song-like closing note. The poem is extended and touched with lyric felicity.

Horace's dream takes place in an affirmed present: 'iam captum teneo, iam volucrem sequor' (line 38; 'now I hold you: now I follow you in flight'.) Pope, again, extends this sense of the here and now through double repetitions: 'Now, now I seize ... And now you burst'; 'Now shown ... And now'. Pope's vision resounds with the voice of longing, of yearning for beauty. In short, Pope transfigures his imitation into a love poem, in which only at the very end is the tantalizingly present scene 'snatched away'. The mood of those poems of the 1710s, the *Epistle to Miss Blount, with the Works of Voiture* and the *Epistle to Miss Blount, on her Leaving the Town, after the Coronation*, written 'in the gentle reign of my Queen Anne', returns for one last time. And the poet knows it will be the last, which is why this tender lyric is also an acknowledgement of, and a meditation on, the nature and experience of time passing, time passed.

21. *The Second Epistle of the Second Book of Horace Imitated*

Examples: Lines 72–79, 198–205

This imitation initiates a sequence of four of Horace's *Epistles* published between April 1737 and March 1738: a glorious year, indeed. The last of the 1737–38 imitations is addressed to Bolingbroke, so bringing the cycle back to the beginning of *An Essay on Man* ('Awake, my St JOHN! leave all meaner things / To low ambition, and the pride of kings') and to where the idea of writing imitations of Horace began. As we noted in Chapter 16, it was Bolingbroke who suggested that Horace's *Satire*, book 2, number 1 applied neatly to Pope's own current situation.

In a letter to Jonathan Swift dated 20 April 1733 (cited in Sherburn 1956, III, pp. 365–67), Pope observed that 'You call your satires, libels; I would rather call my satires, epistles. They will consist more of morality than wit, and grow graver, which you will call duller'. Pope may have been deliberately downplaying the more forthright elements of his poems of the 1730s, but there is nonetheless some truth in the contrast he makes between himself and his fellow-Scriblerian. His distinction, at any rate, indicates that he has in mind an intention to align his current work with philosophical and ethical aims.

It is perfectly possible to argue, in any case, that there need be no strict demarcation between the personal pursuit of philosophical enlightenment and the politico-social endeavour of satirical observation. Maynard Mack writes, in the context of Pope's embarking on his essays in Horatian imitation, of how, 'though their immediate political vein runs deep, the poems of the 30's are enabled to be political in a larger sense of that term' (Mack 1969, p. 187). The personal is the political and vice versa, given that poetry operates, for both writer and reader, within the 'polis', within society. Pope's embrace of the epistolary mode is a sign of his belief that an extensive series of 'moral' essays will add up to a humane and thoughtful meditation on ideas and experiences of general as well as specific and topical interest.

Lines 72–79

> Years following years, steal something every day,
> At last they steal us from ourselves away;
> In one our frolics, one amusements end,
> In one a mistress drops, in one a friend:
> This subtle thief of life, this paltry time,
> What will it leave me, if it snatch my rhyme?
> If every wheel of that unwearied mill
> That turned ten thousand verses, now stands still.

This four-couplet paragraph is Pope's version of just three lines in Horace's epistle (55–57): 'singula de nobis anni praedantur euntes; / eripuere iocos, venerem, convivia, ludum; / tendunt extorquere poemata; quid faciam vis?' (As the years go by they rob us of one thing after another. They have snatched away jokes, love, banquets, sports. They are trying to wrench poetry away. What shall I do then?).

Pope's line 72 is a close rendering of Horace's line 55; the second couplet is an equivalent of line 56, but with an emphasis on human contacts through extension of one form of relationship in Horace, sexual love ('Venerem'), into two ('mistress', 'friend'); line 77 effectively expresses Horace's third line. Thus, the other lines in Pope's paragraph (73, 76, 78, and 79) bring in additional ideas which intensify time's destructive power, and Pope's self-identification as a man whose life has been committed to writing poetry. The result is a verse-paragraph of considerably more emotional weight than Horace's relatively economical and pointed three lines. It amounts to 'a short, but powerful elegy on time, loss, and the self' (Stack, 1985, p. 126).

Time lies at the heart of the lines. This is thanks not only to the central positioning of the abstract noun itself but because of the rhetorical repetition in the opening phrase, 'Years following years', and the appositional phrase, 'This subtle thief of life', which extends the force of 'time' across an entire line. Pope thus gives the paragraph an air of philosophical observation, albeit a conventional enough one, rather than Horace's more epigrammatic vigour.

However, Pope's definition of his life as being—or having been—entirely given up to poetry constitutes his ultimate and strongest addition. The idea is planted at the opening. 'At last they steal us from ourselves away' fills out an entire couplet whose first line by itself is sufficient to render Horace's first line. The repetition of the verb links the two lines, the duplication echoing that of 'years' and glancing at the core idea of regular reiteration. The final 'stealing' us from ourselves points to mortality, which is the topic of the second couplet. But the second half of the paragraph opens up another meaning, another sense in which our self is stolen from us: loss of our craft, our vocation. A vowel pattern is woven into the poem's movement, guiding us to the key note, of the passage and of the entire epistle: 'steal', 'thief', 'leave', 'wheel'. A wheel in constant motion would, to an initial view, suggest the unvaried tedium of unremitting labour. But this mill—the /l/ consonant links back to 'wheel' as well as forward to its rhyme-word, 'still'—is 'unwearied'. The task of churning out ten thousand verses sounds intimidating and onerous, but it is lack of motion, 'stillness', that is really frightening.

The entire verse-paragraph is, however, kept in a state of rhythmic dynamism by means of Pope's characteristic masterly but lightly-worn command of variety, and by the expressive appropriateness of his line and couplet structures. 'At last they steal us from ourselves away' is one seamless sweep of inevitable movement. The dominant monosyllabic simplicity of its language renders the gesture airily unavoidable, as if it is saying, 'there's no point making a meal of this: time passes until there is no more to pass'. The second couplet, in contrast, divides itself into four clearly demarcated half-lines, so expanding and adding weight (but not so much as to disturb the conversational tone) to Horace's four nouns ('iocos, Venerem, convivia, ludum'). The repetitions of 'one' count out the pleasures even as each is subjected to the simple finality of the verbs: 'end', 'drops'.

In the second half of the paragraph, the theme word 'time' is announced as the climax of a line more strongly marked than the preceding lines by plosive consonants, a derogatory adjective ('paltry') and an accentuated caesura. This is the poet starting to stand up against, or at least object to, the unstoppable march of the years. The second line of the couplet moves more rapidly. The caesura is lighter, and is placed at the syllabic mid-point of the line, whereas line 76 divides six and four, so throwing the weight onto 'this paltry time'. The more plaintive tone of line 77 may look like a confession of weakness, but it nonetheless ends by setting the next key term, 'rhyme', in appropriately rhyming contrast to 'time'. The final couplet retains its one real break until almost at the end. The 'wheel', that is, maintains its motion—the motion of time and of the writer's tireless activity—until those three final, equally strongly stressed, monosyllables 'now stands still'. The danger, the emptiness into which the paragraph stares, is that of ultimate and irreversible cessation.

Yet, the entire paragraph is a virtuosic if self-depreciatory display of Pope's art. The lines may speak about a poet being deprived of his calling, but they actually attest to the continuing vitality of that artistic endeavour. Pope's momentum—and, after all, there is plenty of the poem left—is at odds with, and so represents an implied rebuke to, the destructive power of time to disarm the writer. Pope's wheel is, for now, far from 'still'. The question implicitly posed ('if I can no longer write, do I still exist?') is stark and potentially final, but the existence of the poem we are reading constitutes, at the very least, a distinct protest. This is Pope at the height of his powers, not about to enter that good night. In his hands, this *Imitation* becomes a study of what writing really means. It is no mere 'amusement' or 'ludum', nor even just a trade; it is the poet's whole existence.

Pope proceeds to match Horace with a witty and sardonic survey of all the present impediments to writing. 'People ask me to write different kinds of poetry, so I end up displeasing most of them' (lines 80–87). 'How on earth can I possibly compose amidst the noise, business and mess of London?' (lines 88–107). 'Poets who flee to the country end up as eccentrics and objects of mockery' (lines 108–26). The next pause for reflection and escape from these and other irritations seems at first sight to represent an acceptance of the inevitable.

> Well, on the whole, plain prose must be my fate:
> Wisdom (curse on it) will come soon or late.
> There is a time when poets will grow dull:
> I'll e'en leave verses to the boys at school:

> To rules of poetry no more confined,
> I learn to smooth and harmonize my mind,
> Teach every thought within its bounds to roll,
> And keep the equal measure of the soul.
>
> lines 198–205

'Trying to write poetry is, in any case, a childish activity.', Pope seems here to say, 'There comes a point where one needs to grow up, look inwards, and concentrate on getting one's mind and thoughts in order.'

The paragraph begins with a shrug of the shoulders accompanied by a choice of the linguistic silence-fillers adopted by those who have either run out of things to say or cannot find a way of saying them clearly: 'Well, on the whole'. The phrase 'plain prose' sets the bar pretty low for what lies ahead, even if Pope weakly tries to dramatize the moment ('my fate') and to elevate it ('Wisdom'). The parenthesis ('curse on it') is equally unconvincing. This has the air of a poet who has run out of energy and ideas. Indeed, there is 'a time when poets will grow dull', and now looks like that time.

The second half of the paragraph begins no more encouragingly. If 'rules of poetry' are to be seen as ways of confining, of imprisoning, thought, then let us release ourselves from them. Let us re-train ourselves. Hence Pope adopts the language of education: 'I learn ... Teach every thought'. But what, actually, is he now setting himself to learn? To 'smooth and harmonize my mind' does not seem that far from the purposes he is ostensibly putting behind him. Is harmony not one of a poet's principal aims; and does not poetry with philosophical ambition seek to bring form and function together in the productive way that, for example, so many passages in *An Essay on Man* do? And where 'Teach every thought within its bounds to roll' may sound uneasily like an acceptance of another form of confinement (one now willingly entered into), its partner line in the couplet ensures that the ending of the paragraph is a long way from its beginning. 'And keep the equal measure of the soul' may retain the generally quiet, decidedly unrhetorical, level of Pope's writing here, but its language and rhythm strike a much more positive note than the earlier one of resignation to the inevitable. 'Soul' fills out the earlier 'mind'; 'measure' sets 'harmonize' within a poetic semantic field; and 'equal' strikes a chord that resounds with Pope's other uses of a word whose relationship with its Latin root in 'aequus' invests it with genuine philosophical weight. It is indicative that Pope introduces 'equal' here when Horace does not use 'aequus', even though both employ a musical metaphor. (On the significance for Horace of 'aequus', see the *Imitations* of *Satires* book 2, nos. 1 and 2, to Fortescue and to Bethel: Chapters 16 and 17, above.) Horace's equivalent line (144) is 'sed verae numerosque modosque ediscere vitae' ('but to learn the rhythms and measures of a true life'). Pope's version determinedly includes an unobtrusive but clear pointer towards Horace's world-view: more Horatian than Horace.

This verse-paragraph is also one whose combined force is greater than that of its parts. Pope achieves this through adopting a style rarely noted in his verse because it avoids characteristics, rightly celebrated for their intellectual power, to be found in many of his sharper, more satirical, didactic, or ironic poems. The master of the divided line, of the shifting caesura, of the antithesis, of the aphoristic style, avoids all of these in favour of a series of lines flowing with easy grace. This is the quality of the three couplets beginning with 'There is a time'. Pope artfully sets them up by allowing them to play off against the awkward and stuttering first couplet, with its self-consciously mock disgruntlement in an unrhythmical parenthesis '(curse on it)'. The impact of the lines is partly cumulative, in tune with the gentle growth of significant vocabulary leading up to the line, 'And keep the equal measure of the soul'. Natural-sounding euphony lends lyrical support. Vowels tend towards length, notably the long /e/ sounds in 'o'er', 'leave', 'teach', 'keep', 'equal', but also marked in other vowels, such as 'smooth' and, ultimately, 'soul'. The whole passage phonically conveys a move to 'smooth and harmonize'. The sound is the sense.

Herein lies Pope's implicit counter-argument to his ostensible subject, his inability to write more poetry. This is certainly not 'plain prose'. It brings something Pope is not usually recognized for: sheer lyrical beauty. A reader alert to the poem's origins in Horace will get his point forcibly. Horace's poem is an apology for not writing specifically *lyric* poetry. Julius Florus, his addressee here (as he was of the third of his first book of *Epistles*), has complained that the poet has let him down by not sending the 'carmina' ('odes', line 25) he promised. It was after completing his first three books of odes that Horace took up epistles as a form.

The fundamental principle underlying both Horace's *Epistle* and Pope's *Imitation* is that *all* good poetry is the result of artistry. Lines 106–125 of the Horace and lines 153–179 of Pope's imitation take this as their direct subject. Writers of poor 'carmina' (line 106), 'bad rhymers' in Pope's version (line 153), are a joke, and yet they take themselves so seriously. Real artists, those who wish to produce a poem of genuine quality ('qui legitimum cupiet fecisse poema', line 109), take care to be rigorously self-critical and studious of appropriate style: 'Their own strict judges, not a word they spare / That wants or force, or light, or weight, or care' (Pope, lines 159–60). The full verse-paragraph—at 27 lines the longest in the poem—marks its significance by, for example, introducing a relative rarity in Pope's poems, though a common feature of Dryden's, a triplet:

> Pour the full tide of eloquence along,
> Serenely pure, and yet divinely strong,
> Rich with the treasures of each foreign tongue.
>
> lines 171–73

The triplet nobly stretches out to be inclusive, in both its praise of stylistic range and its embrace of the international quality of the English language. Not inappropriately, then, does Pope conclude with a couplet that, taking its cue from a dance metaphor in Horace (line 125), looks back to his own earlier definition of true artistry:

> 'But ease in writing flows from art, not chance;
> As those move easiest who have learned to dance.'
>
> lines 178–79

Pope simply substitutes 'But' for 'True' (in order to fit the sense in context) in his definition of good style in *An Essay on Criticism*, lines 362–63.

The paragraph we have been examining puts these principles in play, with the nonchalance derived from genuine artistry. Yes, we do need to 'learn' (lines 179 and, now, 203) both how to write and how to live. Truly philosophical poetry—as opposed to poetry which attempts to look self-important by writing *about* philosophy—embodies truth within form. Pope's imitation of Horace's *Epistle* is a justification and definition of poetry in the guise of an apology for not writing poetry. The three

Imitations which follow are addressed in turn to 'Augustus'; William Murray; and Henry St John, Viscount Bolingbroke: that is, King George II; the future Lord Chief Justice, Lord Mansfield; and the politician and philosopher whom for years Pope has admired and respected. The realms addressed could be no higher or more important: royalty, the law, and philosophy. These three poems are among Pope's finest, and triumphantly embody the power of poetry at its summit.

22. The First Epistle of the Second Book of Horace Imitated. To Augustus

Examples: Lines 81–83, 95–102, 107–14, 189–200

Pope's *Imitation* of the first *Epistle* of Horace's second book was published on 25 May 1737, a month later than his version of the second *Epistle*. However, the poem seems to have been written during the year 1736. George II, whose second name, Augustus, made him an irresistible candidate for a version of Horace's address to his Emperor, left England for Hanover and his new mistress, Madam von Walmoden, on 22 May 1736. George's lengthy visits to his Electorate were a cause of significant displeasure among opposition politicians in his kingdom. Pope waits only as far as his second couplet before seizing his prey, celebrating how you 'Your country, chief, in arms abroad defend, / At home, with morals, arts and laws amend' (lines 3–4). It would have taken no subtle cynic to read Pope's couplet as a satirical swipe at George's absence from home and the 'arms abroad' he was enjoying. Another reason to date the poem to 1736 is that Pope made one of his frequent visits to Bevis Mount, near Southampton, in the spring of that year. He had maintained for many years a friendship with Charles Mordaunt, Earl of Peterborough, a military man who had retired on the accession of George I. His connections with Bevis Mount appear to have continued after Peterborough's death in 1735. Pope wrote to his friend William Fortescue on 21 September 1736, 'there [Bevis Mount] … [I] began an Imitation of the finest [*Epistle*] in Horace this spring; which I propose to finish there this autumn' (cited in Sherburn, IV, 1956, p. 33). Jonathan Swift wrote to Pope, thanking him for his complimentary lines (lines 221–28), on 9 February 1737. This suggests that Pope had sent him at least these lines, if not the whole poem, in either late 1736 or early 1737. So, it looks as though Pope was writing *Epistle* II, 1 around the same time as he was writing *Epistle* II, 2. The two *Imitations*, then, quite likely constituted a joint project. They are, after all, two of only three epistles in Horace's second book, and the third is the celebrated *Ars Poetica*. All three are about writing, the role of poets within contemporary society, and the ethical tradition they inherit. Why should their work be taken seriously? How do they relate to their predecessors, and what is their place in the present?

Epistles II, 1 is a substantial poem, easily the longest of the Horatian *Imitations*. It would, surely, be irreverent to address the monarch in any slighter form? Its argument, therefore, is leisurely, extensive, and sustained. Poets have 'some weight', line 203 politely suggests, even if not everyone might be easily persuaded. George II himself was notoriously impervious to learning and literature (Mack 1967, p. 130). Pope's *Epistle* has traditionally been read as an ironic attack on George, with the emperor Augustus serving as a model for comparison and contrast. But some critics have argued that reservations about the Roman Augustus were held in the eighteenth century: he may have been regarded as more like George than once assumed. On this debate, see Weinbrot (1978), Erskine-Hill (1983), and Stack (1985, chapter 8). It is certainly the case that poetry and those in power have not always been natural bedfellows. Poets, therefore, need to be humble supplicants for a little attention from their monarchs; and a vein of modest self-depreciation runs appropriately through the poem. If some readers might be tempted to read into this attitude a degree of ironic self-consciousness, let it be upon their own heads, shall we say? Pope's argument is, broadly, as follows. 'People tend to consider writers of earlier ages superior to those of the present; yet why should that be the case? After all, even the supposed greats of the past were not without their faults and failings. These days, it is true, anyone seems to think they can be a poet. However, there is no need to be concerned about this, since poets are pretty harmless creatures. May I, though, respectfully propose that we poets may be of some use, even if tastes seem to have declined over time. Some monarchs, indeed, have encouraged the arts. I, therefore, am here writing this to you, and I would dearly love to be good enough to rise to a level fit for your great status. Alas, I fear I may not be.'

Lines 81–83

The public fame of acknowledged great writers of the past is regularly based on truisms or clichés:

> In all debates where critics bear a part,
> Not one but nods, and talks of Jonson's art,
> Of Shakespeare's nature, and of Cowley's wit.

These attributes had become, by Pope's time, almost automatically attached to their names. Milton's *L'Allegro* (1645) is the classic instance:

> Then to the well-trod stage anon,
> If Jonson's learned sock be on,
> Or sweetest Shakespeare, fancy's child,
> Warble his native wood-notes wild.
>
> lines 131–34

Pope gently subjects the terms to an implied critique. The passage's quality of a mechanical list is part of this undermining and is supported by his diction. 'Nods' is a gesture intending—on the part of the nodder—to show sagaciousness, but Pope is aware of the word's other connotations. He had used the verb twice in the finale to book 2 of the 1729 *Dunciad Variorum*, where a pair of clerks read aloud from the works of John ('Orator') Henley and Sir Richard Blackmore in response to the goddess Dulness's challenge to her acolytes to try to keep awake. None, alas, can resist the soporific power of 'my Henley's periods, or my Blackmore's numbers' (line 338):

> Thus oft they rear, and oft the head decline,
> As breathe, or pause, by fits, the airs divine:
> And now to this side, now to that they nod,
> As verse, or prose, infuse the drowsy god.
>
> lines 361–64

> Who sat the nearest, by the words o'ercome
> Slept first, the distant nodded to the hum.
>
> lines 369–70

Later, in the 1742 fourth book of *The Dunciad*, Pope would employ a similar double dose as Dulness leads a complete lapse into unconsciousness:

> More she had spoke, but yawned—all nature nods:
> What mortal can resist the yawn of gods?
>
> lines 605–06
>
> Wide, and more wide, it spread o'er all the realm;
> Even Palinurus nodded at the helm.
>
> lines 613–14

So, the implication of 'Not one but nods' in line 82 of the present poem is that everyone signals thoughtless assent to the recitation of 'Jonson's art', 'Shakespeare's nature', and 'Cowley's wit', as if they were responding in their sleep. It certainly is not much of a 'debate' where all so readily concur with the commonplaces. The monosyllabic chiming of the simple clause 'Not one but nods' adds to the banality and shows critics' inability even to consider what the generalized nouns 'art', 'nature', and 'wit' actually mean. Proper literary criticism, including Pope's own in his *Essay on Criticism*, has spent considerable time examining the shades of meaning of these complex terms. Explication and amplification, qualification, and questioning—these are what real debate would require.

In any case, Pope's argument proceeds, the people are prone to unthinking and unreliable judgements. 'All this may be; the people's voice is odd, / It is, and it is not, the voice of God' (lines 89–90). Such an observation does seem, prima facie, to point in the direction of an irresolvable scepticism, putting into question the possibility of arriving at any kind of conclusion, however notional. Pope, however, at once probes such nihilism. It is possible to meet between the trenches if the public would admit that the old writers were giants of literature in their own way but are not above critical scrutiny.

Lines 95–102

> But let them own, that greater faults than we
> They had, and greater virtues, I'll agree.
> Spenser himself affects the obsolete,
> And Sidney's verse halts ill on Roman feet:
> Milton's strong pinion now not Heav'n can bound,
> Now serpent-like, in prose he sweeps the ground,
> In quibbles, angel and archangel join,
> And God the Father turns a school divine.

These are not just Pope's judgements. His assertion about Spenser's language echoes the Ben Jonson he has cited as himself a victim of standard evaluations: 'Spenser, in affecting the ancients, writ no language' (Johnson, *Timber: or Discoveries* (1640), ed. by Parfitt 1975, p. 428, lines 2237–38). His reservations about Milton's *Paradise Lost* (1667) follow on from Dryden's preface to *Sylvae* (1685): 'Milton's *Paradise Lost* is admirable; but am I therefore bound to maintain that there are no flats amongst his elevations, when 'tis evident he creeps along sometimes for above an hundred lines together? Cannot I admire the height of his invention, and the strength of his expression, without defending his antiquated words, and the perpetual harshness of their sounds? 'Tis as much commendation as a man can bear to own him excellent; all beyond it is idolatry' (Watson 1962, I, p. 32). In a passage which is carefully looking for a *via media* between extremes of absolute judgement, between ancient and modern, between popular and tempered views, Pope is linking his present ideas to those of his predecessors. Reconciliation and tradition are locked within a vibrant poem; the contemporary shakes hands with the past.

Pope's lines absorb the language and metaphors of past judgement ('affect'; 'sweeps the ground'), but refresh them into his own distinctive style. Thus, the balance of 'now ... Now' in the third couplet introduces the strongest of antitheses in 'heaven ... serpent-like' within a clear and economical metaphor of height and depth. The whole couplet is, meanwhile, harmonized by the 's' and 'p' reiterations. In a stylistic variation, the fourth couplet is structured by a chiasmus of bathos. A 'school divine' engages in scholastic theology, a study which had accrued connotations of dogmatic, tediously meticulous scrutiny; while 'quibbles' imply legalistic and pedantic attention to purely verbal ambiguities and arguments. Proficients of both activities really belong not in an epic poem but in the mock-epic world of *The Dunciad*. In Pope's couplet, these demeaning terms trap within them the notional *personae* of Milton's heroic poem. These are sharp, even acerbic, but witty and snappy judgements within an overall poised syntax and couplet form. It is possible, the verse tells us, to be critical without losing sight of the value of measured commentary. It is not the least of poetry's achievements to conduct itself in a civilized manner.

Lines 107–14

> But for the wits of either Charles's days,
> The mob of gentlemen who wrote with ease;
> Sprat, Carew, Sedley, and a hundred more,
> (Like twinkling stars the miscellanies o'er)
> One simile, that solitary shines
> In the dry desert of a thousand lines,
> Or lengthened thought that gleams through many a page,
> Has sanctified whole poems for an age.

Literary history, like any other category, can produce its own golden-age mythologies. One such is that of the 'cavalier' poet, penning his (it is always 'his') lyrics with spontaneity and nonchalance, whether in reaction to puritan sclerosis or loss of authority during the 'commonwealth', or in response to Restoration liberty. Here is another subset of the meanings of 'wit': not so much the sharp thrusts of informed opinion ('wit' as deriving from *witan*, the Old English verb 'to know') as the self-appointed clowns of lightly-worn ignorance. Pope spears them in a single line: 'The mob of gentlemen who wrote with ease'. The *OED* cites the line under its definition of 'mob' (*sb*. 1. 4), as signifying a 'promiscuous assemblage of people; a multitude or aggregation of persons regarded as not individually important'. The implied lack of discrimination is apposite: compare the goddess Dulness's welcome to the unthinking use of images in writing, 'She sees a mob of metaphors advance' (*The Dunciad*, 1729, book 1, line 65, 1743, book 1, line 67). But 'mob'—a late seventeenth-century coinage of an abbreviated 'mobile vulgus'—also carries the sense of 'lower orders; the uncultured or illiterate as a class' (*OED*, 'mob', *sb.*, sense 1. 2). That tends to be the general 'cavalier' view of the rest of the population, whether the base illiterates or the solemn professionals as disparaged by the true 'amateur' who has no vulgar need to think of money when putting pen to paper. Pope reverses the terms: the 'gentlemen' constitute the real 'mob', all equally indistinguishable and undistinguished. They write 'with ease', with 'facility as opposed to difficulty' (*OED* 'ease', *sb*. 4.b, under the general definition of 'comfort', 'absence of pain or trouble': Pope's line is again included as a citation). But 'with ease' also implies 'in comfort', unrestrained by any need to work for a living. These are the sons of privilege, complacent in their inviolability. Pope, we recall, had to make his writing pay in order to maintain a living, as did Samuel Johnson, who was making his way to London to join the ranks of would-be professional journalists and writers even as Pope was writing his *Imitations* of Horace.

Pope turns the tables on such idlers by demonstrating, in these very lines, that the real professional writer can produce 'easeful' poetry—poetry that moves with smooth rhythm, with a genuine stylistic nonchalance—while also being precise and honed to sharp perfection. The 'mob' may come up with one telling simile in their work (on the principle, presumably, of monkeys accidentally hitting the right keys), but Pope can not only turn a simile back on them ('Like twinkling stars'), but throw in a related metaphor while he is at it: the 'dry desert' of dull and lifeless obscurity. The result is a creatively supple piece of comic writing, lines which humorously mimic the mob's facility, subtly undermine its assumed superiority, and demonstrate real wit (humour derived from knowledge). And he can 'ease' the lines into the wider satirical context of his address to George Augustus. 'Don't worry, George,', he seems to be saying, 'poets are just idle nobodies, out of place in the new Hanoverian order, and so of no use or threat; except that I know exactly what I'm doing—if you had the wit to pay attention.'

Lines 189–200

> Yet, sir, reflect, the mischief is not great;
> These madmen never hurt the church or state:
> Sometimes the folly benefits mankind;
> And rarely avarice taints the tuneful mind.
> Allow him but his plaything of a pen,
> He ne'er rebels, or plots, like other men:
> Flight of cashiers, or mobs, he'll never mind;
> And knows no losses while the muse is kind.
> To cheat a friend, or Ward, he leaves to Peter;
> The good man heaps up nothing but mere metre,
> Enjoys his garden and his book in quiet;
> And then—a perfect hermit in his diet.

To paraphrase, 'Now, I don't want you to think that I'm lecturing you. Hence my deferential 'sir'—I hope you noticed. Yet (I know I'm using rather a lot of qualifying conjunctions, but, well, there's quite a lot that needs qualifying). I do want—at the risk of repeating myself—to reassure you that, although the country and the town may be teeming with would-be poets ('one poetic itch / Has seized the court and city, poor and rich', lines 169–70), they are all quite harmless. Indeed, as long as you allow them their toys ('his plaything of a pen'), they will stay out of trouble and be no bother.'

Pope's rhetoric here is directed at diminishing the status of poets and poetry. Writing, he wants to persuade George Augustus, is a childish pursuit. To prove the point, he makes up his own address with easeful lines, often stripped of awkward caesuras ('Allow him but his plaything of a pen'), and pointed by significant phonic echoes. So 'plaything of a pen' is succeeded in the following line by 'plots', as the work of 'other men'. These others are disruptive types, such as the 'cashier' of the South Sea Company, Robert Knight, who, after the notorious Bubble burst, fled the country upon being found guilty of breach of trust by the House of Lords. They are 'mobs' in a more sinister sense than the old 'mob of gentlemen'. The Hanoverian dynasty had scarcely begun when the 1715 first Jacobite rebellion was hatched, and rumours of plots were—like mobs—never far from fearful apprehension.

Poetry, by contrast, need cause no concern. A disparaging adjective 'mere' (line 198) both qualifies and phonically merges into 'metre', a noun that, in any case, reduces poetry's status to mechanics of prosody. The phrasal verb 'heaps up' further demeans poetry by implying that writing is simply a matter of piling up words by the shovelful. No skill or artistry is required. The rhyme with 'Peter' emphasizes by antithesis poets' harmlessness. The real villains are the Peter Walters of this world, who accumulate wealth, heap up gold, by deceitful and even criminal means. Pope had earlier referred to this common butt of satirists in *The First Satire of the Second Book of Horace Imitated*, line 3, and in *The Second Satire of the Second Book of Horace Imitated*, line 168 (see Erskine-Hill 1975). 'You do not need to concern yourself about mere poets.'

Harmlessness is a value lying at the core of the final couplet of this verse-paragraph, as it is frequently in Pope's self-projection in his Horatian *Imitations*. The paragraph's concluding rhyme, 'quiet / diet', links repose and innocence to lack of excess in lifestyle. It is a retirement myth, of course, and, as such, is open to accusations of being yet another of those poses adopted by poets to present themselves in a favourable, modest light. It is just what a wary but gullible monarch would wish to hear. Pope knows full well that this is the case, and he wants a really alert reader to gather the force of his irony. Now is the time for Pope to move on and speak to the truly intelligent and worthy in his final two *Imitations*, which are addressed to the lawyer William Murray and the statesman Viscount Bolingbroke. The first opens 'Not to admire', a literal rendering of Horace's 'nil admirari'. This was also the motto on Bolingbroke's coat of arms. Thus, Pope deftly unites two meritorious friends from different generations, the young aspiring barrister and the mature philosopher. 'Meaner things' can be left to the 'pride' of mere 'kings', as Pope earlier declared to Bolingbroke in the opening couplet of *An Essay on Man*.

23. *The Sixth Epistle of the First Book of Horace Imitated. To Mr Murray*

Examples: Lines 1–4, 14–15, 18–27, 46–53, 95–96

Pope's last *Imitations* were published in the early months of 1738, followed by two dialogues with the joint title of *Epilogue to the Satires* in May and July of that year. These poems thus represent the culmination and conclusion of his engagement with Horace as a model. Their composition took place during a concerted parliamentary drive by the opposition to Robert Walpole after the death of Queen Caroline in autumn 1737. The failure of that movement was no doubt reflected in the downward momentum of optimism the poems as a whole express. Nonetheless, these works also stand clear as final meditations on the central ethical questions to which Pope's poetry of the 1730s is largely dedicated.

The *Sixth Epistle of the First Book* was the earliest, being published on 23 January 1738 and then included in the *Works* later in the year. The subtitle, 'To Mr Murray', was added only in William Warburton's 1751 edition but there is no reason to doubt its authenticity. Murray had already figured in Pope's version of Horace's 'Intermissa, Venus' ode (see Chapter 20), and, as a rising young lawyer who became Pope's executor, he is a suitable recipient of an epistle that meditates on the value of ethical contributions to public life. After Pope's death, Murray went on to achieve respect and renown as the Earl of Mansfield, Lord Chief Justice and presider over the celebrated 1772 case of the American slave James Somersett, in which Mansfield's conclusion that Somersett should be discharged was based on his judgment that the state of slavery is 'so odious' that it is 'incapable of being introduced on any reasons, moral or political' (*Howell's State Trials*, XX, 1816, cols 1–6, 79–82).

Lines 1–4

> 'Not to admire, is all the art I know,
> To make men happy, and to keep them so.'
> (Plain truth, dear Murray, needs no flowers of speech,
> So take it in the very words of Creech.)

Thomas Creech's 1684 translation of Horace was the standard version at the time. Pope actually improves on Creech's rather pedestrian opening triplet in his own sharper couplet, but he retains Creech's crucial literal translation of Horace's keynote word: 'Nil admirari prope res est una, Numici, / solaque quae posit facere et servare beatum' [Not to be surprised at anything is about the one and only thing, Numicius, that can make and keep a person happy]. 'Admirari' is pretty much untranslatable without recourse to some sort of paraphrase. It is, of course, the root of the English word 'admire': hence Creech and Pope take the shortest cut. In effect, the entire poem that follows is Pope's illustration of its full and complicated meaning. The best guarantee of happiness, Pope proposes, is not to be carried away to extremes, to the excesses and temptations that life offers, but to maintain a position of moderate and well-considered detachment. 'Admire' carried a connotation of foolish wonderment. Pursuit of wealth, of political power, of good eating, and of love can each be taken too far. The word 'admire' runs through Pope's poem: lines 11, 21, 28 and twice each in lines 41 and 68).

Lines 14–15

A single deft couplet can be sufficient to puncture the allure of some attractions. The verse, as it were, contemptuously brushes them aside. Should we admire:

> Or popularity, or stars and strings?
> The mob's applauses, or the gifts of kings?

Should we go for popularity? But the second line is set out in a vertical apposition (a term which normally defines placing one substantive or pronoun after another) to the first. Popularity is nothing but the 'mob's applauses'. Or should we aim socially higher, indeed to the very highest, and look for 'the gifts of kings'? What are these gifts? Well, nothing more than 'stars and strings', the truth of those medals and ribbons that constitute decorations of supposed honour. The effect of the couplet is to degrade, to belittle the rewards gained from both ends of society. And because the demeaning phrases occupy either end of different lines, the couplet itself points both up and down. There's no escape from Pope's rhetoric. All 'honour' is equally valueless.

A couplet from an earlier poem, *An Epistle to Cobham* (1734), demonstrates how contrary impulses—aiming high and aiming low— can co-exist in a single person, in this case Philip, Duke of Wharton: 'Though wondering senates hung on all he spoke, / The club must hail him master of the joke' (lines 184–85). This is an intriguingly complex couplet. How do the two lines relate to each other? It reads as bathos: of course, entertaining the club with jokes is a less worthy occupation than delivering speeches to parliament. But, at a subtler level, is there any real difference *ethically*? Do both exhibit a fundamental flaw, desire for 'applause' wherever one goes? Vanity may be an impulse behind either or both, even if one situation is more honourable than the other. What is true (and this is Pope's main point in his depiction of Wharton's character) is that to want both is to demonstrate lack of discrimination.

Lines 18–27

> If weak the pleasure that from these can spring,
> The fear to want them is as weak a thing:
> Whether we dread, or whether we desire,
> In either case, believe me, we admire;
> Whether we joy or grieve, the same the curse,
> Surprised at better, or surprised at worse.
> Thus good or bad, to one extreme betray
> The unbalanced mind, and snatch the man away;
> For virtue's self may too much zeal be had;
> The worst of madmen is a saint run mad.

The second repetition of the opening 'admire' occurs in this verse-paragraph, in which Pope most explicitly sets out the argument illustrated by successive examples. He advances the idea that, if the pleasure we gain from pursuing our desires is disappointingly insubstantial, apprehension of not achieving them is as feeble. Wishes and fears are equally paths of folly. We are left in a state of dissatisfaction, torn one way or another. Extremes bring the madness of an unbalanced mind.

To express these ideas within the texture of the poetry, Pope enacts a series of mirror-images, trapping us in cages from which there is no escape. In the first couplet, this is effected by repetition of 'weak' at either end. Whichever way you turn, do not expect anything satisfying. The rhyme words—in the second line the only word, save its indefinite article, left dangling after the 'weak / weak' repetition—themselves forge a feeling of disappointment. Hope may 'spring', but is always destined to the feeble anticlimax of 'a thing'.

The following four lines are threaded through with repetitions of 'whether' and near-synonyms: 'In either case', 'the same'. These couplets leave the most devastating repetition till the end: 'Surprised at better, or surprised at worse'. Warburton at once spotted this. 'Surprised' is a recurrence to the poem's keynote word 'admire', reflecting a good way of translating or glossing Horace's 'nil admirari': do not be surprised at anything. But it also, in line 23, conveys the idea of being taken by surprise, being overcome by something unforeseen. Our deficiencies, our inadequacies, hold us captive wherever we look (Erskine-Hill 1964, p. 141n).

The, well, surprising element of Pope's proposition here is that 'good'—the absolute which can be derived from 'better'—can be just as much a trap as 'bad'. Surely, we might protest, you cannot go wrong seeking tirelessly for whatever we deem good? Oh yes you can, our stern philosopher retorts: if you seek over-zealously for some ideal of virtue, madness may that way lie. As 'admire' can imply folly, so zeal carries connotations of excessive fervour in a cause. Such extremism can lead to destructive conflict: compare *An Essay on Man*'s 'For modes of faith let graceless zealots fight' (see Chapter 11). Sainthood may be its own mark of an unbalanced mind.

Lines 46–53

William Murray is currently in the early stages of a legal career which will lead to considerable fame and honour. Pope here, consciously or not, foresees what in Murray's case will turn out to be, by any measure, a quite dazzling degree of success.

> And what is fame? the meanest have their day,
> The greatest can but blaze, and pass away.
> Graced as thou art, with all the power of words,
> So known, so honoured, at the House of Lords:
> Conspicuous scene! another yet is nigh,
> (More silent far) where kings and poets lie;
> Where MURRAY (long enough his country's pride)
> Shall be no more than TULLY, or than HYDE!

These eight lines conclude a passage about pursuit of success in the legal profession. To achieve renown requires a lengthy period of strenuous study and practice from 'morn to night, at senate, Rolls, and Hall' (line 36). For what? For 'fame' (line 39)? This key word provides Pope with his climactic couplets, announced by the rhetorical question in line 46. The fulcrum of the passage lies at its mid-point, the colon at the end of line 49. The first two couplets define a moralist's double perspective, that even highest achievers can attain only temporary eminence. 'Blaze' perfectly captures the intensity of radiance together with its impermanence: the brighter the flame, the shorter its life. The second couplet then translates 'blazing' energy to the sphere of Murray's career, specifically to the bar of the House of Lords where he had taken early steps towards eventual eminence by pleading on Scottish appeals. The topography of Westminster allows Pope to move adroitly to the nearby Abbey. The gift for 'words', which Murray shares with past heroes of oratory such as Cicero and the Earl of Clarendon (Edward Hyde, historian of the English Civil War and Charles II's Lord Chancellor), is poignantly juxtaposed to the 'silent' tombs that are, now, all that remain of former greatness. The whole passage thus appears 'enigmatic' (Stack 1985, p. 212). There is no questioning Pope's genuine tribute to his friend's talent and ardour, but he sounds a deep note of scepticism which questions the ultimate value of such principled commitment. Is this the fate of extreme virtue in an imperfect world? Should even the highest good be shunned for a more tranquil moderation? Or is this yielding to treacherous indifference? How can we judge?

Lines 95–96

> If wealth alone then make and keep us blessed,
> Still, still be getting, never, never rest.

This couplet concludes a paragraph (lines 63–96) on pursuit of money as a source of pleasure and status. The word 'wealth' here makes its fourth appearance in the passage, and the couplet serves as an answer to its first occurrence: 'Is wealth thy passion?' (line 69). If wealth is your passion, if you believe that 'wealth alone' can 'make and keep us blessed', the rest of the couplet follows logically. Dogged repetitions in the last line ('still, still'; 'never, never') express restlessness, the frenetic continual activity incurred by a task that cannot be completed. There is always more to be made, more to add to what Pope calls 'thy golden mountain' (line 73). The endless task goes on; there is no rest for the fixated.

The phrasing of the first line also picks up the poem's opening couplet: 'To make men happy, and to keep them so'; 'make and keep us blessed'. Such linguistic repetitions are a notable feature of this *Imitation*. They represent the obsessiveness with which the whole poem is imbued, and their failure ever to attain a satisfactory conclusion demonstrates the fatuity of the endeavour. There is scepticism at the heart of this poem: a warning to the great in however honourable pursuits.

24. The First Epistle of the First Book of Horace Imitated. To Lord Bolingbroke

Examples: Lines 17–22, 23–34, 35–46, 132–33, 177–88

Pope's friendship with Henry St John, Viscount Bolingbroke (1678–1751), dated back to the days of the Tory administration under Queen Anne. Their precise influence on each other's intellectual development and social thought remains a cause of debate and may well have varied over time. However, of Pope's high regard for his distinguished if controversial senior there can be little doubt. *An Essay on Man* is addressed to him. He also pointed out that the first satire of Horace's second book fitted Pope's present circumstances. The *Imitation* Pope wrote as a result includes an eloquent and warm tribute to him as one who 'mingles with my friendly bowl / The feast of reason and the flow of soul' (lines 127–28). This poem initiated the sequence of *Imitations* that runs through the 1730s. It is fitting, then, that this final *Imitation* should be addressed directly to him. Pope declares this in his opening couplet: 'St John, whose love indulged my labours past, / Matures my present, and shall bound my last! 'As we shall see, Pope closes the poem with another invocation of Bolingbroke, this time in more quizzical fashion, as befits a work that is both probing and marked by self-doubt.

Horace's *Epistle* opens up a new phase in his writing. The early satires and three books of odes behind him, he now dedicates to his patron Maecenas a poem which declares his resolve to turn to matters philosophical and the study of his own self. Pope's *Imitation*, however, marks rather more strongly a sense of an ending. It is not by any means his last work, but those that lie ahead—the two dialogues of the *Epilogue to the Satires* and the fourth book of *The Dunciad*—hark back rather than look forward and present an unsettlingly dark conclusion to his life's work.

Pope's poem is in three broad but clear sections. Lines 1–64 form a farewell to poetry and a turn to philosophy. The middle third (lines 65–133: 69 lines in all) consists of an attack on the values and practices of contemporary society. The last fifty-five lines (134–88) focus on 'consistency and the self' (Stack, 1985, p. 265), and sign off with a self-depreciatory joke.

Lines 17–22

> Farewell then verse, and love, and every toy,
> The rhymes and rattles of the man or boy;
> What right, what true, what fit we justly call,
> Let this be all my care—for this is all:
> To lay this harvest up, and hoard with haste
> What every day will want, and most, the last.

Pope is alive to the paradox here: a farewell to verse takes the form of a new poem. Indeed, he wittily enforces and drives it home. Each of his couplets is equivalent to a line in Horace:

> Nunc itaque et versus et caetera ludicra pono;
> quid verum atque decens, curo et rogo et omnis in hoc sum;
> condo et compono quae mox depromere possim.

lines 10–12

> [So now I lay aside verses and other trifles;
> my study and my pursuit are what is true and becoming, and to that I am wholly dedicated.
> I am putting by and composing stores I can draw on later.]

Pope transliterates 'versus' as 'verse' but then extends Horace's 'caetera ludicra' into two nouns, 'rhymes and rattles'. Pope's lines say that verses are merely toys, and his rhymes are only rattles, noisy baubles, or empty chatter. These are not a proper study for a grown man. His additional phrase, 'of the man or boy', points the moral. In similar fashion, the second couplet amplifies Horace's two adjectives, 'verum' and 'decens', into three, and triples his single 'quid' [what]. 'For this is all' provides a summative version of Horace's 'omnis in hoc sum', forging a strong sense that nothing matters but pursuit of the true and the proper, that all the rest is infantile and trivial.

The third of Horace's lines fuses the literary and the agricultural to express his new resolution of preparing for his future needs. 'Condo' has a range of meanings, from building a city to composing poems to storing up food. 'Compono'—literally 'place together'—contains a similar variety, from composition of verses to dressing properly. Both verbs develop senses of the Latin 'versus', which include a furrow in a field and a line of poetry. In his third couplet, Pope's noun 'harvest' makes the metaphor explicit. The alliteratively breathless 'hoard with haste' anticipates, and is morally reinforced by, the strong final adjective, 'the last'. This note, that all things are moving towards an ending, intensifies the necessity of putting one's life in order. Pope's imitation thus lengthens the Horatian original and gives it added urgency.

Lines 23–34

> But ask not, to what doctors I apply?
> Sworn to no master, of no sect am I:
> As drives the storm, at any door I knock:
> And house with Montaigne now, or now with Locke.
> Sometimes a patriot, active in debate,
> Mix with the world, and battle for the state,
> Free as young Lyttelton, her cause pursue,
> Still true to virtue, and as warm as true:
> Sometimes with Aristippus, or St. Paul,
> Indulge my candour, and grow all to all;
> Back to my native moderation slide,
> And win my way by yielding to the tide.

The relationship between Pope's *Imitation* and the equivalent passage in Horace now becomes dynamically different. The first three lines follow the original stage by stage. Horace begins with the same reported question form: 'ac ne forte roges quo me duce, quo lare tuter?' (line 13) [and indeed lest you should ask who is my leader, in what home I shelter?]. To make his version fit into a single line of English, Pope actually cuts Horace's two nouns to one, instead using the plural form ('doctors', that is, learned people) to introduce the several possibilities that follow. Phonetically, 'doctor' is close to 'duce', so shadowing the original. Horace's second line, 'nullius addictus iurare in verba magistri' [bound to swear by the words of no master] has achieved cultural significance through its adoption as the Royal Society's motto. Pope again uses a single line, following Horace's grammar and diction in his adjectival past participle ('sworn') and a literal translation ('master'). Pope also takes his storm metaphor from Horace's 'tempestas'.

However, this linear restraint on Pope's part now gives way to expansion. The nine lines which follow and complete the paragraph are his version of four lines in Horace. Whereas Horace presents just two alternatives, Pope unleashes a series of contrasting possibilities. Horace's lines are balanced in form and structure. To paraphrase: now (Latin 'nunc') I am a man of action and plunge into the waves of civic matters. Now ('nunc' again) I slip back quietly to the teachings of Aristippus, and try to make things conform to me, not me to things. Aristippus was a fourth-century philosopher from Cyrene in North Africa, whose doctrine was that pleasure of the moment constituted the greatest good. So, Horace exemplifies his versatility of attitude through two directly opposed modes of life—devoting himself to matters of state or retreating to subjective hedonism: public versus private, external versus internal, subjection to a higher good versus self-indulgence.

Pope begins with a contrast between two kinds of philosophical writer. Montaigne's essays are inquiring, exploratory, and varied; Locke's *Essay Concerning Human Understanding* (1689) is systematic, organized, and focussed. Montaigne writes as an amateur, a man engaging in argument out of a love of thinking for its own sake; Locke is a professional philosopher whose aim is to produce a full and structured analysis based on sound principles and with clear goals. For Pope, political commitment is more specific than simply acting on behalf of an abstract virtue. To be a 'patriot' in the 1730s was to be independent, detached from a compromised government and inevitably oppositional. For example, George, Lord Lyttelton was a prominent figure in the Opposition to Walpole, strongly associated with the group around Lord Cobham and with the Prince of Wales. He was a friend of Pope and also on good terms with other writers, notably James Thomson of *The Seasons* (1726–30) fame. Pope retains Horace's Aristippus but, daringly—and, for some commentators, outrageously—sets this pagan philosopher alongside the Christian St Paul, who asserted that 'I am become all things to all men' (I *Corinthians* 10. 33) and that 'I also please all men in all things' (*Philippians* 4. 5). However different their ethical stances might have been, both evoke Pope's 'candour': his disposition to kindness and good intentions. Throughout, he presents himself as easy-going and open-minded.

In these lines, then, Pope advances well beyond incorporation of Horace's ideas to a high level of detailed augmentation. He saves his fullest departure from Horace for his concluding couplet:

> Back to my native moderation slide,
> And win my way by yielding to the tide.

Horace's gloss on Aristippus is that hedonism involves subjecting everything else to one's own desires rather than submitting to the demands of external commitments. Pope reverses such egocentricity by claiming a more understanding and politically sensitive method of entering socio-political waters. It is not studied confrontation that succeeds, but the ability to recognize and work with the flow of opinion: nothing by extremes, everything by self-control; measured and not excessive. Pope is now advancing significantly beyond the bounds set by his model: the poem is taking on a life of its very own.

Lines 35–46

> Long, as to him who works for debt, the day;
> Long as the night to her whose love's away;
> Long as the year's dull circle seems to run,
> When the brisk minor pants for twenty-one:
> So slow the unprofitable moments roll,
> That lock up all the functions of my soul;
> That keep me from myself; and still delay
> Life's instant business to a future day:
> That task, which as we follow, or despise,
> The eldest is a fool, the youngest wise;
> Which done, the poorest can no wants endure,
> And which not done, the richest must be poor.

Having explored their philosophical eclecticism, Pope and Horace both now emphasize how important the task of enquiry remains, despite their varying degrees of certainty and uncertainty about how to proceed. In his *Imitation*, Pope also maintains and strengthens his intensification of Horace's poem.

Pope's opening progression from day to night to year echoes Horace, though Horace's order is actually 'nox', 'dies', 'annus' (night, day, year). But he goes one better rhetorically by converting Horace's adjectival succession of 'longa', 'longa', 'piger' [slow] into a trio of 'long'-s, each of which is put at the beginning of the line. This emphatic use of anaphora and consequent reversal of iambic metre to trochaic give his lines a quality of remorseless plodding, appropriately slowing the tempo even before he reaches, in line 39, his equivalent of Horace's 'sic mihi tarda fluunt ingrataque tempora' [so slow and thankless for me flow the hours]. Repeated long vowels ('So slow … moments roll') add yet further resonance and sonorously usher in the line which concludes at the mid-point of the whole paragraph: 'That lock up all the functions of my soul'. Pope's phrasing here is ominously imprecise, but undeniably negative in a manner beyond anything in Horace. Indeed, negativity is, perhaps, as much a consequence of imprecision as of the image of locking up. The poet needs to escape from the day-to-day routine which gets in the way of a proper examination of his modus vivendi, of his inner self, as surely as his writing here needs to advance from its restrictive and tentative present inactivity to something that can give meaning to his existence now, rather than put it off to some vague future.

Pope saves up his most extreme intensification of the original for the last two couplets. Horace's lines are measured and controlled:

> Aeque pauperibus prodest, locupletibus aeque,
> Aeque neglectum pueris senibusque nocebit.
>
> lines 25–26

> [[The task that calls Horace] 'benefits equally the poor, equally the rich;
> and neglect of it will harm equally the young and the old.']

This is classical rhetoric at its purest and calmest. The first line forms a model chiasmus: 'equally / poor / benefits / rich / equally'. These are just five words in the format a/b/c/b/a; nothing spare, nothing wasted, all in perfect balance. The second line, also of five words, completes a trio of 'aeque', concisely juxtaposes 'pueris senibusque', and comes to rest on the verb 'nocebit' [harm], which sets off the first line's 'prodest' [benefit]. Horace's style and tone propose and express a state of mind and command of language ideally adapted to the measure required to render a philosophical attitude.

Pope doubles Horace's length, rendering each line in a couplet, as he did in lines 17–22. But he reverses the order of Horace's opposites, putting old and young before rich and poor, and his first couplet is a more complicated, denser type of chiasmus than Horace's first line:

> That task, which as we follow, or despise,
> The eldest is a fool, the youngest wise;

Pope is saying that if you pursue the philosophical task, you are wise even if you are very young; if you despise it, you are a fool even if old. So, 'follow' relates to 'youngest wise', and 'despise' relates to 'eldest... fool'. There is neither a steadying central term equivalent to Horace's 'prodest', nor the concise balance of 'aeque pauperibus ... locupletibus aeque'. Pope's final couplet is also a wordier version of Horace: 'Which done, the poorest can no wants endure, / And which not done, the richest must be poor'. Where Horace simply juxtaposes opposites in two words ('pueris senibusque'), Pope sets opposites over two lines ('Which done' / 'Which not done'; 'the poorest' / 'the richest'). In both couplets, Pope transforms Horace's nouns and adjectives into superlatives ('eldest', 'youngest'; 'poorest', 'richest') so that the ideas come across as more extreme. His verse has a more strained feel to it, an intensity suggesting struggle rather than Horatian equipoise and effortful enquiry rather than calm reflection. Semantically, Pope transforms Horace's assurance that the task will profit everyone, rich and poor alike, and his warning that its neglect will harm young and old alike. For Pope, pursuit or neglect of the task will actually alter people. Achievement will make the poor rich and the young mature; lack of accomplishment will make the rich poor and the old foolish. There is an added urgency in Pope's lines. Philosophical inquiry is necessary because failure will be disastrous; while success would be a positive transmutation. There is an awful lot hanging on the outcome.

Lines 132–33

When we reach the middle section of the poem, Horace's satire is aimed at the materialism of the Roman state and people. 'o cives, cives, quaerenda pecunia primum est; / virtus post nummos' (lines 53–54) [O citizens, citizens, the first thing to seek is money, virtue after cash]. Pope has a similarly sardonic view of the city of London. 'Get money, money still! / And then let virtue follow, if she will' (lines 79–80). That little additional subordinate clause, 'if she will', just adds an extra cynical turn to Horace's original irony. By so doing, it initiates a gradual and ultimately climactic intensification of attitude.

Horace observes the workings of a financial system which divorces rewards from merit or even endeavour: 'multis occulto crescit res faenora' (line 80) [for many, fortunes grow by the hidden growth of interest]. Pope turns this into a devastatingly judgmental couplet:

> While with the silent growth of ten per cent,
> In dirt and darkness hundreds stink content.

Horace is detached, a distant observer of the absurdity of a society based on crude monetary principles. Pope's couplet digs down into the filth. This is not merely an abstract contemplation of 'silent growth', the equivalent of 'occulto crescit'; it is precisely concrete ('ten per cent') and vehemently condemnatory. Society operates in not only hidden ways, but modes that are actively foul and soiling. You cannot escape the consequences: you, too, will end up malodorous. And, what is worse, you are quite happy to do so. Pope's plosive consonants ('dirt', 'darkness', 'stink', 'content') spit out contempt.

Lines 177–88

Where, then, is Pope going to see a path out of the mire when he finds it so difficult to maintain philosophical stability? The poem at its end turns back to where it, and all his *Imitations of Horace*, began.

> Is this my guide, philosopher, and friend?
> This, he who loves me, and who ought to mend?
> Who ought to make me (what he can, or none,)
> That man divine whom wisdom calls her own;
> Great without title, without fortune blessed;

> Rich even when plundered, honoured while oppressed;
> Loved without youth, and followed without power;
> At home, though exiled; free, though in the Tower:
> In short, that reasoning, high, immortal thing,
> Just less than Jove, and much above a king,
> Nay, half in heaven—except (what's mighty odd)
> A fit of vapours clouds this demigod.

The phrase 'my guide, philosopher, and friend' is quoted from *An Essay on Man*, 'Epistle 4', line 390. This *Imitation* thus shadows the *Essay* precisely, an address to 'St John' in both first lines and the same resonant acknowledgement of Bolingbroke's significance in Pope's intellectual life in each poem's finale. Pope is clearly signalling that these poems of the 1730s are all part of the same philosophical project: an extensive and free-ranging investigation of our place in the social and ethical world of Enlightenment ideas.

At the end of the present poem, the question 'Is this my guide, philosopher, and friend?' is a response to the first part of the verse-paragraph (lines 161–76). This expresses the idea that, if I turned up dressed all over the place, looking slovenly and disorganized, you would—rightly—laugh at me. But no such odd outward appearance is half as incoherent as my mind. My intellectual confusion—the other side of the coin of that philosophical eclecticism celebrated earlier?—you nevertheless treat as entirely normal. Is this the right reaction of the man to whom I look for guidance, for amendment? Pope's appeal is evidently predicated on the assumption that Bolingbroke alone possesses the power, influence, and intellectual rigour to make the poet into a truly wise man, a 'man divine whom wisdom calls her own'. We might observe that such subservience sits uncomfortably alongside the philosophical independence Pope has claimed and celebrated. Perhaps that proves the point: beneath all the bravado and apparent assurance displayed elsewhere in the poem, notably where he is scathingly critical of the corrupt and morally bankrupt materialism of large parts of contemporary society, Pope is not as intellectually confident as he can pretend to be. We might further note that the use of the adjective 'divine' in line 180 suggests either worrying self-aggrandizement on Pope's part or—more likely if we are familiar with Pope's habitual tendency to self-mockery through bathos—that he is setting himself up for a fall.

The question is: what actually constitutes a wise man? The answer given in the remainder of the paragraph is a figure that brings together features of Bolingbroke himself and of others in Pope's circle of associates. 'Great without title' reminds us that Bolingbroke had been divested of his noble honours when he went into exile following accusations of involvement in Jacobite intrigues. 'Plundered' perhaps recalls the confiscation of Bolingbroke's estates in 1715. 'Free, though in the Tower' does not apply to Bolingbroke, but it does to Robert Harley, his partner in the Tory administration before 1714, who did spend time confined in the Tower of London.

As these resounding assertions of the supreme nature of wisdom and consequent rhetorical paradoxes ('At home, though exiled') proceed, so the passage advances in the level of its claims. Pope appears to be elevating his ideal figure to extreme and even impossible heights, culminating in the daring and riskily vainglorious line, 'Just less than Jove, and much above a king'. Our suspicions are confirmed when Pope draws the curtain on his poem with as sudden and as comic a bathos as any in his work: 'Nay half in heaven'—steady on, Alexander—'except (what's mighty odd) / A fit of vapours clouds this demigod'.

This joke Pope adopts from Horace, where the Latin poet's finale, though much, much shorter and somewhat less irreverent than Pope's, is not without its absurd overstatement and consequent fall:

> ad summam, sapiens uno minor est Iove, dives,
> liber, honoratus, pulcher, rex denique regum;
> praecipue sanus—nisi cum pituita molesta est.
>
> lines 106–08

> [In brief: the wise man is second only to Jove, rich,
> free, honoured, handsome, indeed, a king of kings;
> above all, healthy—unless he's suffering from a cold.]

Horace here characteristically punctures the excessive claims of Stoicism to be able to rise above all human ills. His conclusion reaffirms him as a poet of irony and awareness of the limitations of being a mortal. Horace seems to say, 'just because you think you're a Stoic superman doesn't mean you don't catch colds'. Pope, however, outdoes his Roman model in self-depreciation by aiming the joke at the ideal he has built up of himself (or his own aspirations) rather than at others' ethical idealism.

24. The First Epistle of the First Book of Horace Imitated. To Lord Bolingbroke 255

Pope's linguistic skill and stylistic command are with him to the end of his *Imitations*—note the relapse into colloquialisms and wittily ironic 'mighty' in 'what's mighty odd'—and so, too, is his habitual self-consciousness. All does not bode well, though, for a successful conclusion to his decade-long search for intellectual certainty.

25. *Epilogue to the Satires: Dialogues I and II*

Examples: *I*, lines 29–32; *II*, lines 12–15, 78–93, 208–13

The first of this pair of poems was published on 16 May 1738 under the title of *One Thousand Seven Hundred and Thirty Eight: A Dialogue Something like Horace*. The second followed just two months later. The two were printed together in the 1739 *Works* as *Epilogue to the Satires: Dialogue I and Dialogue II*. Together, they constitute something of an *envoi* to Pope's 1730s poems and his engagement with Horace. Indeed, they represent a stage close to the end of his career. The only major poem to come was the fourth book of *The Dunciad*, in 1742.

Can they, then, be called a culmination or a retrospective? In the form of dialogues between *P.* and *Fr.* / *F.* [Friend], they debate numerous questions that confront an eighteenth-century writer. These include whether satire should be general or actually name names, whether the stance taken should be cautious and ingratiating or forthright and aggressive, and what, finally, should be the role and function of satire in a socio-political environment that appears, from the perspective of the Opposition to Robert Walpole's government, to be entering a dark phase. Signs of cultural twilight were the passing of the Licensing Act in 1737, regarded by opponents as an attempt to stifle free speech by submitting new theatrical works to prior scrutiny and the collapse of attempts to defeat Walpole in parliament. On a personal level, the 21 May 1738 marked Pope's fiftieth birthday: a time for reflection?

Dialogue I, lines 29–32

Pope's friend advises him to be more delicate in his dealings with those in power. To paraphrase: after all, your Horace was discreet in his satires, thanks to his 'sly, polite, insinuating style' (line 19), which gave pleasure at the imperial court. Why not go and see Sir Robert? Pope replies:

> Seen him I have, but in his happier hour
> Of social pleasure, ill-exchanged for power;
> Seen him, uncumbered with the venal tribe,
> Smile without art, and win without a bribe.

These are delicately balanced lines, reflecting his friend's advice to be cautious in calm and controlled language and verse-structure. As many contemporaries, however critical of Walpole's political actions, conceded, he could be as gracious as anyone would wish at the private level. When both were younger men (Walpole was the elder by twelve years), he had responded positively to Pope's application on behalf of another man. (See *TE*, IV, 2nd edn, 1953, pp. 299–300n.). Pope scrupulously distinguishes between Walpole's 'happier hour / Of social pleasure' and his later political presence. The real villains, Pope implies, are the 'venal tribe': a case of power being corrupted by those lesser people attracted to it. Yet, the last of these four lines is devastating in its satirical thrust. Bribery was notoriously rife in government circles in the 1730s, though it was hardly unique in that respect. Everybody knew this, but to state it so bluntly in a couplet that makes 'bribe' the final, rhyming word is another matter. The uncertain textual status of that couplet shows Pope's consciousness of his audacity or, at least, risky forthrightness. Omitted from the first printed version, 'bribe' was restored in the *Works* edition. The accusation is, however, stated in a manner which actually looks back to a lost time of innocence rather than dwelling on present corruption. But one implies the other: the past is viewed through the prism of the present. That is the couplet's own 'art', its graceful phrasing of disgraceful actuality.

Dialogue II, lines 12–15

Dialogue I argues temperately for satire's value in condemning the growth of corruption, of villainy, in the body politic, concluding with a resounding personal commitment on Pope's part: 'Yet may this verse (if such a verse remain) / Show, there was one who held it in disdain'. *Dialogue II* proceeds to justify the adoption of such an assertive and challenging manner. The first question the new poem addresses is whether it is right and effective for satirical writing to draw attention to specific individuals as examples of corrupt behaviour. His friend adopts a cautionary approach, telling Pope that 'none but you by name the guilty lash' (line 10), and advising him:

> F. Spare then the person, and expose the vice.
> P. How, sir! not damn the sharper, but the dice?
> Come on then, satire! general, unconfined,
> Spread thy broad wing, and souze on all the kind.

The first couplet economically sets the poet's reply alongside the friend's recommendation. Its balanced form invites a reader to see equivalence between two pairs of short clauses: 'Spare ... the person' / 'not damn the sharper'; 'expose the vice' / '[damn] the dice'. Syntactic and metrical echoing of this kind is characteristic of Pope's mode of expounding an argument. This, I observed in the Introduction, is a thoughtful procedure: argument by concurrence, by reflective harmony. A voice of reason is expressed through balanced structure. The mind, like the poetry, is at ease with itself. But exactly the same kind of structure can be used antithetically, to draw attention to circumstances in which terms reinforcing or closely shadowing each other are replaced by incompatibility. Such dissonance can range from lesser to greater, from the introduction of some qualification to outright contradiction. We have only to turn to, say, the extraordinary opening paragraph of the second epistle of *An Essay on Man* to see such rhetoric in powerfully expressive action. Rhymes now take on an ironic resonance, their auditory consonance being disturbed by internal semantic disharmony.

Interpretation, then, of structural patterning involves us in two simultaneous activities: recognition of form and questioning of meaning. The context within the specific poem adds a further dimension. Individual couplets, particularly end-stopped couplets, will frequently contain their own self-sufficient rationale. But they will also usually be enhanced or qualified by the couplets that precede and succeed them. Here the relationship between the echoing terms in the two lines seems to represent an organized counterpoint. It is as if the first speaker knocks a ball over the net into the second speaker's court; and the latter responds by knocking it directly back again. We at once understand that they are taking different sides, but also that they are doing so under the rules of the game. So 'person' is answered by 'sharper'—a person, that is, who cheats another by taking advantage of simplicity or innocence—and 'vice' is answered by 'dice'—gambling with dice being a form of activity of, let us say, dubious moral quality and one open to a sharper's manipulation. The friend and the poet are taking different sides: one for restraint in keeping the 'person' anonymous, the other for revealing names. But they both agree on the framework within which such difference of opinion operates. We may, perhaps, expect the passage as it proceeds to elaborate propositions on either side until one wins the point by virtue of superior weight of evidence or deployment of argument.

However, Pope's response actually shifts the terms of reference. 'Sharper' is not simply anyone, but someone who engages in vicious activity. By using the word in place of the friend's neutral 'person', Pope imports 'vice' into the noun. 'Dice' are left to represent a metonymy, the material objects of the gamester's trade. By means of this sleight of hand, the line 'How, sir! Not damn the sharper, but the dice' itself exposes the inadequacy of the friend's proposition. It also addresses what had become something of a commonplace in ethical writing. For example, the Latin epigrammatist Martial had claimed that the method of his works was to 'spare the person and speak of vices' ('parcere personis, dicere de vitiis', *Epigrams*, book 10, no. 33). Such a formula, Pope implies, lets the person off too lightly and reduces satire to bland statements of the obvious, bordering on tautology: to attack a vice for being a vice. Far from merely knocking the ball back over the net, Pope's reply changes the angle and wins the point.

The second couplet then forces home his advantage. Its image is that of a hawk swooping on its prey, to 'souze' (or 'souse', as it is more commonly spelled) being defined by *OED* as 'to stoop down; to descend with speed and force' ('souse', v 3, sense 1). To argue in favour of 'general' satire is to advocate attacking 'all the kind' or the 'genus', that being the Latin root of the word 'general'. The image exposes the absurdity of such an action: a hawk actually swoops on a particular victim. Satire, then, can only be effective if it can seize individual examples of the kind or genus.

Pope goes on to tease the friend by tempting him into exposure of his share of natural, if not entirely admirable, human curiosity. Pope does this by setting off a series of unnamed figures:

> P. The poisoning dame—F. You mean– P. I don't. F. You do.
> P. See, now I keep the secret, and not you!
> The bribing statesman—F. Hold, too high you go.
> P. The bribed elector—F. There you stoop too low.
>
> lines 22–25

By now, the friend's strait-laced recommendation of general commentary lies in the pieces comically dramatized in the chopped-up lines. Game, set, and match.

Dialogue II, lines 78–93

Pope restores dignity and seriousness to the poem by turning satire on its head to show its principled alternative: praise of those participants in public life who have maintained, and who do maintain, the finest traditions of social engagement and ethical standards.

> Oft, in the clear, still mirror of retreat,
> I studied SHREWSBURY, the wise and great:
> CARLETON's calm sense, and STANHOPE's noble flame,
> Compared, and knew their generous end the same:
> How pleasing ATTERBURY's softer hour!
> How shined the soul, unconquered in the Tower!
> How can I PULTENEY, CHESTERFIELD forget,
> While Roman spirit charms, and Attic wit:
> ARGYLE, the state's whole thunder born to wield,
> And shake alike the senate and the field:
> Or WYNDHAM, just to freedom and the throne,
> The master of our passions, and his own.
> Names, which I long have loved, nor loved in vain,
> Ranked with their friends, not numbered with their train:
> And if yet higher the proud list should end,
> Still let me say, 'No follower, but a friend.'

In this passage, the first three couplets salute four names from the immediate past, the second three couplets acknowledge present politicians, and the final two couplets round off the lists by defining Pope's personal attitudes and relationships to them.

Charles Talbot, Duke of Shrewsbury, had figured significantly in the invitation to William of Orange to take over the crown, and served in various ministerial roles under William and Mary, and then under Queen Anne. He also voluntarily resigned from such posts, indicative of his creditable lack of personal ambition and his desire to balance private and public life. Henry Boyle, Lord Carleton, uncle of the third Earl of Burlington, also served under William and Anne. James, Earl Stanhope, took part in proceedings against those guilty of corruption in the South Sea Bubble scandal. They were all moderate politicians, whether of Whig or Tory leanings. Francis Atterbury, Bishop of Rochester, was acknowledged for his dignified and resilient behaviour when imprisoned in the Tower of London for his Jacobite sympathies. He was associated with the Scriblerus Club, and Pope was called as a defending witness in his trial in the House of Lords.

William Pulteney was widely acknowledged for his oratorical powers in the House of Commons. Philip Dormer Stanhope, 4th Earl of Chesterfield, was an active politician in the reigns of George I and George II, gaining particular acclaim for his speeches in the House of Lords. In 1737 he led an unsuccessful attack on the Licensing Bill for restricting the liberty of the theatre. Later, in 1741–42, both Stanhope and Pulteney were influential in the eventual fall of Walpole. Chesterfield was also author of the famous *Letters to his Son* (written from the 1730s, published 1774). John Campbell, Duke of Argyle, had fought under Marlborough (hence 'the field'), was prominent in securing the Act of Union with Scotland, and was in the current Opposition to Walpole. Sir William Wyndham had been Chancellor of the Exchequer under Queen Anne and was a leader of the Tory Opposition and an ally of Bolingbroke, Pope's mentor and friend.

The historical details (of which the above is just a sketch) are important because they explain how and why Pope selects them for his roll of honour, and because their qualities and achievements (and failures) demonstrate that it is possible, indeed praiseworthy to take part in political activity at the highest level while attracting a considerable degree of general recognition and respect, even when some activities are controversial in nature.

Pope's conversion of this political capital into a dignified and orderly succession is the poetic equivalent of that dignity, that worthiness. He achieves this through various means, linguistic, structural, syntactic, rhythmical. Thus, the capitalization of the names awards them a textual prominence to match their public station. The allocation to figures of the past of eulogistic but concise epithets ('wise', 'calm', 'noble', and the like) echoes the restrained language of proper epitaphs. The lines are throughout carefully structured yet, under strict limits, varied. So, whereas the first couplet names Shrewsbury within its second line as a man whose wisdom makes him a fitting object of study in Pope's retirement, the next couplet inverts the syntax by balancing two names and their attributes ('CARLETON's calm sense, and STANHOPE's noble flame') before bringing them together in harmonious relationship ('the same').

The third couplet, on Atterbury, changes the tone from scholarly to exclamatory and sets off a trio of anaphoric 'How'-s. That rhetorical gesture links the first list, of those former greats now departed, to the second list, of present heroes. The two contemporaries distinguished for their powers of oratory are joined together as inheritors of classical virtues: 'Roman spirit', 'Attic wit'. In the middle couplet of the second list, Argyle, a soldier and statesman, is given an appropriately dramatic (but still highly economical) metaphor: 'the state's whole thunder'. Finally, Wyndham is accorded a description ('The master of our passions, and his own') that reflects what Pope, in a note, defines as Wyndham's 'ability and eloquence'—his power to affect *our* emotions—and his 'utmost judgment and temper'—his power to control *his own* emotions.

The quartet that rounds off the passage, and the whole verse-paragraph, is topped and tailed by key nouns, 'Names' and 'friend'. 'Friend' is given added impetus by line 91, which carefully distinguishes the ideal, mutual relationship that Pope is asserting from another kind of relationship, that of a follower in a 'train'. That alliterative contrast—'follower', 'friend'—is the 'proud' and assertive climax where Pope dares to, as it were, ennoble himself through his association with a powerfully distinguished set of individual men who have served, and are serving, the state in just causes and the exercise of due virtue.

Friendship is a theme that runs consistently through Pope's work. It plays a prominent part in his early masterpiece, *An Essay on Criticism*;

it connects his epistles to Teresa and Martha Blount; it is there in his tribute to his instructor in painting, Charles Jervas; it is central to the three-way relationship between poet, addressee and subject of common mourning in the *Epistle to Robert Earl of Oxford*, written as a tribute to Thomas Parnell for inclusion in a volume of Parnell's works. It is also there in the entire Scriblerus Club of which Robert Harley, Parnell, and, of course, Pope himself were members. It binds together the epistles of the 1730s, which form a major element in the separate but interrelated poems of that decade; it underpins particularly the *Epistle to Dr Arbuthnot*: 'Friend to my life! which did not you prolong, / The world had wanted many an idle song' (lines 27–28) and it gratefully and gracefully brings together the large span of *An Essay on Man* and the finale to Pope's set of *Imitations of Horace* under the aegis of dedication to Henry St John, Lord Bolingbroke as 'my guide, philosopher, and friend'. Pope is widely known as a satirist, and he accumulated many enemies; but it is equally important to observe that he attracted many friends, and frequently celebrated friendship in his poetry.

Dialogue II, lines 208–13

> Yes, I am proud; I must be proud to see
> Men not afraid of God, afraid of me:
> Safe from the bar, the pulpit, and the throne,
> Yet touched and shamed by ridicule alone.
> O sacred weapon! left for truth's defence,
> Sole dread of folly, vice, and insolence!

Winifred Nowottny comments on the first couplet of this extract that 'such a remark if made in real life would be unlikely to be received with anything other than social embarrassment'. Her fundamental point is that poetic diction—and, indeed, the use of vocabulary in any oral or written situation—is affected by the context in which we encounter it. However, on top of that basis, she observes that poetry enjoys a set of freedoms not available to people in real life. Many and complex restraints surround how we behave in social situations. 'A poem, in so far as it is a fiction uttered by a poetic 'I', is not tied to any context save the context the poet himself articulates in the poem' (Nowottny 1962, pp. 41–42). In addition, poetry, by virtue of its history, of the expectations that our previous reading of it brings, and of its capacity for independent and surprising interjections under the conditions of contemporary contexts and the experience of the individual writer, is particularly charged with an electric force. That is what makes it so exciting to read.

In the *Dialogues* constituting the *Epilogue to the Satires*, Pope has built up a powerful set of pressures on the quality of contemporary public life and on the ethical duty and responsibility of writers (and, indeed, all of his readers) to respond judiciously, creatively, and—if and when necessary—heroically. All of this energizes the assertive voice of the climax formed by these lines. They attribute failure to the regular instruments of social polity: the legal system, organized religion, and political consensus at the highest level. These derogations have left only ('alone', 'sole') that shaming power of vigorously challenging language as a defence of 'truth'. Pope declares his own total commitment to that challenge—hence the remarkable degree of personal exposure and affirmation enacted here. 'Pride', a term which in other contexts can invoke moral condemnation (as in the exordium of *Epistle* 2 of *An Essay on Man*), becomes a moral necessity, an inspiration, and a badge of honour. The 'weapon' possessed by the 'I' addressing us now is language alone, but language at its powerful height. Similar conditions have charged many writers in our tradition, and may again. Poetry, as the voice of tradition and the individual, exercises its own unavoidable call to arms. It is no surprise that the major poem left for Pope to write, the fourth book of *The Dunciad*, will have language itself as its principal subject.

26. The Dunciad

Examples: A-text book 1, lines 27–42, B-text book 1, lines 29–44; A-text, book 1, lines 61–66, B-text book 1, lines 63–68; A-text, book 1, lines 153–54, B-text, book 1, lines 175–76; book 2, lines 1–6; A-text, book 2, lines 57–64, B-text, book 2, lines 61–68; A-text, book 3, lines 59–64, B-text, book 3, lines 67–72; book 4, lines 149–74; book 4, lines 293–334; book 4, lines 421–36; book 4, lines 627–56

In 1725, Pope's subscription edition of Shakespeare was published by Jacob Tonson, the bookseller who had instigated Pope to take on the project. It was not a success, and it prompted Lewis Theobald, a prolific and versatile writer and translator, to bring out a substantial volume entitled *Shakespeare Restored* (1725).

Jonathan Swift, close friend of Pope's from the 1710s and now Dean of St Patrick's in Dublin, paid two visits to England in 1726 and 1727. He arrived in England trailing clouds of glory from his victory in the affair of 'Wood's halfpence', a proposed minting of copper coins in Ireland under a licence granted by the Walpole government and with *Gulliver's Travels*, his own major contribution to the spirit of Scriblerus, ready for publication. Swift's arrival may well have encouraged Pope to write up satirical materials he had been collecting over time with the working title of 'The Progress of Dulness'. *The Dunciad. An Heroic Poem. In Three Books* duly appeared in 1728.

In 1729, Pope re-issued the poem with extensive preliminaries, 'testimonies of authors' and the like, large numbers of hoax notes, and many gaps in names filled in. This *Dunciad Variorum* increased the burlesque of literary and critical pedantry while maintaining the principal satirical message:

> Books and the Man I sing, the first who brings
> The Smithfield Muses to the ear of Kings.
>
> book 1, lines 1–2

One of Pope's notes explains: 'Smithfield is the place where Bartholomew Fair was kept, whose shews, machines, and dramatical entertainments, formerly agreeable only to the taste of the rabble, were, by the hero of this poem and others of equal genius, brought to the theatres of Covent-Garden, Lincolns-inn-Fields, and the Haymarket, to be the reigning pleasures of the court and town.'

The poem celebrates transfer of sovereignty from Elkanah Settle, a poet and dramatist who had charge of the pageants acted on the Lord Mayor's Day (and who had died in 1724) to Tibbald. Pope is making tacit allusion to the coronation of George II and Queen Caroline after the convenient death of George I in 1727: 'Still Dunce the second reigns like Dunce the first' (I, line 6). The mock-heroic framework burlesques the removal of Troy to Latium in Virgil's *Aeneid*, parodied in the third book's vision vouchsafed by Settle to Tibbald in the underworld. The poem triumphantly installs the tastes of squalid quarters in the sites of 'court and town'.

The Dunciad Variorum of 1729 is denominated *Dunciad A* by the *Twickenham Edition*. In 1742, Pope returned to the work to add a fourth book, *The New Dunciad*. In 1743, the full four-book version appeared, with Colley Cibber replacing Tibbald as king of the dunces. [Cibber had been appointed Poet Laureate in 1730 and published a much-derided *Apology* for his own life in 1740.] Amendments were made, some small, some more significant, for this final version, called *Dunciad B* in the *Twickenham Edition*. I follow this nomenclature. Pope's revised fourth book represents a culmination of the vision of the Dunces' triumph set out in book 3. Various aspects of culture, learning, and science are gathered up around Dulness's throne. A final paragraph detailing the descent of darkness with which the A-text book 3 ended is transferred to become the finale to the B-text book 4, where its impact is all the stronger for the preceding dramatization of the extinction of knowledge.

A-text book 1, lines 27–42; B-text book 1, lines 29–44

A-text:

> Where wave the tattered ensigns of Rag-Fair,
> A yawning ruin hangs and nods in air;
> Keen, hollow winds howl through the bleak recess,
> Emblem of music caused by emptiness:
> Here in one bed two shivering sisters lie,
> The cave of poverty and poetry.
> This, the great mother dearer held than all
> The clubs of quidnuncs, or her own guildhall.
> Here stood her opium, here she nursed her owls,
> And destined here the imperial seat of fools.
> Hence springs each weekly muse, the living boast
> Of Curl's chaste press, and Lintot's rubric post,
> Hence hymning Tyburn's elegiac lay,
> Hence the soft sing-song on Cecilia's day,
> Sepulchral lies our holy walls to grace,
> And new-year odes, and all the Grub Street race.

Dulness's place of choice, her natural home, is a ramshackle ruin of a house set in a ramshackle district. Pope takes care to name the area explicitly in the first line of the paragraph; and he enforces the point by supplying his own succinct note: 'Rag-fair is a place near the Tower of London, where old cloaths and frippery are sold'. This marketplace for the sale of rags, of used and torn linen—all proudly flying in the wind in a mockery of banners of state and dignity—Dulness values more highly than she does the 'clubs of quidnuncs, or her own guildhall'. This juxtaposition in line 34 contains its own process of belittlement: the City's house of civic authority (and the place from which the Lord Mayor's parade traditionally set out) is another of Dulness's favourite spots ('her own'), of equivalent value to any tavern or other haunt of gossipy newsmongers. A 'quidnunc' was, in recent jargon (*OED*'s first citation is from Richard Steele's *Tatler* in 1709), someone who asked 'what now?', that is, an inquisitive seeker after the news of the moment. But Rag Fair beats them both, its torn and frayed scraps and remnants being both the appropriate tatters for its hard-up inhabitants and suitable descriptions of the scraps of paper produced by Grub Street poets. How fitting that

Dulness foresaw that it would be the site of the Tower of London: the 'imperial seat of fools' is set up 'at the heart of a notorious hotbed of vice and penury' (Rogers, 1980, p. 39).

The second half of the paragraph is taken up by a list of the varieties of these poetic torn and tatty creations: weekly journals, elegies for condemned criminals on their way to execution at Tyburn Hill, odes for St Cecilia's day (the patron saint of music), mendacious epitaphs on tombs, predictable odes for the new year from the poet laureate and pretenders to his throne—in fact, the entire production of what has come to be called 'Grub Street', as 'Fleet Street' in the twentieth century signified all journalists. These are the works churned out by booksellers' printing-houses—the traders in second-hand ideas, stories, and other falsehoods (we shall meet Curl and Lintot again in book 2).

Pope's poetry ironically sets off by contrast the haphazard and chaotic mess of everything to do with Rag Fair—what is for sale, those who sell it, those who make it. This he does in two principal ways: through structure and language. Firstly, this entire verse-paragraph is carefully shaped and measured. It is in two broad but clear parts (place, then products) held together by a succession of correlated adverbs. The opening 'where' introduces two groups of organizing words: 'here' in lines 31, 35, and 36, and then 'hence' in lines 37, 39, and 40. These are clearly delineated, but Pope positions them with an eye to varying the overall structure to allow a sense of freedom within the pattern. So, the ternary set of 'here' packed into the single couplet provides particular emphasis at the heart of the passage at a distance from the earlier 'here'; and the ternary anaphora of 'hence' moves from alternate to following lines. Within this structure, phrases and clauses fall naturally into balancing pairs: 'poverty and poetry', 'stood her opium ... nursed her owls', 'Curl's chaste press ... Lintot's rubric post'. The subject-matter is disordered; the syntax is ordered.

Secondly, Pope applies to his language a level of euphony which exposes the discordance of what it is describing. 'Keen, hollow winds howl through the bleak recess' agreeably sustains long vowels with close shadowing of consonants ('hollow', 'howl'). 'Poverty and poetry' phonically suggest themselves as bed-partners, nearly an anagram apart. 'Springs' accords creative vitality to the products of the 'muse'. The 'soft sing-song' of the odes to St Cecilia impishly extends alliterative sibilants to near-parodic extremes. It is as if Pope wants to dress his catastrophic cityscape in the language of pastoral. Indeed, the entire paragraph can readily be conceived as a type of anti-pastoral, as the entire poem is a form of mock-epic. A classical form holds barbaric content, with burlesque and derisive results.

B-text:

> Close to those walls where Folly holds her throne,
> And laughs to think Monroe would take her down,
> Where o'er the gates, by his famed father's hand
> Great Cibber's brazen, brainless brothers stand;
> One cell there is, concealed from vulgar eye,
> The cave of poverty and poetry.
> Keen, hollow winds howl through the bleak recess,
> Emblem of music caused by emptiness.
> Hence bards, like Proteus long in vain tied down,
> Escape in monsters, and amaze the town.
> Hence miscellanies spring, the weekly boast
> Of Curll's chaste press, and Lintot's rubric post:
> Hence hymning Tyburn's elegiac lines,
> Hence *Journals, Medleys, Merceries, Magazines*:
> Sepulchral lies, our holy walls to grace,
> And New Year odes, and all the Grub Street race.

Between 1729 and 1743, Dulness's 'cave of poverty and poetry' has changed its address. It has moved from Rag Fair, near the Tower of London, to a spot 'Close to those walls where Folly holds her throne'. This is the Hospital of St Mary of Bethlehem, originally founded as a priory and, after the Dissolution of the Monasteries, granted to the mayor and citizens of London and then incorporated as a foundation for the reception and cure of the mentally deranged. It became popularly called 'Bedlam' and was rebuilt in 1676 just outside London Wall at its north side, near the parish of St Giles, Cripplegate (see *OED*, 'Bedlam' sb, sense 2). By happy chance, as Pope's note on line 31 explains, two statues over the gates of Bedlam were the work of Caius Gabriel Cibber, father of Colley Cibber, poet laureate since 1730. Hence 'Great Cibber's brazen, brainless brothers stand' and take their place in a spectacular outbreak of plosive alliteration. James Monroe (line 30) was then physician to Bedlam hospital.

These lines on Bedlam replace much of the first half of the A-text verse-paragraph. The euphonious 'cave of poverty and poetry' and the couplet describing the howling winds survive: the change of address has not resulted in an improvement to home conditions. The references to quidnuncs, the guildhall, and the imperial seat of fools are transferred to a place later in book 1 (lines 269–72). In the second half of the passage, some of the products of what are now called the 'bards'—the inspired poets—of Dulness's house remain the same. Others, though, are changed. We now have 'miscellanies' (that is, anthologies of poetry) and a new profusion of '*Journals, Medleys, Merceries, Magazines*'. Pope's explanatory note on these fresh products is relentless in its no-holds-barred way:

> Miscellanies in prose and verse, in which at some times new-born nonsense *first is taught to cry* [an anticipation of line 60]; at others, dead-born Dulness appears in a thousand shapes. These were thrown out weekly and monthly by every miserable scribbler; or picked up piece-meal and stolen from anybody, under the title of papers, essays, queries, verses, epigrams, riddles, etc. equally the disgrace of human wit, morality, and decency.

Good stuff, then.

The concluding couplet of the two texts remains unaltered, so that the paragraphs come to rest on the same place: 'all the Grub Street race'. Grub Street had long been a general term for poor and hack writers: *OED*'s first citation is 1630. But now, in the 1743 *Dunciad*, the street name emerges as literal as well as metaphorical. The actual Grub Street lay in Cripplegate Ward, and so was very close to Bedlam. The grubs have found their natural habitat. The bards live in Grub Street and its environs, infesting an area long known for its poor (in every sense) writers and conveniently located near a hospital ready to receive and treat them. Colley Cibber's father has shown the way for his son and all his fellow scribblers (see Rogers 1980, pp. 56 ff).

A-text, book 1, lines 61–66; B-text book 1, lines 63–68

Some things never change. Wherever she sets her home, Dulness looks out onto the same 'chaos dark and deep' (A-text, line 53; B-text, line 55) and beholds the same confused and garbled verbal universe:

> Here one poor word an hundred clenches makes,
> And ductile dullness new meanders takes;
> There motley images her fancy strike,
> Figures ill paired, and similes unlike.
> She sees a mob of metaphors advance,
> Pleased with the madness of the mazy dance.

The lines establish words as the local habitation for this vision of chaos. *The Dunciad* does, throughout, have a broad, universal frame of reference, but its centre is always language in its varieties, from literary to journalistic. The context may be macrocosmic, but the focus is the microcosm: the fundamentals from which meaning is constructed.

Here Pope rapidly encompasses types of verbal expression, like stars within a dark background. A 'clench' is an archaic term for 'a play on words, pun, quibble'. *OED* cites this line among examples of usage from the seventeenth century to the nineteenth. Pope's couplet connects this with a superficially attractive image of dullness as a river being channelled through various windings. Again, *OED* cites the line under 'ductile'.

The second couplet moves to contradiction. Images don the fool's parti-coloured dress, and similes clash with a contradictory adjective to form a nullifying collision: 'similes unlike'. In the third couplet, the promiscuity implied in 'Figures ill paired' spills over into the chaos of crowds, as metaphors threateningly 'advance' in forms of movement well suited to—in the B-text—nearby Bedlam. Throughout, motion spirals into anarchy. Like the meandering stream, dance takes on the form of random, purposeless motion.

A-text, book 1, lines 153–54; B-text, book 1, lines 175–76

> And lest we err by wit's wild dancing light,
> Secure us kindly in our native night.

Having built a pyre of dull books and his own vain writings, Tibbald (in the A-text) and Cibber (in the B-text) send up a prayer to the goddess Dulness. This couplet from their lengthy invocations gets to the core of *The Dunciad*'s central irony. To employ verbal irony is to say something one does not mean, usually in the form of a statement or a word that is the opposite of, or very different from, what one does mean. In *The Dunciad* as a whole, the creativity at the heart of responsible and imaginative use of language comes disguised in the shape of a triumph of dull, dead, and unimaginative language. But the true subject of ironic writing is that which is implied: the opposite of what is being said. This couplet works by a still further irony. In beseeching one desired outcome, Tibbald and Cibber actually state the contrary, which is, for Pope, the actual truth. In praying for the security of their 'native night' as protection from the error of 'wit's wild dancing light', the kings of Grub Street conveniently and accurately define the stark alternatives. They sound the right notes but not in the right order.

The security they seek is the dark chaos of their primitive and natural environment. It represents the safety of obscurity, a return to the pre-natal state of thoughtlessness, even as 'security' implies a form of imprisonment. 'Wit's wild dancing light' represents the opposite: a release of the mind's potential to embrace knowledge and enlightenment. This is not a 'mazy dance' but a dance of vitality. The antithesis within the couplet is indeed a matter of life or death.

Pope himself supplies a crucial additional level to the irony. It is not enough simply to state the alternatives: his lines actually breathe the energy that the invocation seeks to suppress. 'Wit's wild dancing light' modulates between short and long vowels: 'wĭt / wīld / dance / ĭng / līght. The adjective 'wild' demands rhythmic stress through its long vowel, giving the half-line extra energy: 'wít's wild dancing líght'. 'Wild' thus adds its sense of vehemence and freedom—rather than mere lack of control—to the dance of light. The force so established expands into the second line's ironic 'kīndly ... nīght' so that the succession of open vowels vigorously plays throughout the couplet. The rhythm of the whole transcends the semantic difference of the parts, pulling the two sides of the antithesis into a single expression of the will to live—the very opposite of Tibbald and Cibber's purpose. Pope's poem embodies a riposte to what it is apparently narrating. This is the whole method of *The Dunciad*: it constitutes its own answer to the ostensible victory of Dulness and the dunces.

A- and B-text, book 2, lines 1–6

High on a gorgeous seat, that far outshone
Henley's gilt tub, or Flecknoe's Irish throne,
Or that where on her Curlls the public pours,

> All-bounteous, fragrant grains and golden showers,
> [A-text:] Great Tibbald sate.
> [B-text:] Great Cibber sate.

After Virgil's *Aeneid*, which provides the model for the narrative framework burlesqued in books 1, 2, and 3, the principal point of *The Dunciad*'s allusions is Milton's *Paradise Lost* (1667). Elemental imagery is the common parlance of that epic's depiction of cosmological conflict: 'where eldest Night / And chaos, ancestors of Nature' (II, 894–5). 'I sung of Chaos and eternal Night' (III, 18).

The opening of *The Dunciad*'s second book offers a particularly specific version of Milton's beginning of his book 2, in which Satan leads and directs a debate among the fallen angels:

> High on a throne of royal state, which far
> Outshone the wealth of Ormus and of Ind,
> Or where the gorgeous East with richest hand
> Showers on her Kings barbaric pearl and gold,
> Satan exalted sat.

Pope takes Milton's words and shifts them around: 'High on a gorgeous seat', 'far outshone', 'Flecknoe's Irish throne'. Within the repetitions, Pope substitutes meaner alternatives to Milton's splendour. Satan's 'exalted' (high, but with a smack of self-regarding pretentiousness) state outshines the exotic and barbaric forms of idolatry represented by India and Ormus, a town in the Persian Gulf, famous as a jewel market. Tibbald/Cibber are belittled in contrast by being set alongside the vulgar 'tub' of 'Orator' Henley and the Flecknoe whose 'son', MacFlecknoe, provided Dryden with the butt of his satirical poem. Dryden's *MacFlecknoe* (written in 1676, first printed in 1682, and given an authorized printing in 1684), in which Thomas Shadwell is invested as successor to Flecknoe as chief dunce, is a smaller-scale version of key aspects of *The Dunciad*. Pope's reference is an acknowledgement of his source. Satan's showers of precious stones and metals are more grotesquely demeaned by the 'golden showers' (don't ask) poured on the pilloried Edmund Curll, a publisher of dubious material whom we shall meet later in book 2. Pope imitates Milton's characteristic syntactic rhetoric, the retention of the subject and main clause of 'Satan exalted sat' until four lines have set out the vainglorious objects of the comparisons. But his downgrading of the content of the first four lines renders the rhetoric hollow. Tibbald and Cibber are exposed as shamefully inadequate pretenders to Satanic status: not so much evil as absurd.

A-text, book 2, lines 57–64; B-text, book 2, lines 61–68

Book 2 is devoted almost entirely to a lengthy, uproarious and frequently scatological parody of the celebratory games in book 5 of the *Aeneid*. These 'high, heroic games' (A-text, line 14; B-text, line 18) are called by Dulness to mark the placement of Tibbald / Cibber on his throne as 'antichrist of wit' (A-text, line 12; B-text, line 16). The first game is a race between booksellers ('stationers' as the poem has them) to claim as his own a poet as plump as a partridge. The pursuit begins with Edmund Curll ('dauntless Curll') quick to take the initiative:

> Swift as a bard the bailiff leaves behind,
> He left huge Lintot, and out-stripped the wind.
> As when a dabchick waddles through the copse
> On feet and wings, and flies, and wades, and hops;
> So labouring on, with shoulders, hands, and head,
> Wide as a windmill all his figure spread,
> [A-text:] With legs expanded Bernard urged the race,
> And seemed to emulate great Jacob's pace.
> [B-text:] With arms expanded Bernard rows his state,
> And left-legged Jacob seems to emulate.

Pope's description of Bernard Lintot's halting attempts to keep up with Curll (whose rapid start glances at his reputation for dubious practices and for never giving a rival an even deal) derives from Milton's account of Satan's difficult progress across the 'vast vacuity' of Chaos on his journey towards Earth:

> As when a gryphon through the wilderness
> With winged course o'er hill or mossy dale,
> Pursues the Arimaspian, who by stealth
> Had from his wakeful custody purloined
> The guarded gold: so eagerly the fiend
> O'er bog or steep, through straight, rough, dense, or rare,
> With head, hands, wings or feet pursues his way,
> And swims or sinks, or wades, or creeps, or flies.
>
> *Paradise Lost*, book 2, lines 943–50

Milton's epic simile, one stretched out over several lines to attain or seek a grandiloquence of scale, takes in a range of allusive significance. The Scythian griffin that keeps guard over a hoard of gold, a legend told by Herodotus and Pliny, is a compound monster—half eagle, half lion—whose eventual subordination to Apollo, the Greek sun god, presages the defeat of Satan (the darkness of evil) by Christ (the bringer of light). Such allusions widen the cultural references way beyond the boundaries of the biblical text and so place Milton's poem within an expansive and impressive sense of human myth-making. Doing so has, naturally, been a source of controversy among Miltonic commentators. Does the outrageously pagan context open the author to charges of blasphemy, or should it be seen as contributing to a grandeur befitting Milton's audacious attempt to build a stage fit for the greatest story of all? Milton himself, in his famous exordium to the whole poem, sets out the sheer ambition of his project to write an 'adventurous song, / That with no middle flight intends to soar / Above the Aonian mount, while it pursues / Things unattempted yet in prose or rhyme' (*Paradise Lost*, Book 1, 13–16).

When Pope wrote *The Dunciad*, *Paradise Lost* had firmly established itself as *the* great modern epic: a Christian equivalent of classical epic in its aim to re-define heroism for a new age, an age in which the martial code of Homeric or Virgilian epic has been replaced by a moral code founded on Christ's sacrifice on behalf of erring humanity. So, Pope's relegation of a mythical griffin to a comical dabchick—a waddling little grebe—is of a piece with the diminution of Tibbald's/Cibber's aspirations to greatness exposed in the opening to book 2. Pope picks up some of Milton's vocabulary—'flies', 'wades', 'hands', 'head'—and mixes it up with inapposite and belittling words such as 'hops' and 'shoulders'. Milton's insistent use of asyndeton and lists of nouns and verbs may risk what Ernst Robert Curtius terms 'Mannerist' rhetoric in pursuit of sheer scale and the unparalleled task of venturing through blank chaos (Curtius 1953, chapter 15). But Milton has, at the outset, declared the vast scale of his 'adventurous song'. By limp contrast, Pope's Lintot simply reinforces the absurdity of a publishing world willing to descend to ridiculous depths in pursuit of a money-making opportunity. Whatever previous ages, for good or ill, have sought for through the language of ambition, our modern age converts into shameless degradation.

Such debasement takes a further step as the race between the rival booksellers proceeds. In Virgil's version of the lesser Ajax's losing his footing on cattle-dung in funeral games for Patroclus (*The Iliad*, book 23), Nisus, the race-leader, slips on the blood of bullocks that have been sacrificed as part of the funeral rites. Nisus converts his misfortune into an act of comradeship by raising himself into the path of the pursuing Salius and causing his fall, so that Euryalus, Nisus's friend, can speed ahead. The hero Aeneas, who is presiding over the games, declares Euryalus victor, but honours the unlucky losers by awarding them consolation prizes. It may be difficult for a cynical modern reader to take such 'heroism' entirely seriously in the first place, but Virgil's episode would appear to claim consistency with a code that balances ruthlessness with recognition of honourable actions.

In *The Dunciad*, Curll's fate is to slide on the product of all-too-human natural processes and so allow Lintot to beat him. Pope's mock-serious notes explain at great length how 'Corinna', the producer of the 'lake' on which Curll slips, was the name adopted by a woman who 'procured some private letters of Mr Pope's', then sold them to Curll, who printed them without consent. The po-faced Scriblerian annotator explains and defends the unedifying account with reference to 'the natural connection there is between libellers and common nuisances' and reports that he has 'heard our author own, that this part of the poem ... pleased him least; but that he hoped it was excusable, since levelled at such as understand no delicate satire'. With this, Pope proposes that readers will buy muck so writers are really only giving them what they want. Not for the only time does book 2 of *The Dunciad* sound a very contemporary note as it depicts a world taken over by literary consumerism emptied of anything but hypocritical excuses.

Well, should we view all this as nothing more than the Scriblerian spirit at its least attractive and most juvenile—Pope's sniggering version of the excretory obsessions of some of Swift's writings? Brower, for example, in terms of careful understatement, writes of book 2's 'weakness' in rarely lifting 'our attention to the large moral and aesthetic concerns that give dignity and meaning to the satire of Book IV' (1959, p. 335). Is it the age-old satirical problem of the consequences of immersion in a vulgarized world: that the outcome is as vulgar as that which it purports to satirize? Or should we allow ourselves to row along with a 'sense of high clowning, of an imagination freely frolicking and at times itself entertained, even convulsed, by the rich absurdities to be unveiled when modern dunces are viewed against older traditions they no longer understand or follow' (Mack 1985, p. 467)?

A-text, book 3, lines 59–64; B-text, book 3, lines 67–72

>Ascend this hill, whose cloudy point commands
>Her boundless empire over seas and lands.
>See, round the poles where keener spangles shine,
>Where spices smoke beneath the burning line,
>(Earth's wide extremes) her sable flag displayed,
>And all the nations covered in her shade!

This is the opening paragraph in book 3's main event, Elkanah Settle's vision of the future progress of Dulness vouchsafed to Tibbald/Cibber. The scene is an extended parody of the prophecy granted to Aeneas in book 6 of Virgil's *Aeneid*. He will establish himself in Latium and so initiate the process that will lead to the Roman state and empire, and the reign of the *gens* Iulus (that of Augustus Caesar).

The satire works by playing off the exalted, politically charged manner of Virgil's original against its inverse. Vocatives set the exclamatory tone: 'Ascend', 'See'. Grandeur is maintained in 'commands'—hence the opening line is powerful in its beginning and end—and in 'boundless empire', 'Earth's wide extremes' and 'all the nations'. Doubts are, at first, subtly and ambiguously introduced. The top of the commanding hill is 'cloudy': high up in the clouds is the ostensible meaning; but 'cloudy' in the sense of 'obscure' uneasily picks up on the kind of language associated with Dulness and her chosen king. For example, book 3 has opened with his head resting on the goddess's lap, where 'Him close she curtains round with vapours blue' (B-text, line 3). Right back at the beginning of book 1, Dulness holds court in 'clouded majesty' (B-text, line 45).

By the third couplet, the scene has darkened. As Pope's note tersely observes, 'Almost the whole Southern and Northern continent wrapped in ignorance'. 'Sable' and 'shade' are now the tones, the latter playing off the 'shine' that is the rhyme-word in the middle couplet, where even the bright warmth of the equator is attended by an ambivalent verb, 'smoke'. This range of language points inexorably towards the fulfilment of the entire prophecy, the 'now' of today, the 'here' of the entire world of British letters. But first, in 1742 and 1743, as he re-visits the Scriblerian context of the A-text in the brave new world of book 4, Pope takes his final review of the system of learning to which he has devoted his major poems of the 1730s. The result is more ambiguous than might at first appear.

***

The 1729 text concludes with the fulfilment of Elkanah Settle's vision (A-text, lines 335–56): the descent of universal darkness. Pope's decision to add a fourth book after a decade may be viewed as a confession that all the work of those years (*An Essay on Man*, the *Epistles*, the *Imitations of Horace*) has met with failure, despite its best endeavours to articulate a reasoned response to the key philosophical question of what constitutes the good personal and social life. The old Scriblerian satire of a culturally benighted nation returns with renewed force. Pope's Enlightenment project is back where it started. Such a conclusion does, however, overlook the massive achievement represented by the 1730s poems, both as individual works and as a mutually enhancing entity of progressive thought and expression. It also, arguably, embodies a limited reading of the complex and powerful *New Dunciad*.

The fourth book raises the level of the whole *Dunciad* to that of a small-scale epic. It is worth recalling that Milton's immediate response to the publication of the first edition of *Paradise Lost* was the rapid composition of his four-book *Paradise Regained* (1671). All was not lost. It is also perhaps instructive that the public context for this project was failure: the Restoration had put an end to the English Revolution in which Milton had played a minor but not insignificant part. By the time of the *New Dunciad*, the Opposition to Walpole had signally failed in its mission. 'Dunce the Second' still reigned 'like Dunce the First'. Of course, Pope's brief epic, if such we may call the 1743 text, is of a very different kind. If it is, in some ways, a triumph, it is so in ironic and satirical terms conducive to Pope's restless interplay between ethical assurance and relentless questioning.

The structure of book 4 is that Dulness on her throne, head in a cloud and her laureate son (Colley Cibber) reclining softly on her lap, summons all her children to converge around her. A parade of the nation's great is drawn to her in a vortex. Prominent are those who, by virtue of their roles within the education system, ensure that young people adhere to the poem's central proposition: that words should be ruthlessly kept apart from any kind of meaningful action. Later, a series of 'projectors' from the sciences and philosophy come to demonstrate the inverse: that any kind of action should be kept apart from any rational purpose or purport. Both these aims achieved, Dulness can close down the poem and the world. There is, however, a deeper irony, which follows through on that established in the earlier books: that the poem, the *Dunciad* itself, in its own vigour, imagination, and sheer creative energy, embodies a riposte to what it narrates.

Book 4, lines 149–74

Dr Richard Busby (1605–1695), the well-known, strict, and long-enduring Master of Westminster School, is the man to whom is entrusted the key-note speech in the first part of *The Dunciad*'s fourth book. He enters the poem as a 'spectre' (line 139), garlanded with a mock victor's wreath made of birch rather than laurel, and dripping 'infant's blood and mother's tears' (line 142) rather than abundant leaves. He is number one for inflicting pain and punishment, for causing grief and gashes: the principal purpose of education. To what end? His speech clarifies everything and leaves nothing to be said. He begins with three end-stopped couplets setting out his principles and practice:

> Then thus: 'Since man from beast by words is known,
> Words are man's province, words we teach alone.
> When reason doubtful, like the Samian letter,
> Points him two ways, the narrower is the better.
> Placed at the door of learning, youth to guide,
> We never suffer it to stand too wide.

Each of the couplets works by setting out a premise in the first line followed by a perfect non-sequitur in the second, thereby demonstrating the triumph of logic in the realm of Dulness. Concluding half-lines initiate the process. So, the principle that humans are distinguished from other animals by their possession of words, of articulate and complex modes of creating and storing knowledge, leads to the conclusion that 'words we teach alone'. That words are signs of ideas and objects—a principle most fully explained for the eighteenth century in John Locke's *Essay Concerning Human Understanding* (1689)—dangerously connects words with things. Busby's educational theory depends on separating words from things, lest one thing should lead to another—a desperately progressive danger. The Pythagorean letter 'Y', emblematic of choice between vice and virtue, necessitates steering pupils down the 'narrower' path. The third couplet employs the full weight of a caesura-free second line to develop to illustrate the full meaning of this vital decision: keep the door of learning as narrowly open, as close to closure, as possible in order to restrict access to learning and its perilous fruits. The 'Samian letter', or Pythagorean 'Y', is an appropriate symbol, as it not only implies an ethical dimension to the notion of choice but it also fits with words as the domain of inquiry: 'why'.

The perils of inquiry are at the heart of the following six lines, this time forming one larger sentence unit:

> To ask, to guess, to know, as they commence,
> As fancy opens the quick springs of sense,
> We ply the memory, we load the brain,
> Bind rebel wit, and double chain on chain,
> Confine the thought, to exercise the breath;
> And keep them in the pale of words till death.

The couplets enact a complex process of building up. This begins with three verbal infinitives, which rapidly, monosyllabically, define stages of human growth to knowledge: by asking questions, by hazarding possible answers, and then by coming to some kind of knowledge. The purpose of Busby's education is to cut off that growth at the very beginning, at the moment when the young imagination ('fancy') tries to push open that door, to release the sources ('springs') of understanding: the engagement of a child's senses with the external world of experience and the internal responses that constitute the mind's reception of experience. These are the means by which we, as human beings, come to life ('the quick'). The prospect of rising in this way—as a river rises from its source, as the mind leaps upwards—is cut off by weighting the child's mind down with the lifeless bones of learning, mere objects to memorize rather than experiences to meet. 'Wit'—that is, thinking, knowledge, the source meaning of the word, together with all the connotations which the word has itself accumulated by growth in our language, such as liveliness, vitality, humour—must be bound up, imprisoned. The importance of this in the scheme of education is signified by the linguistic variants defining it: 'ply', 'load', 'Bind', 'chain', 'Confine', 'pale'. Children are left with one sole marker of existence remaining: 'breath', the physical actuality of being, only just, not dead. In practical educational terms, as the text's straight-faced, sardonic note spells out, this means making pupils memorize 'the classic poets by heart, which furnishes them with endless matter for conversation, and verbal amusement for their whole lives' (line 159n). That word 'classic' will be picked up later, in a passage about the Grand Tour, where the young man (one who has unfortunately not passed through the rigorous hands of the redoubtable Busby, but somehow has been allowed access to forbidden fruits) will lose 'all classic learning ... on classic ground' (line 321). He will finally turn air (line 322), meaning, in Pope's parodic conception of Italianate operatic arias ('airs'), he will make meaningless sounds. The young man thereby reverts to the state in which the properly educated pupils of Busby's school are bred to remain. By making the classic poets—the 'quick springs' of modern literature—mere breath, Busby drains them of meaning and significance in order to shortcut any need for later re-education. It is indeed an Orwellian world, in which learning is converted from active process to static state:

> Whate'er the talents, or howe'er designed,
> We hang one jingling padlock on the mind:
> A poet the first day, he dips his quill;
> And what the last? a very poet still.
>
> lines 161–64

Busby is under no illusion about the challenges of his task. Westminster School, unlike other contemporary temples of education, such as Eton or Winchester, is dangerously near to 'yonder house or hall' (line 166)—Westminster Hall and the Houses of Parliament. There, it may be, an occasional product of Busby's care finds an outlet for fruitful action in the body politic, the application of learning to engagement for the public good. Pope's sardonic treatment of Busby is maintained in such deft details as describing Sir William Wyndham, one such escapee from Busby's clutches, as 'truant' (line 167), and lamenting how many Martials—that is, how many masters of the epigram, the shortest form of verse—have been lost when William Pulteney entered the House of Commons and was a principal mover in the opposition to Sir Robert Walpole.

The Dunciad is, of course, so much more—or, at least, so much longer—than an epigram. However, Pope himself was no slouch when it came to the art of turning an epigram; and, to a considerable extent, his couplet art is founded on the capacity of short forms of poetry to resound with intense significance and 'wit'. And, after all, Pope's own artistic relationship with, at any rate, one master of Italianate opera, Handel, makes it clear that the apparent critique of contemporary arts implied in the satiric, inverted world of *The Dunciad* does not tell the whole story. Like an aphorism, itself a form of epigrammatic expression, the ultimately fragmented nature of all expression (according to Francis Bacon—see Chapter 11) acts as a spur to further thought, further investigation. Poetry, however great, must acknowledge its incompleteness. At the heart of even the bitterest satire there must be a grain, or more, of humility.

At the same time as implicitly acknowledging its own inadequacy, Pope's satire is replete with a much more positive message. By allowing Dr Busby to explain his principles and practice in such a clear and well-developed manner, Pope ensures that an alternative vision is equally clearly presented. Busby's intelligence and grasp of the essence of his argument are predicated on confident knowledge of, and respect for, the forces ranged against him. That he should conclude his speech by drawing attention to those dangerous truants and their like gives away his doubts. His capacity to articulate what is ranged against him is impressive:

> To ask, to guess, to know, as they commence,
> As fancy opens the quick springs of sense.

The couplet is worth repeating and reconsidering. The first line, we have seen, is a wonderfully concise enactment of the living process of mental growth. Its syntactic inversion—putting the infinitives before the full verb at the end of the line—highlights that process. This inversion also enables the couplet to take on a chiastic shape. The two parallel subordinate clauses, of time and of causation, 'as they commence, / As fancy opens' occupy the middle ground of the chiasmus. Their grammatical subjects—'they', 'fancy'—bring into parallel the human subjects (the pupils of the school) and the force that infuses them (fancy, imagination: the terms are virtually synonymous in this pre-Coleridgean context). The wings of the chiasmus mirror each other in a combined expression of what that imaginative power can do. The rapid rise from questions to answers in the trio of infinitives is marvellously described in the couplet's concluding phrase with its concentration of vitality and rising, its association of living with the source of a river. Learning is acknowledged by Busby to be a natural force, which can only be stopped by application of extreme and relentless effort, a process that ends with 'death' (line 160). Yes, Busby does represent such a death-force, but he also vividly expresses its opposite. His speech is thus a microcosm of the wider triumph of the whole *Dunciad*. The poem narrates the triumph of Dulness, the return of the world to primeval darkness, but does so in a manner that is comically magnificent, a testimony to Pope's living poetry.

Book 4, lines 293–334

Pope was particularly pleased with his depiction of a young man who has completed his education by a Grand Tour of Europe. According to Spence, he thought his 'travelling governor's speech one of the best things in my new addition to the *Dunciad*' (cited in Spence, I, 1966, p. 150). The governor proudly presents to Dulness the youth whom he has escorted with an oration, which describes places visited (Paris, Rome, Venice) as now emptied of their former cultural values, and proceeds to celebrate his charge's active contribution to their decline. The mutual relationship between Europe and the tourist is summed up in a single couplet:

> Intrepid then, o'er seas and lands he flew:
> Europe he saw, and Europe saw him too.
>
> lines 293–94

'Intrepid' sets up heroic expectations, which soon begin to slide into a downward spiral, the result of which is a perfectly groomed anti-hero. The intimate connection between the youth himself and the continent where he shows himself to such advantage is demonstrated in the second line. Syntactic inversion ('Europe he saw': object/subject/verb) is followed by usual syntactic order (subject/verb/object), so completing a concise reciprocal action. An experience which should enhance both visitor and lands visited is comically transformed into a shared voyeuristic display of shame.

For example, convents, sites of southern Europe's religious orthodoxy, have sunk into wine-soaked sleep:

> To happy convents, bosomed deep in vines,
> Where slumber abbots, purple as their wines
>
> lines 301–02

Pope's pictorial and pastoral language, common to much eighteenth-century landscape poetry, embraces the abbots as easily and effortlessly as falling asleep. Their complexion merges gracefully into their landscape, offering a perfect harmony of colouring and, at the same time, emptying convents of any religious or monastic value. As for the tourist,

> Led by my hand, he sauntered Europe round,
> And gathered every vice on Christian ground
>
> lines 311–12

The ease, indeed nonchalance, of the entire ceremony is precisely captured in the verb 'sauntered': motion emptied of commitment, purpose, and order. Everywhere the youth goes, he enthusiastically declines into one individual and egregious product of modern manners and morals:

> The stews and palace equally explored,
> Intrigued with glory, and with spirit whored;
> Tried all *hors-d'oeuvres*, all *liqueurs* defined,
> Judicious drank, and greatly-daring dined.
>
> lines 315–18

Here the chiastic first couplet—topped and tailed by 'stews' and 'whored'—takes its place in the speech's inexorable accretion of sexual innuendo and corruption, which culminates in the presentation of the 'glorious youth' where his companion 'Venus' ensures that Dulness's reign will be peopled by 'sons of sons of sons of whores' (lines 330–32): a demeaned aristocratic succession is established with the banality of the dull repetition of 'sons'. At the same time, the hero's intrepidity is directed towards his own immersion within carefree sensual indulgence, a process encapsulated in the sarcastic 'greatly-daring dined'.

Pope, meanwhile, is throughout demonstrating his commitment to language as a precisely shaped and expressive means of exposing such emptiness. His speaker, the young man's tutor, ironically skewers his own charge, the supposed object of his educational care, on the spike of exact phrasing. The result is a revelation of the gap between expressive language and that which sinks to the level of the cultural low being satirized. Thus, the poetry replicates the youth's experience: the destruction of cultural values on the very historical site of those values. The youth

> Dropped the dull lumber of the Latin store,
> Spoiled his own language, and acquired no more.
>
> lines 319–20

The goods accumulated over centuries, from the days of the classical language to the present, and stored in the historical transmission that education shares with a sense of place, the *genius loci*, are turned into 'lumber': useless, redundant, and meaningless material fit only for rapid disposal. Pope's verb 'Dropped' captures in its monosyllabic, plosive disdain the youth's thoughtless disregard for what he is losing. 'Spoiled' follows up and is re-emphasised by 'acquired no more': he has given up any attempt at renovation, and so empties his store.

Book 4, lines 421–36

> Of all the enamelled race, whose silvery wing
> Waves to the tepid zephyrs of the spring,
> Or swims along the fluid atmosphere,
> Once brightest shined this child of heat and air.
> I saw, and started from its vernal bower
> The rising game, and chased from flower to flower.
> It fled, I followed; now in hope, now pain;
> It stopped, I stopped; it moved, I moved again.
> At last it fixed, 'twas on what plant it pleased,
> And where it fixed, the beauteous bird I seized:
> Rose or carnation was below my care;
> I meddle, Goddess! only in my sphere.
> I tell the naked fact without disguise,
> And, to excuse it, need but show the prize;
> Whose spoils this paper offers to your eye,
> Fair even in death! this peerless *butterfly*.

A butterfly collector—could there be a more harmless fellow?—presents himself and his great achievement to the goddess Dulness. Consistent with his inoffensive, light being (as light as a butterfly, even) is the pastoral language with which he begins. 'Enamelled' (in the sense of adorned, beautified with extra colours, e. g. , Milton, *Arcades* (1634), line 84: 'O'er the smooth enamelled green'), 'silvery wing', 'zephyrs', 'vernal bower'—these are the very words and phrases of that innocent genre. Characteristic, too, is the continuing anthropomorphism of 'race', 'swims', 'child'. Human-centred language used to describe another creature is at the heart of a common eighteenth-century vision of the inter-connectedness of the various parts of creation. Pope himself had, in earlier days, availed himself of this vein of expression, as in the pheasant passage in *Windsor Forest*, where a 'whirring pheasant springs' (line 111) before feeling 'the fiery wound' (line 113). Like that pheasant, the butterfly as it moves is 'rising game'.

However, the truest pastorals are not that simple. Pope's set of *Pastorals*, we have seen, follows precedents by exposing more complex emotions, including sorrow. Here, the verse soon descends from circumlocutions into something close to outright comedy. In the lines 427–28 couplet, the collector's reiterative short, sharp clauses ('It fled, I followed'; 'It stopped, I stopped'; 'it moved, I moved again') imitate the butterfly's jerky, sudden, and seemingly random movements. His being led in a merry dance by the object of his chase humorously enacts his unthinking enthralment to his quarry and his obsessive submission to the single object of his attention. Dedication to his task, yes; but at what cost to his dignity and supposedly superior place in the chain of creation?

Far from feeling a tinge of shame, or even self-consciousness, the collector glories in his reduction to one singular and isolated task. He does not even distinguish between the flowers on which the butterfly settles. 'Rose or carnation was beneath my care', he boasts, oblivious to the teasing ambiguity of 'care'. The suggestion is, both, 'no, it was no concern of mine' and 'no, such inferior elements of creation'—plants being below animals in the standard lists of the chain of creation—'were of no interest to me, and, indeed, did not merit the same degree of care which I dedicated to my work'. The collector has his own 'sphere' of thought and action. He is what we would call a specialist, as a modern academic may proudly speak of his or her 'field': a handy and seemingly incontrovertible defence of ignorance elsewhere. Such limitations of endeavour fail, fatally, to contextualize, to see the wider picture which alone gives shape and scale to its parts. The butterfly collector is, in his own way, the natural history equivalent of the literary critic exemplified by Aristarchus earlier in book 4. There, Aristarchus vaunted his reduction of vision to the minutiae of literary texts, to 'disputes of *me* or *te*, of *aut* or *at*' in orthography (line 220). Such endeavours are part of his life's work, the scholiast's unwearied task of making 'Horace dull'—just as Dulness herself would, of course, want. It is a triumph of pedantry, of the kind that makes us would-be literary critics wake in a cold sweat. 'Turn what they [poets such as Horace and Milton] will to verse, their toil is vain, / Critics like me shall make it prose again' (lines 213–14).

And where does it all end? In the 'prize', like that proposed for victors in the singing games so loved by rustic inhabitants of pastoral poetry: the 'spoils this paper offers to your eye, / Fair even in death! this peerless butterfly'. The harsh recurrent lesson of true pastoral is 'Et in Arcadia ego': even in the earthly paradise am I, Death. Pursuit of a single object of knowledge ripped from its context—here the wide world of natural creation, in literary works the teeming vitality of language positively and expressively displayed—ends in death. Life depends on the maintenance of connection, the whole not the parts. As Pope puts it in the Stowe passage in his *Epistle to Burlington*, 'Parts answering parts shall slide into a whole' (line 66). Dulness is concerned with division, the separation of parts from parts that leads to desiccation and mortality. What is true of nature, the environment we inhabit, is equally true of human works of creativity.

Book 4, lines 627–56

> In vain, in vain,—the all-composing hour
> Resistless falls: the Muse obeys the power.
> She comes! she comes! the sable throne behold
> Of *Night* primeval, and of *Chaos* old!
> Before her, Fancy's gilded clouds decay,
> And all its varying rainbows die away.
> Wit shoots in vain its momentary fires,
> The meteor drops, and in a flash expires.
> As one by one, at dread Medea's strain,

> The sickening stars fade off the ethereal plain;
> As Argus' eyes by Hermes' wand oppressed,
> Closed one by one to everlasting rest;
> Thus at her felt approach, and secret might,
> Art after Art goes out, and all is Night.
> See skulking Truth to her old cavern fled,
> Mountains of casuistry heaped o'er her head!
> Philosophy, that leaned on heaven before,
> Shrinks to her second cause, and is no more.
> Physic of Metaphysic begs defence,
> And Metaphysic calls for aid on Sense!
> See Mystery to Mathematics fly!
> In vain! they gaze, turn giddy, rave, and die.
> Religion blushing veils her sacred fires,
> And unawares Morality expires.
> Nor *public* flame, nor *private*, dares to shine;
> Nor *human* spark is left, nor glimpse *divine*!
> Lo! thy dread empire, CHAOS! is restored;
> Light dies before thy uncreating word:
> Thy hand, great Anarch! lets the curtain fall;
> And universal darkness buries all.

The dramatic finale of the revised *Dunciad* needs to be read in its entirety for its full effect to be exerted. Pope clearly intended it to be a rhetorical *tour de force*. He expanded the twenty-two lines of the A-text equivalent verse-paragraph (book 3, lines 335–56) into thirty, retaining many lines, revising others, and adding more. So, the sequence of couplets describing the suppression of stars in the night sky, leaving all in complete darkness, is retained (A-text, lines 341–46; B-text, lines 635–40). These lines offer mythological grandeur: Medea, priestess of Hecate, has darkly supernatural powers, and Hermes used his caduceus (his 'wand') to kill Argus, the hundred-eyed monster. These analogies are presented in parallel, and they resolve themselves into the starkly monosyllabic 'Art after Art goes out, and all is Night'. The sublime, as eighteenth-century aesthetics never tired of pointing out, best expresses itself in the language of night. For example, 'night [is] more sublime and solemn than day (Edmund Burke, *A Philosophical Enquiry into the Origin of our Ideas of the Sublime and Beautiful*, ed. by Adam Phillips 1990, p. 75). Pope repeats the line 'Daughter of Chaos and eternal Night' in A-text, book 1, line 10 and B-text, book 1, line 12. In this finale, he also repeats the line 'Art after Art goes out, and all is night' (A-text, book 3, line 346; B-text, line 640).

On the other hand, Pope extends the A-text's list of spheres of knowledge extinguished or displaced by the power of darkness. To philosophy, physic (that is, natural science), metaphysics, and mathematics, he adds religion and morality. These lines widen the passage's reach to include social and personal ethics, central concerns of Pope's 1730s poetry, and so gather them into Dulness's destructive vortex. Further, he defers a revised version of the earlier couplet 'Lo! the great Anarch's ancient reign restored, / Light dies before her uncreating word' (A-text, lines 339–40) to follow, rather than precede, this passage, so that it becomes a climactic penultimate couplet: 'Lo! thy dread empire, Chaos! is restored; / Light dies before thy uncreating word' (B-text, lines 653–34). The striking and sacrilegious oxymoron of 'uncreating word' is thus accorded extra prominence. Its significance lies in its encapsulation in a single striking phrase of the *Dunciad*'s most serious idea. In the New Testament, the Greek 'Logos' is rendered 'Word' as a designation of Jesus Christ. Christian theologians then employed it as a title of the Second Person of the Trinity ('God the Son') (see *OED*, 'Logos'). This is the poem's most resonant justification of its central premise. *The Dunciad* is, fundamentally, about the destructive misapplication of language. If words are abused, misused, mangled, even extinguished, then all knowledge and all enlightenment die.

In this finale we have reached the most sonorous vindication of all the elements of the *Dunciad*, from the depths of its satirical mud-flinging to the heights of its declamatory grandiloquence. Misuse of the faculty of reason and of its means of expression is, in the poem's dystopian vision, endemic and triumphant. The place of the fourth book in affirming and expounding the high seriousness of the poem's mission is best examined and explained by Aubrey L. Williams, in chapter 5 of his definitive study, *Pope's Dunciad* (1955).

But this is not quite all. The present chapter's analysis of passages has, from time to time, sought to bring to the fore one significant element of the *Dunciad*'s aesthetic and expressive presence, the very nature and fact of its existence—in our century as well as Pope's own. Thy *'uncreating word'* (my italics): the oxymoron pulls contraries into a single oppositional phrase. The result, for the reader, is not a nihilistic obliteration of meaning, or even a fusion of elements, but, on the contrary, a reduction which retains—perhaps even enhances—its potential for a more powerful re-emergence. The paradox, like the irony of 'wit's wild dancing light' being termed an error, is replete with creative possibilities.

And where do we find such creativity? In the *Dunciad* itself, the words we are reading. The vigour, power, and imagination of Pope's writing and its riotous humour and cutting wit act as an energetic and vital counter to the 'story' it tells. It is possible, even in the darkest times, to keep the flame of meaning alight. Just because the last line claims that 'universal darkness buries all' ('covers all' in the A-text of 1729, another example of a telling alteration, bringing in, as it does, the idea of extinction) does not bury the poem we have in our hands.

In a last dramatic gesture, Dulness's hand 'lets the curtain fall'. This is, in one sense, an act marking finality, darkness, and obliteration. But the metaphor is in the full sense 'dramatic'. The curtain falls on a stage. In this case, it is a stage of Pope's creation, where the poor players strut and fret their hour, but are not annihilated. They can be heard again by the simple process of re-reading. Worse societies than Pope's (and, in any case, *The Dunciad*'s vision of England in the 1730s and 1740s is, self-evidently, a hyperbolic one) have sought in vain to ensure that literature is heard no more. Think of the theatrical metaphor, and another vision suggests itself: that of the writer creating his own *dramatis personae* in the puppet-show of a dramatic performance.

Read in this way, the rhetorical expansiveness of *The Dunciad*'s final paragraph is a magnificent display of exaggeration, all suddenly brought down in Pope's final act of bathos, of sinking in poetry: his reduction of the world to a stage. Like Falstaff at the end of Verdi's opera, we may conclude that 'tutto nel mondo è burla' ('all the world is a joke'). And *The Dunciad* is, actually, fully as much a comic romp as it is an excoriating vision of cultural emptiness. Pope's genius throughout his work has tended to the comic. Satire may not change the world, but it can illuminate it with the glare of its own absurdity. Pope's wit—in every sense—has the last dance.

Bibliography

This bibliography is in no way exhaustive or authoritative. It lists references made in the text and selected additional titles. Its aim is simply to point readers towards some useful editions and critical/biographical works. The following authors may be especially recommended for new readers and as being outstanding or definitive: Rueben Arthur Brower, David Fairer (1984, 1989), Maynard Mack (1969, 1985), David B. Morris, Winifred Nowottny, A. D. Nuttall, Pat Rogers (all items), Felicity Rosslyn, John Sitter (all items), Frank Stack, Aubrey L. Williams. *The Cambridge Companion to Alexander Pope*, edited by Pat Rogers (2007) contains excellent short essays on many aspects of Pope and serves as a useful indicator of the range of writing on Pope in the early twenty-first century.

Archer-Hind, L., ed. and intro., *Lives of the English Poets*, 2 vols, by Ben Jonson (London: Dent, 1925)

Audra, E., and Aubrey Williams, eds, *Alexander Pope: Pastoral Poetry and An Essay on Criticism* (1961), vol. 1 of 11 of *The Twickenham Edition of The Poems of Alexander Pope* (London: Methuen, 1939–69)

Ault, Norman, ed., *The Prose Works of Alexander Pope* [vol. 1]: *The Earlier Works, 1711–1720* (Oxford: Blackwell, 1936)

Barnard, John, ed., *Pope: The Critical Heritage* (London: Routledge and Kegan Paul, 1973)

Bateson, F. W., ed., *Epistles to Several Persons (Moral Essays)*, vol. 3, part 2 (1951) of *The Twickenham Edition of the Poems of Alexander Pope* (London: Methuen, 1939–69)

Bond, Donald F., ed., *The Spectator*, 5 vols (1711–14) (Oxford: Oxford University Press, 1965–1987)

Brower, Reuben Arthur, *Alexander Pope: The Poetry of Allusion* (Oxford: Clarendon Press, 1959)

Brownell, Morris R., *Alexander Pope and the Arts of Georgian England* (Oxford: Oxford University Press, 1978)

Bullard, Paddy, ed., *The Oxford Handbook of Eighteenth-Century Satire* (Oxford: Oxford University Press, 2019), https://doi.org/10.1093/oxfordhb/9780198727835.001.0001

Bulloch, A. W., 'Hellenistic Poetry', in *The Cambridge History of Classical Literature*, 2 vols (Cambridge: Cambridge University Press, 1982–85), I: *Greek Literature*, ed. by P. E. Easterling and B. M. W. Knox (1985), pp. 541–621

Burke, Edmund, *A Philosophical Enquiry into the Origin of Our Ideas of the Sublime and Beautiful*, ed. by Adam Phillips (Oxford: Oxford University Press, 1990)

Butt, John, ed., *Alexander Pope: Imitations of Horace (1939; 2nd edn, 1953), vol. 4 of The Twickenham Edition of The Poems of Alexander Pope* (London: Methuen, 1939–69)

—— *The Poems of Alexander Pope* [a one-volume version of the *Twickenham Edition*] (London: Methuen, 1963)

Cousins, A. D., and Daniel Derrin, eds, *Alexander Pope in the Reign of Queen Anne: Reconsiderations of his Early Career* (New York: Routledge, 2021)

Rosemary Cowler, ed., *The Prose Works of Alexander Pope* [vol. 2]: *The Major Works, 1725–1744* (Oxford: Blackwell, 1986)

Curtius, Ernst Robert, *European Literature and the Latin Middle Ages* (London: Routledge and Kegan Paul, 1953)

Damrosch, Leo, *Jonathan Swift: His Life and His World* (New Haven: Yale University Press, 2013)

Edwards, Thomas R., *This Dark Estate* (Berkeley: University of California Press, 1963)

Elwin, Whitwell, and William John Courthope, eds, *The Works of Alexander Pope*, 10 vols (London: John Murray, 1871–79)

Empson, William, *Seven Types of Ambiguity*, 3rd edn (London: Chatto and Windus, 1953)

Erskine-Hill, Howard, *The Augustan Idea in English Literature* (London: Arnold, 1983)

—— 'Pope and the Poetry of Opposition', in *The Cambridge Companion to Alexander Pope*, ed. by Pat Rogers (Cambridge: Cambridge University Press, 2007), pp. 134–49

—— *The Social Milieu of Alexander Pope* (New Haven: Yale University Press, 1975)

Fairer, David, *The Poetry of Alexander Pope* (Harmondsworth: Penguin 1989)

—— *Pope's Imagination* (Manchester: Manchester University Press, 1984)

Foxon, David, *Pope and the Early Eighteenth-Century Book Trade*, ed. by James McLaverty (Oxford: Clarendon Press, 1991), https://archive.org/details/popeearlyeightee0000foxo

Griffin, Dustin H., *Alexander Pope: The Poet in the Poem* (Princeton: Princeton University Press, 1979)

Hagstrum, Jean H., *The Sister Arts: The Tradition of Literary Pictorialism and English Poetry from Dryden to Gray* (Chicago: University of Chicago Press, 1958)

Halsband, Robert, *The Rape of the Lock and its Illustrators 1714–1896* (Oxford: Oxford University Press, 1980)

Harris, John, *The Palladian Revival: Lord Burlington, His Villa and Garden at Chiswick* (New Haven and London: Yale University Press, 1994)

G. B. Hill, ed., *Samuel Johnson: Lives of the English Poets*, 3 vols (Oxford: Clarendon Press, 1905)

Homer: The Iliad, trans. by E. V. Rieu (Harmondsworth: Penguin, 1950; rev. by Peter Jones with D. C. H. Rieu, 2003)

Hone, Joseph, *Alexander Pope in the Making* (Oxford: Oxford University Press, 2021), https://doi.org/10.1093/oso/9780198842316.001.0001

Honour, Hugh, *Neo-Classicism* (Harmondsworth: Penguin, 1968; rev. edn 1977)

Horace: Satires and Epistles; Persius, Satires, trans. by Niall Rudd (Harmondsworth: Penguin, 1979)

Hutchings, William, *Living Poetry: Reading Poems from Shakespeare to Don Paterson* (Basingstoke: Palgrave Macmillan, 2012)

Johnston, Arthur, ed., *Francis Bacon: The Advancement of Learning and New Atlantis* (Oxford: Clarendon Press, 1974)

Jones, Edmund D., ed., *English Critical Essays (Nineteenth Century)* (Oxford: Oxford University Press, 1916)

Jones, Peter, 'Introduction', in *Homer: the Iliad*, trans. by E. V. Rieu (Harmondsworth: Penguin, 1950; rev. by Peter Jones with D. C. H. Rieu, 2003), pp. ix–xlvi

Jones, Tom, *An Essay on Man* (Princeton: Princeton University Press, 2016)

Kerby-Miller, Charles, ed., *Memoirs of the Extraordinary Life, Works, and Discoveries of Martinus Scriblerus* (New Haven: Yale University Press, 1950; reissued 1966), http://name.umdl.umich.edu/004809278.0001.000

Kirk, G. S., 'Homer', in *The Cambridge History of Classical Literature*, 2 vols (Cambridge: Cambridge University Press, 1982–85), I: *Greek Literature*, ed. by P. E. Easterling and B. M. W. Knox (1985), pp. 42–91, https://doi.org/10.1017/CHOL9780521210423

Langer, Susanne K., *Feeling and Form* (London: Routledge and Kegan Paul, 1963)

Le Faye, Deirdre, ed., *Jane Austen's Letters*, 3rd edn (Oxford: Oxford University Press, 1997)

Leranbaum, Miriam, *Alexander Pope's 'Opus Magnum' 1729–1744* (Oxford: Clarendon Press, 1977)

Lonsdale, Roger, ed., *The Poems of Thomas Gray, William Collins, Oliver Goldsmith* (London: Longman, 1969), https://archive.org/details/poemsofthomasgra00gray_0

_____ *Lives of the Poets*, 4 vols, by Samuel Johnson (Oxford: Clarendon Press, 2006)

Lynch, Jack, ed., *The Oxford Handbook of British Poetry, 1660–1800* (Oxford: Oxford University Press, 2016), https://doi.org/10.1093/oxfordhb/9780199600809.001.0001

McLaverty, Jim, *Pope, Print and Meaning* (Oxford: Oxford University Press, 2001)

Mack, Maynard, ed., *Alexander Pope: An Essay on Man* (1950), vol. 3 (Part 1) of *The Twickenham Edition of The Poems of Alexander Pope* (London: Methuen, 1939–69)

Mack, Maynard, *Alexander Pope: A Life* (New Haven and London: Yale University Press, 1985)

_____ *Collected in Himself: Essays Critical, Biographical, and Bibliographical on Pope and Some of His Contemporaries* (Newark: University of Delaware Press, 1982)

_____ *The Garden and the City* (London: Oxford University Press, 1969)

_____ *The Last and Greatest Art: Some Unpublished Poetical Manuscripts of Alexander Pope* (Newark: University of Delaware Press, 1984)

Marshall, Ashley, 'The Myth of Scriblerus', *Journal for Eighteenth-Century Studies*, 31 (2008), 77–99, https://doi.org/10.1111/j.1754-0208.2008.00005.x

Morris, David B., *Alexander Pope: The Genius of Sense* (Cambridge: Harvard University Press, 1984)

Nichol, Donald W., ed., *Anniversary Essays on Alexander Pope's The Rape of the Lock* (Toronto: University of Toronto Press, 2016), https://doi.org/10.3138/9781442669673

Nowottny, Winifred, *The Language Poets Use* (London: The Athlone Press, 1962 and 1965)

Nuttall, A. D., *Pope's Essay on Man* (London: Allen and Unwin, 1984)

Osborn, James M., ed., *Observations, Anecdotes, and Characters of Books and Men*, 2 vols, by Joseph Spence (Oxford: Oxford University Press, 1966)

Oswald, Alice, *Memorial: An Excavation of the Iliad* (London: Faber and Faber, 2011)

Ovid: The Erotic Poems, trans. by Peter Green (Harmondsworth: Penguin, 1982)

Panofsky, Erwin, 'Et in Arcadia Ego: Poussin and the Elegiac Tradition', in *Meaning in the Visual Arts* (Harmondsworth: Penguin, 1970), pp. 340–67

Parfitt, George, ed., *Ben Jonson, the Complete Poems* (Harmondsworth: Penguin, 1975)

Ricks, Christopher, *Milton's Grand Style* (Oxford: Clarendon Press, 1963)

Rogers, Pat, *The Alexander Pope Encyclopedia* (Westport, CT: Greenwood Press, 2004)

Rogers, Pat, ed., *Alexander Pope: The Major Works* (Oxford: Oxford University Press, 2006)

_____ *The Cambridge Companion to Alexander Pope*, (Cambridge: Cambridge University Press, 2007), https://doi.org/10.1017/CCOL9780521840132

_____ *Essays on Pope* (Cambridge: Cambridge University Press, 1993)

_____ *Grub Street: Studies in a Subculture* (London: Routledge, 1972)

_____ *Hacks and Dunces: Pope, Swift and Grub Street* (London: Methuen, 1980) [a shortened version of *Grub Street*]

_____ *An Introduction to Pope* (London: Routledge, 1975)

_____ *A Political Biography of Alexander Pope* (London: Routledge, 2016)

_____ *Pope and the Destiny of the Stuarts: History, Politics, and Mythology* (Oxford: Oxford University Press, 2005)

_____ 'Pope in Arcadia: Pastoral and its Dissolution', in *The Cambridge Companion to Alexander Pope*, ed. by Pat Rogers (Cambridge: Cambridge University Press, 2007), pp. 105–17

Rosslyn, Felicity, *Alexander Pope: A Literary Life* (London: Macmillan, 1990)

Rudd, Niall, *Horace: Satires and Epistles; Persius: Satires*, revised edition (Harmondsworth: Penguin, 1979)

_____ *The Satires of Horace* (Cambridge: Cambridge University Press, 1966)

Rumbold, Valerie, *Women's Place in Pope's World* (Cambridge: Cambridge University Press, 1989)

_____ 'Pope and Gender', in *The Cambridge Companion to Alexander Pope*, ed. by Pat Rogers (Cambridge: Cambridge University Press, 2007), pp. 198–209

Rumbold, Valerie, ed., *The Dunciad in Four Books*, Longman Annotated Texts (London: Routledge, 1999)

Sherburn, George, ed., *The Correspondence of Alexander Pope*, 5 vols (Oxford: Oxford University Press, 1956)

Sitter, John, ed., *The Cambridge Companion to Eighteenth-Century Poetry* (Cambridge: Cambridge University Press, 2001), https://doi.org/10.1017/CCOL0521650909

_____ *The Cambridge Introduction to Eighteenth-Century Poetry* (Cambridge: Cambridge University Press, 2011)

_____ *The Poetry of Pope's 'Dunciad'* (Minneapolis: University of Minnesota Press, 1971)

_____ 'Pope's Versification and Voice', in *The Cambridge Companion to Alexander Pope*, ed. by Pat Rogers (Cambridge: Cambridge University Press, 2007), pp. 37–48

Stack, Frank, *Pope and Horace: Studies in Imitation* (Cambridge: Cambridge University Press, 1985)

Thomas, Claudia N., *Alexander Pope and his Eighteenth-Century Women Readers* (Carbondale: Southern Illinois Press, 1994)

Tillotson, Geoffrey, *On the Poetry of Pope* (Oxford: Clarendon Press, 1938)

_____ *Pope and Human Nature* (Oxford: Oxford University Press, 1958)

_____ *Augustan Studies* (Oxford: Oxford University Press, 1961)

Warton, Joseph, *An Essay on the Genius and Writings of Pope*, 2 vols (London: printed for M. Cooper, 1806 [1757, 1784]), https://books.google.co.uk/books?id=OBcfAAAAMAAJ

Watson, George, ed., *John Dryden, Of Dramatic Poesy and other Critical Essays*, 2 vols (London: Dent, 1962)

Weinbrot, Howard D., *Alexander Pope and the Traditions of Formal Verse Satire* (Princeton: Princeton University Press, 1982)

_____ *Augustus Caesar in 'Augustan' England* (Princeton: Princeton University Press, 1978)

_____ 'Pope and the Classics', in *The Cambridge Companion to Alexander Pope*, ed. by Pat Rogers (Cambridge: Cambridge University Press, 2007), pp. 76–88

Willey, Basil, *The Seventeenth Century Background* (London: Chatto and Windus, 1934), https://archive.org/details/in.ernet.dli.2015.458724

_____ *The Eighteenth Century Background* (London: Chatto and Windus, 1940), [1950 edn:] https://archive.org/details/eighteenthcentur0000will

Williams, Aubrey L., *Pope's Dunciad: A Study of its Meaning* (London: Methuen, 1955)

Williamson, Paul, 'Gray's Elegy and the Logic of Expression', in *Thomas Gray: Contemporary Essays*, ed. by W. B. Hutchings and William Ruddick (Liverpool: Liverpool University Press, 1993), pp. 39–72

Index

Addison, Joseph 5, 7, 8, 39, 59, 113, 116–120, 190, 207, 212–213. *See also* Pope, Alexander: Poems: *To Mr Addison*
Arbuthnot, John 12, 15, 113, 169, 175, 207–209, 214–215. *See also* Pope, Alexander: Poems: *Epistle to Dr Arbuthnot*
Argyle, John Campbell, Duke of 262–263
Aristotle 142
Atterbury, Francis 261–263
Atticus 210
Audra, E. 24, 42
Austen, Jane 77–78

Bacon, Francis 134, 284
Bateson, F. W. 165, 178
Bentley, Richard 195
Bethel, Hugh 197–203, 226. *See also* Pope, Alexander: Poems: *The Second Satire of the Second Book of Horace Imitated. To Mr Bethel*
Blackburne, Lancelot 204
Blackmore, Sir Richard 25, 190, 231
Blount, Martha 15, 79, 83, 165, 169–170, 173–178, 180, 218, 264. *See also* Pope, Alexander: Poems: *Epistle to Miss Blount, with the Works of Voiture*; *See also* Pope, Alexander: Poems: *An Epistle to a Lady*; *See also* Pope, Alexander: Poems: *Epistle to Miss Blount, on her Leaving the Town after the Coronation*
Blount, Teresa 83, 169, 173–174, 264
Boileau, Nicolas 39, 63, 74, 183, 185
Bolingbroke, Henry St John, Viscount 15, 52, 121, 125–126, 144, 181, 194, 221, 228, 237, 245, 253–254, 262, 264. *See also* Pope, Alexander: Poems: *The First Epistle of the First Book of Horace Imitated. To Lord Bolingbroke*
Bridgewater, Elizabeth, Countess of 82–83
Broome, William 99, 121
Brower, Reuben Arthur 55, 75, 168, 278
Budgell, Eustace 189–190, 192–193
Burlington, Richard Boyle, Earl of 122, 146–150, 152, 153, 154, 155, 157, 165, 197, 262. *See also* Pope, Alexander: Poems: *An Epistle to Richard Boyle, Earl of Burlington*
Busby, Richard 143, 281–285
Byron, George Gordon, Lord 205

Carr, John 202
Caryll, John 59, 119, 170
Charteris, Francis 186–187
Chesterfield, Philip Dormer Stanhope, Earl of 262
Cibber, Caius Gabriel 271–272
Cibber, Colley 121, 190, 268, 271–277, 279, 281
Cicero, Marcus Tullius 123, 181, 207, 243
Cowper, William 107, 109
Craggs, James 118–120. *See also* Pope, Alexander: Poems: *Epitaph on James Craggs, Esq*
Curll, Edmund 271, 275–276, 278
Curtius, Ernst Robert 277

Denham, Sir John 100–104, 106, 198
Dryden, John 36, 39, 45, 76, 79–80, 118, 183, 185, 227, 233, 275
Dufresnoy, Charles Alphonse 79, 82, 118

Edwards, Thomas R. 83
Eliot, Thomas Stearns 135
Empson, William 73, 127

Fenton, Elijah 99, 121
Fielding, Henry 186
Forster, E. M. 78
Fortescue, William 182, 187–190, 202, 213, 226, 229
Fox, Henry 191
Fox, Stephen 191

Garth, Samuel 74
Gay, John 12, 18, 113, 174
George II 159, 189, 228–230, 235–236
Gibson, Edmund 204
Granville, George, Baron Lansdowne 33, 83
Gray, Thomas 50, 97
Griffin, Dustin H. 134
Guernier, Louis Du 59

Hagstrum, Jean 80, 89–90
Handel, George Frederick 24, 284
Hardy, Thomas 217
Hervey, John, Baron 187, 213–214
Homer 37, 60, 62, 75, 99, 101, 105–106, 110, 113, 119, 121, 212. *See also* Pope, Alexander: Poems: *Homer, The Iliad*
Honour, Hugh 40
Horace (Quintus Horatius Flaccus) 17, 18, 26, 29, 39, 52, 141, 145, 147, 151, 153, 164, 181–185, 187–190, 192–195, 197, 200– 205, 207, 213, 217–224, 226–227, 229–230, 235–237, 239–240, 242, 245–252, 254, 257–258, 264, 280, 289. *See also* Pope, Alexander: Poems: *Epitaph on James Craggs, Esq*; *See also* Pope, Alexander: Poems: *The First Epistle of the Second Book of Horace Imitated. To Augustus*; *See also* Pope, Alexander: Poems: *The First Ode of the Fourth Book of Horace: To Venus*; *See also* Pope, Alexander: Poems: *The First Satire of the Second Book of Horace Imitated*; *See also* Pope, Alexander: Poems: *The Second Epistle of the Second Book of Horace Imitated*; *See also* Pope, Alexander: Poems: *The Second Satire of the First Book of Horace. Imitated in the Manner of Mr Pope*; *See also* Pope, Alexander: Poems: *The Second Satire of the Second Book of Horace Imitated. To Mr Bethel*; *See also* Pope, Alexander: Poems: *The Sixth Epistle of the First Book of Horace Imitated: To Mr Murray*
Hunt, James Leigh 67

Jenyns, Soame 135
Jervas, Charles 79–80, 82–83, 170, 264. *See also Epistle to Mr Jervas*
Johnson, Samuel 8, 33, 46–47, 50–51, 61, 78, 134–135, 175, 213, 233, 235
Jones, Inigo 146, 150, 154
Jones, Peter 106
Jonson, Ben 95, 120, 158, 219, 231–233
Juvenal (Decimus Junius Juvenalis) 187

Keats, John 34, 56
Kit Cat Club 51
Kneller, Sir Godfrey 79–80
Kyrle, John 161–163

Langer, Susanne K. 5
Lee, Nathaniel 192–193
Leranbaum, Miriam 145
Lintot, Bernard 59, 99, 116, 170, 269–271, 276–278
Livy (Titus Livius) 77
Locke, John 13–14, 247–248, 282

Mack, Maynard 25, 35, 51, 113, 116, 121, 123–125, 127–132, 135, 139, 141–142, 156–157, 160, 169, 212, 217, 221, 230, 279
Marlborough, John Churchill, Duke of 16, 55, 57, 83, 262
Martial (Marcus Valerius Martialis) 95, 260
Marvell, Andrew 28, 178
Milton, John 6, 13–14, 44, 61, 135, 138–139, 214, 231–233, 275–277, 280, 288–289
Montagu, Lady Mary Wortley 72, 187, 213
Montaigne, Michel de 135, 191, 247–248

Nowottny, Winifred 26, 67–68, 264
Nuttall, A. D. 71–73

Oswald, Alice 108–111
Ovid (Publius Ovidius Naso) 35, 85, 87, 89, 92, 96
Oxford, Edward Harley, Second Earl of 181
Oxford, Robert Harley, Earl of 113, 115. See also Pope, Alexander: Poems: Epistle to Robert Earl of Oxford and Earl Mortimer

Palladio, Andrea 146, 150, 154
Palmer, Sir Thomas 205
Panofsky, Erwin 34
Parnell, Thomas 12, 113–116, 121, 264
Peterborough, Charles Mordaunt, Earl of 169, 229
Philips, Ambrose 23–24
Pope, Alexander
  Poems
    The Dunciad 5, 14, 26, 75, 114, 121, 141, 143, 149, 152, 154, 190, 231, 233–234, 245, 257, 262, 265, 267–268, 272–275, 277–278, 280–281, 284–285, 290–292
    Elegy to the Memory of an Unfortunate Lady 93, 96–97
    Eloisa to Abelard 85–86, 89, 92, 96
    Epilogue to the Satires: Dialogues I and II 239, 245, 257, 265
    An Epistle to a Lady 79, 160, 169–170, 175, 177–178, 180
    An Epistle to Allen, Lord Bathurst 155–164, 186, 197
    Epistle to Dr Arbuthnot 5, 15, 119, 169, 203, 207–209, 211–212, 215–216, 264
    Epistle to Miss Blount, on her Leaving the Town after the Coronation 79, 169–170, 220
    Epistle to Miss Blount, with the Works of Voiture 79, 169–170, 172, 176, 179, 220

    Epistle to Mr Jervas 79, 81–83, 169–170, 172, 176, 179, 220
    An Epistle to Richard Boyle, Earl of Burlington 6, 13, 15, 47, 122, 145–155, 157, 165, 197, 262, 289
    Epistle to Robert Earl of Oxford and Earl Mortimer 113, 115. See also Pope, Alexander: Poems: An Epistle to Sir Richard Temple, Lord Cobham
    An Epistle to Sir Richard Temple, Lord Cobham 15, 17, 165–168, 212, 241, 248
    Epitaph on James Craggs, Esq 113, 118–120
    Epitaph on Sir Isaac Newton 10–11
    An Essay on Criticism 6, 14, 39–53, 79, 102, 144, 153, 176, 189, 227, 232, 263
    An Essay on Man 9, 15–17, 25, 40, 121–130, 132–145, 147, 155–158, 165–166, 194, 210, 221, 225, 237, 242, 245, 253, 259, 264–265, 280
    The First Epistle of the First Book of Horace Imitated. To Lord Bolingbroke 141, 203, 239, 245–254
    The First Epistle of the Second Book of Horace Imitated. To Augustus 229–237
    The First Ode of the Fourth Book of Horace: To Venus 217–220
    The First Satire of the Second Book of Horace Imitated 153, 181–195, 236
    Homer, The Iliad 60, 62–63, 70, 74, 99–100, 104, 106, 108, 111, 113, 116, 119, 121, 212, 278
    Pastorals 11, 21–23, 32–35, 37, 39–40, 53–54, 79, 90, 99–100, 173, 288
    Prologue to Cato 7–8, 204, 210
    The Rape of the Lock 10–13, 25, 31, 54, 58–78, 83, 99, 111, 170–174, 179, 214
    Sappho to Phaon 35–38, 85, 96
    The Second Epistle of the Second Book of Horace Imitated 221–228

The Second Satire of the First Book of Horace. Imitated in the Manner of Mr Pope 203–205
The Second Satire of the Second Book of Horace Imitated. To Mr Bethel 197–202, 236
The Sixth Epistle of the First Book of Horace Imitated: To Mr Murray 239–244
To Mr Addison 113, 116–120
Windsor Forest 31, 39, 53, 55–58, 79, 100, 288
Prose
The Guardian, no. 40 (On Pastorals) 23, 113
The Guardian, no. 173 (On Gardens) 113, 153
Peri Bathous, or The Art of Sinking in Poetry 12, 114, 190
Stradling versus Stiles 182
Pulteney, William 262, 284

Rieu, E. V. 107, 110
Rochester, John Wilmot, Earl of 18, 204, 262
Rogers, Pat 165–166, 178, 191, 270, 272
Rudd, Niall 182, 184–185, 188

Sawbridge, Thomas 204
Scriblerus Club 12, 113–114, 152, 207, 262, 264, 267
Settle, Elkanah 268, 279–280
Shakespeare, William 68, 214, 231–232, 267
  Antony and Cleopatra 68
  As You Like It 28, 140
  Hamlet 94, 131
Shippen, William 191
Shrewsbury, Charles Talbot, Duke of 163, 262–263

Spence, Joseph 59, 181, 285
Spenser, Edmund 21, 26, 232–233
Stack, Frank 182–183, 188–189, 222, 230, 243, 246
Steele, Richard 80, 113, 269
Swift, Jonathan 12, 18, 113–114, 119, 121, 152, 161, 208, 221, 229, 267, 278

Temple, Sir William 15, 142. *See also* Pope, Alexander: Poems: *An Epistle to Sir Richard Temple, Lord Cobham*
Theobald, Lewis 121, 214, 267
Tickell, Thomas 116, 212
Tillotson, Geoffrey 67, 115
Tonson, Jacob 11, 23, 32–33, 99, 116, 267

Villiers, George, Duke of Buckingham 163
Virgil (Publius Vergilius Maro) 21, 30–33, 36, 39, 53–54, 56, 61, 76, 106, 113, 118, 268, 275, 278–279

Walpole, Sir Robert 17, 125, 182, 186–187, 191, 195, 204, 213, 239, 248, 257–258, 262, 267, 280, 284
Walsh, William 25, 33, 50–51
Walter, Peter 186–187, 191
Warburton, William 12, 165, 203, 207, 217, 239, 242
Warton, Joseph 89
Wharton, Philip, Duke of 167–168, 241
Wilde, Oscar 64
Williams, Aubrey L. 24, 42
Wordsworth, William 5
Wycherley, William 33
Wyndham, Sir William 262–263, 284

About the Team

Alessandra Tosi was the managing editor for this book.

Jennifer Moriarty copy-edited and indexed this book.

Jennifer Moriarty and Anna Mullock proofread the book.

Jeevanjot Kaur Nagpal designed the cover. The cover was produced in InDesign using the Fontin font.

Cameron Craig typeset the book in InDesign and produced the paperback and hardback editions. The text font is Tex Gyre Pagella and the heading font is Californian FB.

Jeremy Bowman produced the PDF and EPUB editions. The conversion was performed with open-source software and other tools freely available on our GitHub page at https://github.com/OpenBookPublishers.

This book has been anonymously peer-reviewed by experts in their field. We thank them for their invaluable help.

This book need not end here...

Share

All our books — including the one you have just read — are free to access online so that students, researchers and members of the public who can't afford a printed edition will have access to the same ideas. This title will be accessed online by hundreds of readers each month across the globe: why not share the link so that someone you know is one of them?

This book and additional content is available at:
https://doi.org/10.11647/OBP.0372

Donate

Open Book Publishers is an award-winning, scholar-led, not-for-profit press making knowledge freely available one book at a time. We don't charge authors to publish with us: instead, our work is supported by our library members and by donations from people who believe that research shouldn't be locked behind paywalls.

Why not join them in freeing knowledge by supporting us:
https://www.openbookpublishers.com/support-us

Follow @OpenBookPublish

Read more at the Open Book Publishers BLOG

You may also be interested in:

Tennyson's Poems
New Textual Parallels
R. H. Winnick

https://doi.org/10.11647/obp.0161

Making the Void Fruitful
Yeats as Spiritual Seeker and Petrarchan Lover
Patrick Keane

https://doi.org/10.11647/obp.0275

Yeats's Legacies
Yeats Annual No. 21
Warwick Gould (editor)

https://doi.org/10.11647/obp.0135

www.ingramcontent.com/pod-product-compliance
Lightning Source LLC
Chambersburg PA
CBHW042043240426
43667CB00048B/2961